Christmas /83

W9-BIU-558

Fighting for your dignity,
Fighting for your cause,
We'd all better stop for a while and pause,
God, with wisdom and love,
gave man the ability to reason.

P. Alward/83 ⊗

"I'm a 2000 man —
And my kids, they just don't understand."

The Rolling Stones
late 60's

MAN
ALIVE:
The Human
Journey

Also by Roy Bonisteel
In Search of Man Alive

Roy Bonisteel

MAN ALIVE: The Human Journey

COLLINS, Toronto

First published 1983 by
Collins Publishers
100 Lesmill Road, Don Mills, Ontario

Canadian Cataloguing in Publication Data

Bonisteel, Roy.
  Man alive: the human journey

ISBN 0-00-217102-3

1. Man alive (Television program). 2. Christian biography.
I. Man alive (Television program). II. Title.

CT120.B67 1983   209'.2'2   C83-099106-9

p. 84 quotation from *Lightning East to West* © 1980 by Jim
Douglas (reissued 1983 by The Crossroad Publishing Co., New
York) is reprinted by permission of the author.

Printed and bound in Canada
by John Deyell Company

To
    Anis
        and
            Ernest

ACKNOWLEDGEMENTS

I would like to thank CBC-TV for permission to quote from transcripts of programs including *Man Alive* and *Take 30*. Thanks also to Frances McFadyen for her assistance in preparing this book.

Special thanks to Ernest Harrison for his encouragement, criticism and expertise, to Anis Harrison for providing more than "just the odd word" and above all, to my wife, Jane, whose name should also be on the cover.

Contents

MAN
ALIVE:
The Human
Journey

PREFACE

As *Man Alive* enters its seventeenth season it becomes more than ever, as one reviewer commented, "an oasis of sanity in a desert of mediocrity". Especially in Canada, where the bulk of our population lives within signal distance of all three of the American commercial networks with their emphasis on entertainment programs, our series which speaks to viewers about values, ethical concerns and responsibility to others stands out and is appreciated.

Many Canadians and some border-dwelling Americans have watched *Man Alive* regularly since it began in the fall of 1967. When they write or when I meet them in my travels, they surprise me with almost total recall of programs or interviews I did years ago and had personally forgotten.

First-time viewers of the program write to me of their delight in discovering a program of substance. Appreciation by the viewers is precious indeed and the many awards won by *Man Alive* on the national and international broadcasting scene are cherished. But perhaps the highest accolade of all is the CBC's decision to continue the program in its schedule each year.

I have been in broadcasting long enough to realize that if *Man Alive* was produced by any other network in North America, it would likely have been discontinued years ago. The reason? Ratings! While many of our programs score extremely high in the weekly head count, others fall short of the acceptable level. Programs dealing with Third World problems, unfamiliar faiths and interviews with theologians do not garner vast audiences, but they are important and certainly part of *Man Alive*'s mandate to explore and report. CBC's commitment to programming, which puts content and quality ahead of popular viewing habits, fulfils its responsibility as a national service for all Canadians.

Readers of *In Search of Man Alive,* published in 1980, will notice a somewhat different approach to the subjects in this book. Rather than devote an entire chapter to a single program or personality, I have combined the material and experiences of several productions into a more thematic approach to issues. Some of the programs mentioned were produced many years ago, the majority are quite recent, but they all, for me, share a common factor — faith. Faith can be something as simple and trusting as a child tossed in the air who knows his father's arms will never fail, as deep and mysterious as a mountain-top revelation or as passionate and forceful as a movement's desire to change the world. For some, faith is elusive. It comes and goes with the vagaries of life. For others, it is a constant force that shapes and directs this life and assures them of joy in the next. Exploring the realm of faith is something that has involved the *Man Alive* producers for many years. Some of the producers whose work is mentioned here have moved on to other endeavors. They include Roz Farber, Kathy Smalley, Tim Bentley, Azza El Sissi and John McGreevy. Current *Man Alive* producers include Louise Lore (Executive Producer), Don Cumming, Tom Kelly, David Cherniack and Ray Hazzan. Producers are the geniuses behind all of our programs and you'll meet some of them in the following chapters. Whether they are named or not, I ascribe to them the credit for the success of our series and the thanks for taking me with them on their human journeys.

VERY SPECIAL PEOPLE

When my three children were in school, the end of term always brought a report card which read that one of them was "not living up to expectations". I could never sort out whose expectations were not being met. Their own? The teacher's? Mine? All three would be a safe bet in most cases.

There are, however, certain young people who never have to worry about carrying around the "expectations burden". These are the mentally handicapped. I have found that few people, including parents, expect much from them and are surprised when they accomplish even the simplest tasks.

Strangely, it is often the medical profession that abandons them first. Time after time, when talking with parents of retarded children, I have heard the tale of some doctor advising them at birth that their child would only be a vegetable and therefore should either be allowed to die or at least be placed in an institution as soon as possible.

The decision to keep the child at home and face the inevitable burdens is a tough one to make. There are, of course, severe cases where institutional commitment is by far the wisest course, both in terms of proper care and for the maintenance of a healthy family life. Yet many parents who have gone against their doctor's advice, and raised their child in the family setting, have told me about a special kind of joy and satisfaction. I'm sure this sense of satisfaction exists partly because their expectations were very low, or even non-existent.

In 1979, the CBC drama department decided to produce a play about a family of five in which the eldest boy had Down's Syndrome, a condition often known as mongolism. The search was on for an actor to play the part. The executive producer, Sam Levene, a former *Man Alive* producer, knew a family whose eldest son actually had Down's Syndrome and, although he admitted it might be a crazy idea, decided to cast this boy in the role. He was sixteen-year-old David, son of Ed and Grace McFarlane of Toronto.

The play, entitled *One of Our Own,* was shown in the *For the Record* series and became an outstanding success. David won top Canadian acting awards for his performance and the resulting *Man Alive* program won many international awards for both David and producer Tom Kelly. It was just one more milestone in the life achievements of this remarkable young man.

Grace is Japanese and, when pregnant with David, often wondered if her baby would be born with her features or her husband's. When she first saw David, his "oriental" features came as no surprise.

Grace told me, "When the pediatrician first came in, he looked at me, then walked out, then came back and finally told me my baby was mongoloid and had very, very poor responses. He said it would be best if we signed the papers to have him placed in an Ontario Hospital for the retarded. When he was two days old, they told me that his responses were so slow that he would never progress, that he would always be a vegetable."

"What were your feelings at that time?" I asked.

"Shock," answered Grace. "I didn't cry in front of the doctors, but I certainly did when no one else was around. And I really cried when the lady in the next bed got her baby to feed and I didn't. They wouldn't bring David to me."

This was the moment of decision for the McFarlanes. The advice of the medical profession was clear. They were soon made aware of the problems, the effort and the heartbreak ahead if they chose to keep David. Lifetime decisions, however, are often made for seemingly insignificant reasons.

"When we finally got to see him, he was making little noises. We played with him and talked to him and he seemed to smile. We thought, 'Hey, a vegetable can't respond like that. This is no vegetable. This is our son!' We took him home."

At that time, the McFarlanes lived in an apartment on the outskirts of Toronto. David developed into a happy and playful baby. The family doctor urged Grace and Ed to have another child as soon as possible, insisting that the chances of retardation happening again were very slight. This time they took the medical advice and a year later Jane was born, perfectly normal. A year and a half after that, Grace gave birth to Scott. Scott worried them for a while because he had a single crease across his palm, a usual sign of Down's Syndrome; but he, too, was normal.

"I must admit it took a while to get used to having a retarded child. It was difficult for me to go out with him, or show him to people. I used to ask Ed to take him out for a walk and fresh air. After a while this passed and, when the time came for him to go to school, we decided to enroll him in the local kindergarten. He had a wonderful time and the school enjoyed him. David would walk to school by himself. Sometimes, when he was late in arriving, the principal would phone and ask if he had left yet. When we said, 'Yes,' he'd say, 'Don't worry; I'll send a couple of grade eights out to look for him.' Then he'd call and say, 'We've found him. He was looking in every garbage can on the way to school.'"

This happy relationship continued until the McFarlanes moved into Toronto itself. Ed explained: "When we put him in the local school in Toronto, they seemed shocked to have him and didn't know what to do with him. They stuck him into a corner away from the other kids and started phoning institutions to try to get him out of the classroom. They told us he shouldn't be in a regular class, that he didn't belong in a regular school and that they just couldn't take having him there any more. David began coming home crying and upset. He stopped talking, began wetting himself and regressing in almost every aspect. A complete change in the space of three months. We finally put him in a special school for retarded children. It was a good move. He started to blossom again."

When I met the McFarlane family, David had just finished the filming of *One of Our Own* and was basking in the glow of praise for a job well done. He also had many other accomplishments to his credit. He was an excellent bicyclist, could ice skate, play basketball and chess and he'd been invited to swim in the special Olympics. Jane, now fifteen and Scott, now fourteen, were obviously very close to their older brother and said they seldom noticed that David looked "different".

"I don't really think about the way he looks," explained Jane, "except when I have guests over and suddenly I notice they are staring at David. Then I look at him and notice that, yes, he does look different. It's funny. You only see it when other people do. I've lived with him since I was born, so he's just my brother David."

I asked Scott if he was ever embarrassed about David. He answered to the contrary and said he was proud of him. "He's very kind, constantly going out of his way to help people. Sometimes he makes me feel guilty because he's so kind. He's not always perfect or anything. He wants people to treat him as a normal person. Really he is. One time he was out jogging when two teenagers on bikes stopped in front of him and jeered at him. He simply went around them and continued jogging. The two boys did it again and again. David patiently went around them. The boys got bored and went away. I think it proved that David could handle himself on his own."

There was no doubt that David had the support and encouragement of a close, loving family, but we found it interesting how he continued to surprise them with his accomplishments. Grace admitted that whenever they asked anyone to teach David something, they always left an "out".

"We would say, 'Would you try to teach David how to do this or that? Would you try to teach him how to skate? If it doesn't work out, that's fine.' We always left an out for that person and maybe for us."

David was determined to succeed in whatever he tackled. Skating was a perfect example. Not only did he learn the fundamentals, but he became extremely confident and adept at intricate steps.

"For a figure eight," Ed explained, "you must balance on one foot only. David would turn half way, then immediately put the other foot down because he was afraid he was going to fall. He would spend hours practising just his figure eight, never being able to complete it, but continually trying it. I remember, after about four months, thinking 'he's never going to be able to do that, why does he keep trying?' Then one day, after a full year, Scott came running over and shouted, 'He did it! He's finally got it!'"

The slow development of a retarded child often leads to omissions on the part of the parents. Grace, for example, had never really thought about David's reaction to puberty. "One day he came downstairs and said to me, 'We've got to talk, very privately.' I said, 'All right.' Then he asked, 'Is it okay to have hairs growing in your private parts?' I said, 'Yes, of course. It just means that you are growing up.' He was so relieved. He said, 'I'm glad, because I've got twenty-seven of them.' It seemed so funny. I could just see him counting them so meticulously."

Bill Fruet, director of *One of Our Own,* worked very closely with David and described him as a natural actor. "He would react naturally to people talking to him. He responded well. Reaction shots are difficult for actors because they must look directly into the camera and often find no motivation for their facial expressions. David had absolutely no trouble with these subtleties. When it came to something like laughing without a good reason, well, David couldn't understand that at all. He solved the problem himself, though. In one scene, where he was supposed to laugh, he asked his stage mother to tickle him, and we have this marvellous shot of him laughing uproariously."

There was concern that David might not be able to handle the complicated action scenes. In one part of the drama, the character gets lost on the subway and ends up wandering through a major department store in awe of the bright lights and colorful displays. Another has him being pushed and shoved by a girl who is trying to resist what she thinks are sexual advances but are only friendly embraces. The producer wisely hired a double, dressed him exactly like David and had him stand by, ready to step in when needed. David was intrigued to see someone who looked just like him and so he approached the actor to find out what he was doing. When the stand-in explained, David told him he could go home, as he wouldn't be needed. He wasn't!

David worked hard during the thirteen days of filming. He made friends with everyone connected with the production. Many found him an inspiration and a challenge to their own professionalism. The days were long. Some lasted from six in the morning to after ten at night. But David was eagerly on the job bright and early, always having learned his lines for that day's scenes.

The glamor of appearing in a major television play, together with the publicity that followed its success, gave David even more confidence. At a special film festival showing *One of Our Own* and the *Man Alive* "David" programs at Toronto's Harborfront, I introduced the various directors and producers to a highly appreciative and responsive audience. While they were speaking, I quietly asked the McFarlanes if they thought David might like to say a few words, or if the excitement might fluster him. After sixteen years of being constantly surprised by this remarkable young man's achievements, they answered, "It's entirely up to him."

David, dressed in blue jeans and a sweater, made his way to the stage. Grinning widely, he thanked the audience for their warm reception. He was perfectly at ease and within a few moments had charmed them with his warmth and obvious self-confidence.

Perhaps Scott said it best in an essay he read to his class: "A common phrase is 'don't judge a book by its cover'. This statement is very accurate when applied to my brother David. At first glance, most regard David as a retarded kid. David's cover is Down's Syndrome, which most people recognize as mongolism. When David was born, the doctor recommended an institution, stating that David would be a vegetable all his life. David is an example of a mentally retarded child who, when given the opportunity, can succeed. I'd like to see the doctor's face who suggested an institution. His vegetable has certainly flowered."

David McFarlane challenges himself and, with the support of his family, succeeds in areas no one had thought possible for him. It is all too easy for us to throw up our hands and say, "it can't be done". It requires courage to try, to risk possible failure. Success is then a richer experience. But courage is not the endowment of the retarded person alone; it is a possession of the family and teachers and friends who can reach beyond their prejudices and help create a full life.

The McFarlanes were able to communicate with David. They were eventually able to understand his needs as he expressed them. This is not always the case. Sometimes a person can be locked away in a world no one else can understand and to persistently try to communicate and push this person onward requires an extraordinary kind of courage.

The Lemkes have such courage.

Joe Lemke has lived in Wisconsin all his life, working in the construction industry. During World War II he had served with the American army in an African hospital unit, then returned to Milwaukee and his old job. It wasn't until 1948 that he met the woman who would end his forty-four years of bachelorhood.

May Pollard was a nurse/governess when Joe met her at a Milwaukee dance. She had trained in England following World War I, which had taken the lives of her father and five brothers. At the age of fourteen, she had been badly burned in the explosion of a munitions factory where she was working. She was hospitalized for many months and doctors claimed that a damaged thyroid caused her to remain a diminutive four foot two.

During World War I, May's family home in England had been a haven for many servicemen looking for a home-cooked meal. After the war, one of them — a Wisconsin farmer named James Pollard — remembered the vivacious young May and began writing to her regularly, finally proposing marriage.

In Wisconsin, May tackled farming and child rearing with her innate enthusiasm and despite floods, tornados, the Depression and finally the death of her husband in 1943, she never lost her courage or her faith in a miracle-working God.

With her sons off to war, May sold the farm and moved to Milwaukee so that her two daughters could finish school. She once again became a nurse/governess and many families still remember the care and devotion she showered on her charges. She married Joe Lemke in 1949.

After her marriage, she divided her time between her work and her new life at Joe's renovated cottage on Pewaukee Lake. Her children were now all out on their own.

One summer day in 1952, a nurse from a Milwaukee hospital called May at home to tell her about a helpless six-month-old baby left in their care. The parents did not want him and all the hospital knew about him was that his name was Leslie. After hearing of the baby's condition, May insisted on seeing him.

"He looked like a withered little piece of humanity," she says. "Gaping eyes — a poor little thing shriveled up in a ball, so skinny, so thin."

He was almost dead when discovered, with eyes that would not open and so infected that they were removed surgically to save what life remained. The doctor then discovered severe cerebral palsy and no noticeable mental function.

May asked to take the baby home. Since nothing could be done for him at the hospital, her request was granted. "The doctors said they couldn't do anything. They said, 'He's gonna die.' I said, 'Oh, shut up. He ain't gonna die if he's with me. Nothing ever dies that comes to me. Some day he'll be something.'"

May is a ninety-pound bundle of dynamite. She talks incessantly in machine-gun bursts of fractured English, imploring her listeners and her God to pay attention. She is always on the move, trotting from room to room, stopping only long enough to push her worn, wrinkled, beautiful face inches from yours to expound on the glory of "the miracle" that would occur with Leslie.

Almost everything is a miracle to May. With producer Tom Kelly and a television crew of three, I spent several days with May, Joe and Leslie in their cramped cottage and May exhausted us all with her explosive energy, her persistent chatter and her continual claims of divine intervention in her life.

After two and a half days of rain, we had filmed just about everything we could inside. "It will be all right after lunch," proclaimed May. "I prayed for sunshine for you this afternoon."

At about two o'clock that afternoon, our camera man set up his tripod to film Joe Lemke against the backdrop of the sun glistening off the sparkling water of Pewaukee Lake. The rest of the crew sighed with relief to be out of the cramped cottage. May looked up devoutly at the rapidly clearing sky and said simply, "Thank ya, God."

At one point during the filming, the key required to open the lid of the Lemkes' piano was mislaid. May searched through a ring of several keys she kept on her belt, but the one for the piano was missing.

"I must have put it down somewhere last evening when I locked up after you fellers left," she said. "Now let's all start looking."

Since we needed Leslie playing the piano for the next segment of filming, there was nothing to do but systematically begin searching room by room.

Joe, in the meantime, had gone to the local store to buy some soft drinks. He returned in about an hour and was surprised to find us all on our hands and knees peering under the furniture and sifting through the trash. May was on her knees too, but for a different reason. I was alone in the tiny kitchen looking through a pile of dishes and snacks that had been prepared for the crew, when Joe came in.

"What's going on?" he asked.

I explained that the filming had been delayed until the key for the piano was found and that we weren't having much luck. A strange look came over Joe's face.

"I know where it is," he said quietly. "It's in my pocket. I didn't put it back on May's ring, because I didn't want to bother her every time you folks wanted the piano opened. What'll I do? She'll be as mad as a wet hen to have had to turn the house inside out because I took the key to the store with me."

"Let us take the blame," I offered. "She's not likely to be so angry."

I called into the living room where the search feverishly continued and explained that the key had been found, saying that it had apparently fallen on the kitchen floor and got covered by our camera and lighting equipment, which was scattered throughout the small room. May appeared in the doorway then, wearing a smug smile.

"Of course you found it! I've just been praying to God to let the key turn up so you could get on with your work, and he showed you where it was hiding. God never fails me."

It was this complete and unswerving faith that had saved Leslie. As a baby, he had no sucking instinct. A bottle was useless.

"There was no movement on his part at all. I would have to put food into his mouth and push it down his throat with my finger. I started sucking on his cheek with my lips over and over again to try and teach him. He made no sound, no noise, no movement. He just lay there like a piece of fluff. In about a year's time, he started to suck and chew on his own."

"You must have spent most of your time holding him," I suggested.

"Sure I did. I used to say, 'Dear Creator, in the name of Jesus, let this little piece of flesh know that it's loved and wanted.' It was years before he made any movement."

Actually, it was seven years before any real progress was noted, seven years of constant caring, working, training and love.

"I had a leather belt with two loops on it so his little hands could go through and I would kind of drag him along behind me, trying to teach him to walk. But all he would do is flop."

"Could he sit in a chair?" I asked.

"No, not at all. I had to prop him up and tie him in because he couldn't hold himself up. Then I got an idea and I said to Joe, 'Take him in the lake. He should enjoy the water.' 'Course the kid's getting pretty old by this time. So I said, 'Take him in the lake and bounce him up and down in the water.' So Joe did and we thought maybe he'd like it, but how could we tell?"

The hours, days, weeks and years went by as they waited for some response. No movement, no emotion, no sound. The only noticeable change was that the baby was growing into a boy and the boy into a young man.

May and I walked outside and strolled along a chain link fence that ran the full length of the property from the street to the edge of the lake. A path about a foot wide had been worn by years of tramping along the edge of the fence.

"I had the fence built after consulting with the neighbors, because I wanted to give Leslie fresh air and I thought the fence would give me something to prop him up against. So Joe would take him in the water and jump up and down with him; then I would wrap him in towels and prop him up by the fence. And he'd promptly fall down. Then one day he showed the first sign of movement. He moved and he stood there and he didn't fall. I shouted to Joe and I ran and got a camera and took a picture. Then he flopped right over on his back. Well, that's the way it was all the time, over and over again, until the day he finally pulled himself up to the fence. He pulled himself up and just stood there hanging on. He was twelve years old."

Three years later, Leslie took his first steps, still clinging to the fence. He could not stand alone and he had never spoken a word.

When he was sixteen, May's biggest miracle took place. "Joe and I had gone to bed and were asleep. It was about three in the morning. I woke up and said to Joe, 'Hey, where's that music coming from?' It was nice music, very soft, but real. I asked Joe if he'd left the television on, but he said no. So I got up and walked down the hall in the dark. And there was Leslie. He was playing the piano. I threw myself down on the floor and said, 'Oh, my God. Thank you, thank you. Thank you, dear Creator. You've really made a miracle this time.' Later, all the neighbors and everybody came running. Oh, how beautiful it was! A child who never moved, couldn't talk or walk — there, playing the piano."

The astounding thing was that Leslie was not simply playing the piano; he was playing Tchaikovsky's *Piano Concerto No. 1*. In the days that followed, he could hardly be taken away from the keyboard. A flood of tunes came pouring out: ragtime, show tunes, marches, hymns, classical music and obscure old English folk tunes that May had crooned to him while he was still a baby. It seemed that every tune the child had heard from his mother or from radio, records or television was etched in his brain and could somehow be transformed by his fingers into a fine piano performance. Hands that could not yet hold a cup or a pencil, flew with dexterity and sensitivity to fill the tiny cottage with music.

What had happened was a miracle for May. But it was soon diagnosed by the medical profession. Leslie was an *idiot savant* — a person, usually male, who is mentally sub-normal, but possesses an island of brilliance. The gifts vary. One might draw brilliantly, another out-perform computers in calculations, another have an exquisite sense of smell. They are sometimes called autistic *idiots savants,* are exceedingly rare and the medical profession seems unable to agree as to the condition's nature or cause.

Autistic children are self-absorbed and cannot differentiate between interior and exterior sensations. They cannot assimilate life experiences, but rather react to sensory stimulation. Repeated phrases are often their only source of communication; their words are repeated rather than understood. Bernard Rimland, psychologist and founder of the National Society for Autistic Children, states that the *idiot savant is* autistic: "My theory is that the *idiot savant* suffers from a laser-like...focus...which he cannot broaden to allow himself to see the relevance of what he is doing...like a man watching a football game through a high-powered telescope. He can count the blades of grass along the fifty-yard line, but can't tell you what's going on."

One case history describes a family taking their *idiot savant* child to the theatre. The child could not describe the drama, but eagerly informed his family as to the number of words spoken and the number of entrances and exits.

Other theories to account for the phenomenon include chemical over-stimulation of one small area of the brain concurrent with under-stimulation of the rest, or an unidentified process whereby the brain exists in complete isolation from the outside world except through one small form of autistic or technical expression. Some believe that *idiots savants* are psychotic from infancy and that they should not be categorized as retarded at all.

The condition is a remarkable one, but one that science has yet to define properly. Leslie's case is even more remarkable since he is also blind and suffers from severe cerebral palsy.

During the filming of the *Man Alive* program with Leslie, I found it very difficult to relate to him as a person. I have been involved in many programs with the retarded and have, over the years, known several personally. I have always been able to communicate on some level and form a relationship of some kind, but with Leslie there was simply no response. He showed no emotion. There was no way to tell if he was happy, sad, angry or content. Words spoken to him were repeated back.

"Are you hungry, Leslie?"

"Hungry."

"Are you full, Leslie?"

"Full."

The procedure at the piano was always the same. He would sit until a tune was requested or an artist mentioned.

Roy: How about Satchmo?

Leslie: Satchmo.

May: Just say Louis Armstrong.

Roy: Louis Armstrong.

Leslie (singing): Hello, Dolly. This is Louis, Dolly.

He began to sing when he was nineteen. From a flat, guttural sound, his voice developed into a rich, vibrant baritone. He still couldn't speak a word on his own, but he could mimic any song he heard. Indeed, many of his mistakes were easily traceable to improper reception or flawed recordings. He simply performed exactly what he heard — and his hearing was superb.

One sometimes tends to forget this and make the mistake of talking as though Leslie isn't in the room. At one point, producer Tom Kelly and I were discussing the placement of music in the program and Tom said, "It would be good at this point to have Leslie play a classical piece." I agreed, adding "I wonder if he knows *Clair de lune.*" From the other side of the room, Leslie said, *"Clair de lune"* and immediately began to play it. There is no interrupting him once he begins and we were treated to hours of performing during our filming.

It's hard to tell, but I assume that Leslie enjoys performing. He never stops on his own, but keeps going until May removes him from the bench to eat or rest or go to the toilet. All of these functions are at May's suggestion, with no indication from Leslie that he requires any of them.

May told us that once, and only once, did Leslie show any emotion. One day he began to cry. "It was just a little over two years ago. He was sitting in his chair and I noticed tears on his cheek. I said, 'Leslie, you're crying.' He said, 'Crying.' And God, did he cry! It flew out of him. I said, 'Oh, come on, boy. Let it out. What you've suffered all your life is coming out now.' He cried as if the whole world was coming out of him. We cried along with

28

him. It poured out like a river. He hasn't cried since."

The Lemkes have been the source of considerable media attention since the "miracle". Newspapers and television have spread the story of Leslie's remarkable talent and his change from a blind, mute, unresponsive creature to a person now able to talk, walk and function on a nearly normal basis. Some of these reports are, I believe, misleading.

It is true that Leslie's vocabulary has increased consistently and is growing every day. Being able to say words, however, does not necessarily indicate that he knows their meaning. I feel that Leslie responds to words he has heard over and over again, but to use those words in the context of a conversation is impossible for him. Certain sentences trigger correct response. His piano playing and singing are echoes of others' performances. He can walk from object to object by hanging on to May or by clinging to his familiar and beloved fence. He does not walk or talk on his own initiative. I saw no evidence of emotion in Leslie. He does not smile or show anger. Sometimes a spasm contorts his face and body, causing one to wonder if he is uncomfortable or agitated. May will stroke his shoulders and coo to him gently. Has this been an emotional upset or a physical reaction to his palsied condition? I hope he experiences joy as his hands and voice produce such beautiful sounds. Surely he must feel the tenderness and care that constantly flow to him from May and Joe.

The real miracle is not that a severely handicapped young man suddenly plays Tchaikovsky; rather, that two simple, compassionate human beings who found each other late in life also found another human being who needed them in order to survive and grow. The day by day unremitting love that May and Joe unselfishly lavish on their adopted son is a manifestation of that miracle.

When May and Joe die, Leslie will be legally transferred into the care of May's daughter Mary, who also lives in Wisconsin.

The miracle of love and devotion will continue.

Three per cent of Canadians are born mentally retarded. The best chance for most of them is employment in a "sheltered workshop", confined to simple, repetitive tasks, resigned to dependency or care from others. A few rise to unexpected levels of ability because of the love and care of their families or because of teachers whose guidance is rooted in respect for individuals capable of directing their own lives, accepting responsibility for

29

their actions and growing to whatever heights their initiative takes them.

I first met the Famous People Players in 1976 in the basement of St. Mary the Virgin's Anglican Church in Toronto. They had been organized then for almost two years. As I watched a rehearsal of their black-light presentation, I would not have guessed that this group of young people would stay together for so many years — nor reach such giddy heights of success and commendation. I wasn't even sure they would survive the rehearsal when I heard and saw their director, puppeteer Diane Dupuy.

I am no stranger to directors and am familiar with the various methods used to wring the best performance from a cast. Some cajole, coax and sweet-talk; others adopt a lackadaisical attitude, pretending to allow the performers to direct themselves; then there are those like Diane who yell, stamp feet, threaten and demand absolute attention at all times. It is a perfectly legitimate method of getting results, but I was surprised and somewhat shocked by its use in this particular situation.

"Should you be yelling at them?" I asked. "After all, these kids are mentally retarded."

"They are performers," she told me. "They have a show to put on. Not one is being asked to do something he or she can't do or hasn't done before. All I demand is that they behave like professionals for the show's sake and for their own."

The Famous People Players use life-size puppets designed with special fluorescent materials in the likeness of celebrities or characters from musical works. In perfect synchronization to live or recorded music, the puppets are brought to life when invisible ultra-violet light is projected on them, while their black-clad animators provide movement to their various parts.

For instance, when the music for "The Impossible Dream" begins, the theatre darkens and from the wings minces a smiling, familiar, outrageously dressed Liberace who walks to a prop piano and sings to an "unreachable" star dangling above his head. After only a few seconds, the magic takes over and the audience is oblivious to the number of silent, blackened young people working Liberace's hands, feet and mouth or adjusting his candelabra. This was the act that gave the Famous People Players their first big break.

When Liberace was playing at the O'Keefe Centre in Toronto in 1975, Diane took the opportunity to tell him about her group. Liberace recalls the incident. "She said they were going to do a special performance at a convention for the mentally retarded and asked me to come along and watch. I went to that performance and was absolutely flabbergasted. It was funny. It was sad. It was serious. It ran the entire gamut of emotions. Then I contacted the people at the Las Vegas Hilton, who went up to Toronto to see them perform and they were immediately booked to be part of my engagement."

Before the Liberace connection, the group had worked hard perfecting their craft in a number of local shows, primarily at the Canadian National Exhibition in Toronto.

"At that time we could only handle about five minutes at a time," explained Diane. "That was about all our minds could hold. Our deal with the C.N.E. was that we had to do sixteen shows a day. It didn't cost them anything because our expenses were paid by an Opportunity for Youth grant. I wanted work training for us and it was good exposure. I also had to perform sixteen shows on my own, so that meant thirty-two shows a day. It was exhausting and we all lost a lot of weight, but we felt so fulfilled at the end of the day that I guess if they had asked us to clean up the midway, we would have done it. We had a lot of energy and we were very high on the company. Looking back, they were likely lousy shows we were giving at the C.N.E., but we were so proud. We used to come out and take bows and say, 'aren't we great?'"

Diane is a slim, dark-haired, rather vivacious woman with challenging eyes and an easy, infectious smile. She had been interested in puppetry as a very young girl. She found it a fascinating hobby and was even able to make a little money through local performances.

"I collected puppets like some kids collect stamps," says Diane. "When I was in school in Hamilton, I used to put on plays when I needed extra money. These were hand puppets and I would do political satire about government leaders and their foibles. I was very young and going through that 'what am I going to do with my life?' period, so I moved to Arizona to work in merchandising because I thought I might like to be a fashion buyer and go into the retail business. After two years, I came home realizing that this wasn't for me and went back to puppetry because it was the only thing I could do to make money. One day I put on a show for the handicapped at Sunny Place Centre in Toronto. I was so impressed with these people that I became a volunteer and very much involved. I did volunteer work up in Orillia at the Centre for the Mentally Retarded and that's where I realized that I had much more to offer than toilet training or taking the kids tobogganing. I wasn't fulfilling myself and I didn't think they were either; so I thought, 'Why not puppetry?' That's when I formed the Famous People Players."

Two years at conventions, the C.N.E. and the St. Lawrence Centre helped polish the performance and perfect the intricate techniques of handling life-size puppets in total darkness, but it was still a huge jump to Las Vegas.

In September 1975, with Liberace's support, Diane's no-nonsense direction and a great deal of courageous effort, the youngsters scored a hit and rave reviews in *Variety,* the American show business magazine. Many of the entertainment critics were unaware that most of the performers in the troupe were mentally retarded. As proof of their ability, they were invited back.

It was at this point, in February 1976, that *Man Alive* filmed the group preparing for their second Las Vegas engagement. Full size puppets of Barbra Streisand and Elvis Presley were added to the program. Rehearsals were intensified. Production values became more sophisticated. There was no place now for amateurish mix-ups. Famous People Players were now professional and Diane Dupuy intended to keep them that way.

At breaks in rehearsals I talked to some of the young people. One of them, Brenda — a large, pale girl with blonde hair — told me about her alternatives. She is shy and speaks hesitantly. Her eyes dart from behind her bangs when she's interested. "If Diane didn't lead the company, we would never learn these parts. We probably would be going to the workshop or at home, but I wouldn't like to go to the workshop. I like to come here and perform and do a lot of work."

"What's the workshop?"

"You go in and do shifts like making light fixtures or something. I don't think I would like it as much as Famous People Players 'cause you learn more at Famous People Players than you do in the workshop, I think."

"How old are you, Brenda?"

"I just turned twenty-two."

"Do you realize you're different from other twenty-two-year-old girls?"

"Yes, I understand."

"How would you explain that difference to people who don't know?"

"I would just say that I'm a slow learner and they have to realize that they have to be my friend. I realize that I'm like that, but if somebody can help me, I can do it very well — you know, teach me all the stuff and, if they don't teach me, I won't learn fast."

"And yet this is very exacting work you do here. It requires precise timing and co-ordination. It isn't easy, is it?"

"No, it isn't."

"Yet you're doing it very well. You must be very proud of yourself."

"Yes."

"Are you happy?"

Brenda beamed. "Oh, yes."

Tony looks like many eighteen-year-old boys. His hair is slightly unkempt and he has a promising beard. It is only when he speaks that you realize he is mentally handicapped. For Tony, taking direction in school was much different from taking direction from Diane.

"I always hated going to school. I liked to go out and play and do things my way all the time. I don't like people telling me to do this or that. I hated it. I just wanted to go out and play with my friends and have a good time."

"Most people wouldn't know you have a problem. How would you explain it to them?"

"Slow in reading and stuff like that. If you put a book in front of me, I won't be able to read it. But if you tell me to pick up a box, I probably can pick it up. But to read and to write has really been hard for me. I just can't do it."

"But you are very good working the puppets. It shows that if people take the time to work with you, you can do things well."

"That's what I've thought all the time. I always hated doing what other people said before, but not now."

"You can't do things your own way here. Diane tells you what to do."

"Exactly — and you have to do it."

"What's your role in the Liberace number?"

"The head and the body. There's three that operate the puppet. One does the feet, one does the hands and I stand up and do the body and the head."

"That must be hard, to work the body and the head and the mouth at the same time."

"I do it in a hood so nobody will know what I'm doing underneath. I mouth the words to myself so I can make like the puppet. I make a few mistakes sometimes. Like sometimes the hands will be playing here and I'm still talking there, so I have to move the body quickly."

Brenda, Tony and their fellow performers are in a very tough branch of show business indeed. Diane told me, "It is very hard work, very difficult. Black light is the most difficult technique I've ever experienced. You are working with a blind man's handicap. You can't see where you're going on the stage. You have to go by touch so your body co-ordination has to be almost perfect. It's a very dangerous technique because it's like walking a tightrope. You can't go off balance for one second. It is not easy at all."

The second Las Vegas appearance seemed even more important to Diane. She was extremely excited, her face alternately alive with anticipation and fear. In their dressing room moments before curtain call, she assembled the troupe and laid it on the line. Pacing back and forth, she said, "Now tonight — think! Don't move without thinking. Forethought always wins. Please remember that. Remember what you've been taught. If you go to reach for a prop and it isn't there, don't have a fit on stage. Now this one is very important because the last time you were in Las Vegas, nobody knew the Famous People Players. They didn't know what kind of show you had. They had no idea until that curtain went up what it was going to be like. But now they know. They expect a lot more from you than they did the first time. I know it's really tough because we have no more government support. The only way you people are going to survive from now on is working, getting jobs like this. Either this or you go into a workshop or an institution. So you're fighting for your lives out on that stage. I don't want you to forget that. You've got to please that audience and a Las Vegas audience is the toughest in the world. This isn't the St. Lawrence Centre. I'm telling you right now, this is a very important gig. Now check your props. Double check them. Check and check and check. Now break a leg, guys. Let's go!"

Once again the show was a success. Two shows a day for thirty-five days and rave reviews that left no doubt that this remarkable Canadian group was a highly professional and talented addition to the world of show business.

Back in Canada, however, money was still a problem. Without the massive government grants enjoyed by some other theatre companies, the Famous People Players had to rely solely on paid bookings and private donations to raise the needed funds.

"As the company gets more popular, the funding gets cut off," complained Diane. "You get people here who say, 'Well, you've been to Radio City Music Hall and CBS has assigned you to work in a *Movie of the Week* program and you're going on a trip to China. My God, you must be making a lot of money.' Not so. The National Ballet has done the same things and they're being given all sorts of money. Other people tell me, 'What you need is an elite board of directors like the ones who sit on the board at Stratford. They'll just get on the phone and you'll have all the money you want.' I think that stinks. It doesn't work. I wish people would look at history. We do have those boards in Canada and I see very sad companies. I don't see happy actors. It's a board thing. They manipulate. It's their project. They have no concern for people. They are running a huge deficit anyway, so the big shots must not be doing such a good job."

Though funding may be a problem, that doesn't prevent Famous People Players from risking new ventures. In 1977, they began performing with symphony orchestras across Canada, giving their unique black light magic to productions such as the Saint-Saëns' *Carnival of the Animals*. In 1980, they played Radio City Music Hall; scheduled for the 1983 season is a CBS television movie based on the group and entitled *Black Light: A Love Story*. The tour of China was a dream of Diane's for a number of years. The future, however, is uncertain. Especially for Diane, who explains:

"I'm going through different phases. Right now I feel I have to take a leap in some direction, whether it's with the company or something else. I've found that, if I don't grow, the company doesn't grow. It's especially important for this company to keep growing, so we have constantly to set goals for ourselves. I think we should go for bigger productions and adopt new styles. Perhaps we'll incorporate a live person on stage with the puppets or we'll get in a composer to write new music for a story line. We need to take more leaps and jumps and perhaps think more internationally. You never know whether you've made the right decision with the company until opening night and I get to a point at times where I'm scared to take risks any more. Sometimes I miss the young girl in me, the one who founded the company, the young rebel who had the big mouth, who really didn't care what she said. I do miss her. I guess she's mellowed.

"I think, if I did leave the company, I'd appoint a young nineteen-year-old to run the show. There's a lot to be said for not knowing what you're getting into. All you've got is dreams. As we get older, we have our dreams behind our eyelids, but we do nothing about them and that's sad. You worry when you get older about what other people think and that's not productive."

Diane's philosophy and approach to life has certainly affected the members of her troupe. In conversation they talk about goals and dreams, long range hopes, special wishes. One dreams of learning to read and write. Another's goal is to graduate from operating a puppet's feet to working the head. They all have learned the thrill and satisfaction of achievement through their own efforts and will continue to do so as they perform increasingly difficult acts across Canada and around the world.

Diane Dupuy is a hard taskmaster, but in reality more loving than many of us. While much of society views the mentally retarded as less than human, objects of pity and burdens of charity, she refuses to accept conventional wisdom.

"A common belief," she points out, "is that the mentally retarded are hindered or unable to succeed and not capable of learning. The Famous People Players are no longer hindered, because they have succeeded. They've reached for that 'unreachable star' and in so doing have developed mentally, physically and spiritually. They've proved to themselves that they are capable and it's nice to know they've proven it to others. I can only do so much. Once that curtain goes up, it's out of my hands. It's up to them — and they've never let me down."

When we define the limits of another person's ability, we are always wrong. None of us is wise enough to judge the potential of others. The Davids, Leslies, Brendas and Tonys of this world will always exceed the expectations of those who measure worth by graphs, charts and percentages.

Assistance to the mentally retarded takes many forms. I believe that underlying all our efforts should be the realization that, given a climate of acceptance, understanding and love, their potential knows few bounds.

It is the same for all of us.

LIFE VERSUS
RATIONAL SUICIDE

Throughout history, one of mankind's greatest concerns has been death. Innumerable books, essays and sermons have been written about it and every family has thought deeply about death as it approached a beloved member. And yet, at the very moment that we face its reality, it is as though we want to put it out of sight. We find ourselves embarrassed, almost tongue-tied, and very frightened. We know that we are going to die but we handle the privileged information awkwardly.

Fortunately, several modern writers have brought the subject out of the closet. One of these is Elizabeth Kübler Ross whose *On Death and Dying*, written in the late 1960s, has popularized the phrase "death with dignity" which has been used in seminars and conferences, television documentaries and church sermons around the world.

Our awareness of the subject stems in part from publicity

surrounding certain technical advances that enable doctors to prolong a threatened life. Commonly referred to as life support systems or heroic measures, these modern scientific methods, while increasing our life span, have called into question the quality of that life itself. As Hilaire Belloc succinctly puts it,

> Of old when men lay sick and sorely tried,
> The doctors gave them physic and they died,
> But here's a happier age, for now we know
> Both how to make men sick, and keep them so!

I remember seeing a cartoon in *The New Yorker* magazine which showed an old man in a hospital bed surrounded by medical equipment, attached to wires and tubes, hooked up to various machines and pumps. He was being interviewed by a reporter who leaned over the bed with his microphone to ask, "And to what, sir, do you attribute your longevity?"

A growing number of people today believe that new medical techniques are not prolonging life so much as they are prolonging death. They advocate a speedy, premeditated termination of one's life at a time of one's own choosing and refer to this process as "rational suicide".

In Canada it is estimated that over two thousand people commit suicide each year. How many of these suicides are performed calmly and deliberately to escape prolonged debilitating illness is not known. We do know that organizations are spreading throughout Europe and North America to advise terminally ill people in the techniques of taking their own lives.

Perhaps the best known group is *Exit*, a British organization formerly known as the Voluntary Euthanasia Society. Founded in 1935, it was for many years a quaint, somewhat irrelevant body with constant financial worries and very little political influence. Its purpose over the years was to encourage legislation to allow the incurably ill to die with dignity, its tenet being that such people should not be kept alive by doctors against their will. This passive euthanasia was as far as the original society went. But, in 1977, Nicholas Reed became *Exit*'s secretary and began a much more aggressive campaign. Also joining the society at that time were Dr. Colin Brewer and Derek Humphrey. Dr. Brewer had written an article in *World Medicine* admitting that for humanitarian reasons he had attempted to kill a terminally ill cancer patient, but had failed. The patient subsequently died of the disease. Humphrey had just published *Jean's Way*, a book in which he told how he had helped his wife Jean commit suicide to prevent a lingering and painful death.

Although the Suicide Act of 1961 in England made it no longer illegal to attempt suicide, it is still a criminal offence to "aid, abet, counsel or procure" someone else to do it. The maximum penalty is fourteen years' imprisonment. Brewer and Humphrey were questioned by police and, although they admitted administering drugs to the deceased in both cases, it was ruled that there was insufficient evidence to prosecute either of them.

A division then occurred in *Exit*'s membership between those who advocated passive euthanasia and those who, like Reed, Brewer and Humphrey, pushed for legalizing "mercy killings". The entire issue came to a head and caused sensational press coverage when Reed announced that *Exit* would be publishing a 'do-it-yourself' book on rational suicide. Brewer was largely responsible for the first draft but the booklet had to be published in Scotland, where laws regarding suicide are more lenient than in England.

The booklet gave detailed instructions on preparing for your death, such as selecting appropriate clothes, putting on your favorite taped music or radio program, arranging the time to ensure at least sixteen hours of total privacy and, if doing it in a hotel room, being sure to hang a 'do not disturb' sign on the door and to leave a note nearby thanking the manager.

The booklet highly recommended using drugs and gave a list of lethal sedatives by chemical name, brand name, tablet strength and suggested dose. While admitting they were second choices, the booklet also listed such methods as weed-killers, plastic bags, dropping electrical appliances into the bath water, jumping from tall buildings, shooting and knifing.

It was promptly criticized by the more traditional members of *Exit*, who called it "ghoulish, crude and amateurish". It was, however, a great shot in the arm for the organization. Since only members were allowed a copy, seven thousand new applications came in almost immediately.

Meanwhile, Derek Humphrey, whose book about helping his wife die had become a bestseller in five languages and the subject of a television film, emigrated to Santa Monica, California. He and his second wife, Ann Wickett, formed *Hemlock*, an organization supporting active euthanasia. At the time, Humphrey was quick to point out that *Hemlock* wanted to speak only to the terminally ill or to those individuals who wished to consider the option of planned death. Suicide, he pointed out, is usually a response to severe emotional, traumatic or financial pressures and is a problem better left to psychiatrists and suicide-prevention centres. *Hemlock* is set up to help those who have not long to live and to enable them to die in the manner they choose. He continued: "Of course, in law, what *Hemlock* is talking about *is* suicide, but what validity does that legal definition have in real human terms when a terminally ill person is going to die soon anyway? There is evidence that a growing number of people want to think about whether they should accelerate their deaths."

Humphrey is apparently right. When I talked to him in the fall of 1982, he already had six thousand members in the United States and although he has not encouraged them, over five hundred in Canada. A new book, *A Right Way to Die*, is being sold to members. It deals with the subject in a documentary style and avoids possible lawsuits by not giving direct advice or counsel. Humphrey told me that he was not interested in setting up *Hemlock* in other countries, but remained friendly with Canadian interest groups in Quebec and British Columbia.

Suicide has been a matter of controversy since ancient times. In the sixth century B.C., Pythagoras opposed it. "We are," he said, "chattels of God and without his command we have no right to make our escape." Plato rejected it because: "Man is a soldier of God and must remain at his post until he calls". Aristotle claimed that man had a civic duty and suicide deprived the State of his services. Sophocles was among the first to accept suicide as a release from life's problems and Seneca wrote, "Against all the injuries of life I have the refuge of death. If I can choose between a death of torture and one that is simple and easy, why should I not select the latter?"

The Old Testament, when it records such suicides as those of Saul and his armor-bearer, does so without condemnation. For the first three centuries after Jesus, the Stoic philosophy of suicide prevailed: if a person felt he must leave life, then he should.

Though Josephus, the first century historian, condemned suicide outright in all circumstances, he still counseled that his trapped garrison of forty men draw lots and kill each other rather than be captured by the Romans. He then cleverly drew the last lot and talked his potential killer into surrendering. The mass suicide of the Zealot garrison of Masada in 73 A.D. indicates that not all Jews at that time thought suicide dishonorable. Present-day orthodox Jewry condemns outright any consideration of suicide or euthanasia.

Although neither the Old nor the New Testament condemns

suicide explicitly, the Koran declares it a crime worse than homicide.

Then came Augustine (A.D. 354-430) who stated that suicide was a "detestable and damnable wickedness" on the ground that it prevented man from any possibility of repentance. He maintained that life was a gift from God and suicide rejected that gift. The body of the suicide was refused Christian burial and, in some instances, was buried with stones on the head and stakes through the heart. Thomas Aquinas (A.D. c.1225-74) maintained that it was for God to determine when life should end and, up to the present day, the Roman Catholic church has steadfastly disapproved of suicide.

Attitudes to suicide among Protestants are now less rigid than they were. Certainly the principle of assisted suicide, or passive euthanasia, has been defended by many Protestant churchmen.

After the Revolution in 1789, anti-suicide legislation was repealed in France and most countries soon followed suit. England, in 1961, was the last to do this.

With Japan is associated the custom of sippuko or hara-kiri, ceremonial suicide by dagger, practised by the warrior class when disgraced or sentenced to death. Although compulsory hara-kiri is illegal, voluntary hara-kiri occurs even today.

Buddhism generally condemns suicide except in instances of painful and incurable disease. In *The Dialogues of Buddha*, two cases are related of holy men suffering from incurable disease and who, committing suicide, still reached *nirvana*, a release from the endless cycle of reincarnation. Islamic law leaves no doubt: "Whosoever shall kill himself shall suffer in the fire of hell and shall be excluded from heaven for ever."

There are many old sagas from Iceland, Greenland and Siberia that tell of a society in which suicide is accepted as right when life has no more to offer. The ancient Celts actually believed that those who died of senility or disease went to hell. They called it "spoiling" and, to prevent it, one committed suicide. In 17th-century Brittany, anyone who had an incurable disease could petition the priest for the holy stone. When the family was gathered around, last rites were administered and the oldest relative would then raise the heavy stone above the ailing person's head and let it drop.

Anthropologists tell us about Polynesian, Melanesian, Eskimo, African, Burmese and other communities in which suicide is common and generally acceptable when used to avoid senility and death by disease.

In talking with many doctors privately and in front of the television camera, I have found that most of them have encountered awkward problems of passive euthanasia. Decisions not to resuscitate, not to feed certain newborn infants, not to administer drugs which will hasten death, all involve difficult ethical problems on which there is still no consensus. From an ethical point of view, most doctors have worked out their own individual positions on the matter. However, legal difficulties remain; except in circumstances of extreme necessity, such as saving one's life by taking another, the law quite simply prohibits taking a step deliberately calculated to bring life to an end. This does not mean that active euthanasia is never practised; it is just not admitted and it would be foolish indeed for a doctor to do so.

Dr. Brewer, whose public admission landed him in the courts, implies that the practice is widespread. "There can be little doubt that our present methods [of euthanasia] are clumsy, inefficient and badly organized. This is partly because the subject is not well taught at medical schools, most students having to rely on rather haphazard oral tradition. All I had were a few hints about inducing cardiac failure with a fast intravenous infusion, or large doses of morphine or insulin. The main reason, though, for the inefficiency is probably that about seventy percent of [terminally ill] people die in hospital. If any of them have to be killed, they have to be killed in public — which leads to all sorts of problems. Consequently, the art of killing patients has been somewhat neglected. It flourishes only in general practice where a G.P. attending a terminally ill patient in the privacy of his home can administer a lethal dose without worrying whether half a dozen nurses are looking over his shoulder, and without having to explain why he gave 100 mg of morphine in a single intravenous dose."

There is no doubt that fear of prosecution prevents many doctors from actively assisting patients to die. Lord Donald Soper, the fiery member of Britain's House of Lords, told us he wanted the legal responsibility taken away from the medical profession by enacting protective legislation. "If mercy killing were made legal, it would be a tremendous advance from the ridiculous condition we have now. I believe some mistakes would be made but I also believe it would be a tremendous advance. The responsibility should be shared by those who have to sit by the bedside using medical and professional advice.

Mercy killing is constantly being practised subversively and under cover by the medical profession now. I just want them to be excused from having to play God."

More than any other reason, the moral dilemma of "playing God" is seen to prevent doctors from practising active euthanasia.

On a recent CBC *Take 30* television program, when host Harry Brown asked his guests whether or not doctors were "forcing patients to live", Dr. Michael Gordon of Baycrest Centre for Geriatric Care in Toronto responded with these words:

"It is not so much whether we force people to live by giving treatment so a patient lives or withholding treatment so the patient will die. I think the question is more what will the living consist of, and that is the most difficult question for anybody to answer. There's a tendency for each of us to project our own feelings as to what 'quality of life' is and I've heard young physicians talk about somebody who is unconscious and ask why do we treat that person, because their life has no quality. Well, I don't know what the quality of life is to a person who is unconscious. For all I know they may be listening to Tchaikovsky in their comatose state. It is very hard to project 'quality' and 'usefulness' in terms of determining whose life is worth prolonging.

"I have dealt with many extremely elderly people who have had serious illnesses, especially when there is pain and suffering, who will often say, 'I'm too old, let me go.' Basically I feel what they're saying to me is 'Tell me it isn't so.' That there is still hope and that something can be done. I can give hundreds of anecdotes of people who had requested death, who later survived their illness and who are now probably enjoying life as much as anybody here. I think we have to temper very carefully the particular request for death, what the circumstance is and at what time it is being asked for, especially if it is during a rather acute, sudden illness that has a certain degree of suffering and pain."

On the same program, Eleanor Wasserman, a nurse-clinician from Mount Sinai Hospital in Toronto, talked about the importance of terminally ill patients being allowed to live out their last days at home. Since the primary objective was to deliver the patients from pain, this could be done in the comfort of their own familiar surroundings by self-administered drugs. This brought up an interesting point with regard to self-destruction. "All our patients have lots of drugs and as we go through over two thousand cases, we find very few who had their drugs at home and who went on to commit suicide. I think this says something about the patient's attitude. People don't want to die. When there's life, there's hope and this is very important to patients, even when they have the means [of death] at their bedside."

The accuracy of the remarks made by Dr. Gordon and Eleanor Wasserman was proven to me in a series of interviews I did in the palliative care unit of a Winnipeg hospital, where I talked to the doctor in charge about preparing patients for the inevitability of their deaths.

The hospital staff had worked out a very careful and compassionate system to enable patients to talk openly about their approaching demise. Family members, attending nurses, chaplains and trusted friends were often involved in bringing into the open the subject that, while on everyone's mind, was so often avoided. I asked the doctor if he could recommend a patient for me to interview, who would talk comfortably on camera about death. He recommended an elderly woman whose terminal cancer was at a very advanced stage and who was "completely resigned to the fact" that she would die in a few months.

The interview in her hospital room went like this:

Question: This is quite a place, isn't it?

Answer: Oh, it's wonderful. I've lived right here in Winnipeg all my life and didn't know it existed.

Q: Have you been in other hospitals?

A: Yes, I had my operation about a year ago, then I took care of myself at home.

Q: What's different about this place?

A: I can't give anything specific but they're right here when you want them. Anything you want is done. I had almost given up. I'm pretty near the end of my treatments now and I'm feeling much better. It's a wonderful place.

Q: Tell me how you spend your day.

A: Well, after I wake up and the nurses come in, we have our breakfast and then I read the *Tribune.*

Q: You like to keep up on the news, do you?

A: Oh my, yes. I read everything in the paper. You never know. I read it from front to back. There might be a cure for me that someone has found. I don't want to miss it.

Q: I've talked with your doctor and he said that you and he have had long discussions about your illness. He said you are

44

quite prepared for what's going to happen...that you know there is no cure.

A: Yes, well, he's such a nice person, I don't like to hurt his feelings. I know he doesn't want me to worry. He's so busy and kind, I don't want to worry him either. But you can never give up hope, can you?

This did not sound to me like someone who had resigned herself to her imminent death and I found it interesting that she felt impelled to tell her doctor what she thought he wanted to hear and yet was quite willing to confess to me — on camera — and to a sound man, lighting man, and cameraman that she was actively searching for news of a cure.

For this same program, I filmed a brief interview with a woman who, I had been told, had only a few weeks left. We talked about her illness and the care she was receiving in this special unit. That weekend she expected to spend her last few days at home with her family, so I was very surprised five months later to receive a letter from her, asking when her interview would be going on the air. I wrote back telling her how pleased I was to hear from her and explained that the processing, editing, writing, filming other items and the general preparation of a television program took a great deal of time. Her reply was terse and to the point: "I wish you would hurry up. I've never seen myself on television and you may remember, I haven't got much time."

Later, I was touched to hear from a member of the nursing staff that this patient had indeed watched the program when it was finally aired and was happy to "see herself on television" before she died. A moving testament to one individual's tremendous will to live.

Since it is generally conceded that pain can be controlled in at least 95% of terminal cases, one might wonder why suicide is even a consideration. One reason seems to be the desire to have control over one's life, to be able to opt out when the quality of that life has disintegrated.

In the course of producing a program on rational suicide, *Man Alive* talked with several people who expressed this view. One woman said, "I would like to see the possibility of a death like that of Socrates. You know, the taking of hemlock or the equivalent. You could have all your friends to a lovely party, then quietly retire to your room and take the potion or whatever and die perfectly happy, then go on to the next stage — whatever that may be. That's my ideal for the future."

Another woman told us, "I don't want to be looked after in my old age — to have my bottom wiped — not to be able to move — humiliated — standing around naked in the nursing home — pushed around — and being a nuisance to other people. I would want then to die. I've written out a statement and I've told my children — please don't keep me alive when I'm a nuisance."

One man who supported suicide told us we would understand if we had seen his mother as she approached death. "Every morning she would wake up and say, 'Oh, God, you haven't let me go yet'. That went on for two years. It was very hard to watch."

It is indeed hard to watch someone suffer. Yet there are those who see worth in suffering, value in pain. The noted Austrian psychoanalyst, Viktor Frankl, maintains that "suffering and trouble belong to life as much as fate and death. None of these can be subtracted from life without destroying its meaning. To subtract trouble, death, fate and suffering from life would mean stripping it of its form and shape. Only under the hammer blows of fate, in the white heat of suffering, does life gain shape and form. There is achievement in suffering."

This may be so, but in our modern society we prefer not to suffer if we can avoid it. Doctors pride themselves on eliminating pain from our final days, so that most debates about euthanasia centre around the idea of a "good death" — one without pain or suffering. If pain can be eliminated from approaching death, we must again ask why it should be desirable to hasten the end.

Most of us who have visited hospitals, nursing homes or geriatric residences have heard the statement, "I just don't want to be a burden to anyone." Our institutions are filled with people who feel they would be a burden to others if they remained at home. There was a day when this burden was accepted by many families as a normal responsibility.

I believe that the fear of being a burden causes more thought of suicide on the part of the elderly than any physical pain and that the practice of both passive and active euthanasia is more tolerated today by relatives and the medical profession because they, too, want the burden lifted either from themselves or from society in general.

During the production of our program on rational suicide, I visited the Royal Victoria Hospital in Montreal. One unit of the hospital is devoted to the care of the terminally ill of all ages. Here life is not prolonged artificially but patients *are* given the most effective pain control available. Carefully trained volunteers and hospital staff work with the patients, who remain living at home as long as possible. It was there I met a most remarkable woman, Jean Cameron. Jean had helped found the unit and was for many years a social worker with patients and families coping with death. When I met her, she had already known for three years that she, too, had terminal cancer and though under massive doses of morphine to control pain, still counseled and gave advice about a subject she now knew only too well.

Later, in her small but comfortable apartment, over a plate of her fresh-baked cookies, I asked if at this advanced stage of her illness she had ever considered ending her life, or asking someone else to end it.

"I wouldn't have done anything myself to end it," she affirmed, "so I wouldn't have asked anyone else to. By committing suicide I might have taken one kind of burden away from the people who are caring for me, but it would be a small burden in comparison to what I might leave them. When you commit suicide, you leave a kind of legacy of guilt, of self-reproach. I find in my work that when there is a suicide in the family, this guilt can last a lifetime. I wouldn't want to do that to anybody."

"But, Jean, you are terminally ill. You're dying of cancer. How does one handle the knowledge that death is imminent?"

"It takes time to come to terms with this news. It comes gradually. First of all comes the disease, then the hope that the disease isn't going to spread. But when the disease does spread, you have to work through all your feelings. You feel first of all that this can't be true. I was working in a palliative care unit among people who were dying of cancer the very day I had my own diagnosis. It was very difficult for me. I just couldn't believe it. Here I am among these people. I looked around the ward and thought, 'Am I going to end up in one of these beds too?' I didn't really believe it."

"There must come a moment when you know it is true."

"Yes, there came a time when I was told there would be no hope of a cure. It was difficult to take but I was fortunate in a way. You see, because of my work I have seen people die. I know death *can* be easy, it *can* be peaceful. There are times when it is painful, but it doesn't have to be, even when one is dying of cancer."

"You obviously don't think much of these groups that advocate rational suicide. What do you think their increasing popularity says about our society?"

"I think it's rather a terrible and terrifying thing. I think it distorts all our values. It distorts what is important in life, what is beautiful, what is good. I think when you love people, you want to help them. I don't think you want to hasten their departure from the world."

"These groups and their members consider hastening the dying's departure as a loving thing to do."

"From a healthy distance, I suppose these things in theory seem practical. I can understand a person saying, 'I don't want to live through a terminal illness, I don't want to become a burden, I don't want any of these things.' But, you know, it's a bit like old age. A younger person does not want to get old or feeble. Maybe some would rather end life than reach that stage. But the older we get, the more distant that becomes and we don't feel old just yet, a little later perhaps. I think an awful lot of it is fear of things we don't know. We have this awful bogey about people dying of cancer. Almost all of us can remember an older relative who has died in excruciating pain. We have this mental image still. But this was before the use of powerful pain killers, before there was enough knowledge to help people with symptom control."

"Cancer itself has a horrible image, hasn't it? Some people seem to feel it's catching. A person with cancer is almost treated like a leper."

"Yes, I've encountered this. I had rheumatic fever when I was young. I've also had a heart attack. I could talk quite freely about that to people and be accepted fine, but when I developed cancer there was a completely different reaction; there was a drawing back. There were people who avoided contact with me. It was their fear and it is a terrible thing. I heard about this from patients and I wondered about it and then it was happening to me. They avoid you because they are afraid and I think how terrible it is for them. You feel as though you want to help them with their fear, even though you are distressed yourself, because some day something like this may happen to them."

"What part does your faith play in all this? I can see a person asking, 'God, why me?' Some would feel a betrayal by God."

"I think it's the very opposite for me. I think it has given me a challenge to prove my faith. It has given me a task to rise above it all. There are times when I am very depressed. I don't want to give the idea that I'm floating on some cloud of happiness in this state. There are times when the task is very difficult and the days are very dark. These days do pass and when I come out on the other side, through the worst of them, I've learned a little."

I was very impressed by Jean's calm and optimistic demeanor. This vital woman who was now reduced to shuffling slowly around her apartment in a walker, whose hands had become almost black from her disease, still nourished a considerable amount of hope for the future. I asked her, "How can you maintain hope? Here you are with this terminal illness. You know you are going to die soon. Where is the hope?"

"Hope does not die, Roy. Hope is something that changes from time to time through the different experiences that one has. At the beginning of my disease I did hope that it wouldn't spread, but it did. Now hope has to be something different."

"What is it for you now?"

Jean smiled. "Hope is what happened a few weeks ago. I was planting bulbs in my garden just the way I have done for many years, although now the holes were being dug by a kind friend because with these hands I couldn't quite manage it. Other friends came by, looked at me. One said, 'Why on earth are you doing that? You know you're too sick. You know you're too weak. Why are you still planting bulbs?' "

"It was a fair question. You may not see them come up."

"Aha! That was the very thing they were thinking, but not saying. But the answer to that is very simple. I love the garden. I love the flowers that grow there and I know they will come up in the spring and that they will be beautiful. If I'm there to see them, it will be a joy, a gift and I'm looking forward to that. But even if I'm not there, other people will see them. Other people will enjoy them. I helped to make that possible and that gives me a special kind of feeling. This is the kind of hope that I have."

"Do you feel the pressure of time?"

"Throughout my illness I have felt the pressure of time. I've felt there may not be much time and I've become impatient about doing things. I've had to learn not to be. I have begun to look at time in a different way. I've begun to appreciate the time I have. I have more time now. I have time to sit at my window and feed the birds and the squirrels. I have time to appreciate things in a way I never did before. The first time I noticed this was quite soon after I was told I was going to die. It was early spring and there was the last unexpected snowfall of the season. I looked out the window at the snow and I felt this tremendous urge to rush outside. I stood in the snow and felt and saw the snowflakes drifting down on me and it was a beautiful experience. I was enjoying it in a way I never had before and somehow this registered in my mind. I can still remember that particular day very vividly. I think of it sometimes when things are going wrong or something is distressing me. I remember that it was something special and, you see, if I hadn't had cancer, if I hadn't known I was going to die, I wouldn't have given that snowstorm a second glance."

"You'll be leaving behind so much because of the lives you have touched. You have helped so many people over the years. This must give you a certain amount of satisfaction."

"It works both ways. I carried on with my bereavement work even after I became quite ill. People would say to me, 'How can you keep doing this? Don't you find it terribly depressing?' It was the exact opposite of that. You see, when you are faced with dying, you are faced with the loss of not just one person, but of everyone and everything that is precious and dear in your life. This is one of the very hard things about dying, having to say goodbye. As death comes closer, you notice that people who care are looking increasingly sad and this is an added burden. I used to feel, 'What on earth am I doing to these people? I'm powerless to prevent it, but I'm devastating people's lives.' I was quite egocentric about them. I felt *they* would never recover. Yet I've worked with people who have been bereaved. I've listened to them over a long period of time. Sometimes months, sometimes years, and I've seen that they do recover. I've seen them take up new activities again, start new interests, recall old ones. I've also realized that they don't forget the person who has died and this is good as far as I'm concerned. But life for those who are left can also be good again. They can gradually stop thinking about that brief time in life that is illness and dying. They can remember the good things that happened, the joyful things and, when they do that, they recover. Grief is a price we pay for having loved somebody. Love is worth the price of pain and so pain is not so terrible after all."

"What are our responsibilities as relatives or friends of a dying person? What should we do?"

"I think the most important thing is to let them know that

you care. Many people are afraid to approach someone who is dying, because they're embarrassed. They don't know what to say. It doesn't matter what you say. It matters that you care. Once we know somebody cares for us, that's the most important thing of all."

"This may be a hard question to answer, Jean, but what is it that sustains you from day to day?"

"Love, faith, trust. I never know what tomorrow may bring, any more than you do. Sometimes it brings all kinds of joyful things still in my life. I didn't know that I was going to meet you and that is a joyful thing that has happened today. Who knows what tomorrow will bring?"

After the *Man Alive* program on rational suicide — entitled "Leaving Early" — was broadcast, the CBC conducted a survey among our viewers. A number of statements were made about the subject and the audience was asked to agree or disagree.

It was interesting to discover that only 28% thought that people should have the right to choose when to end their lives but that 49% thought terminally ill people should have this privilege; 38% said that people who are asked by another person to help end his or her life should not be held legally responsible for that person's death, but 56% said that only the laws of nature can decide when a person's life is to end; 70% thought that the decision to end a person's life must involve that person's family and doctor and 73% said that the trouble with suicide advocacy groups is that some people may be persuaded to end their lives when they are mixed up or confused; 61% did think that a service such as *Exit* provides would be useful to many terminally ill persons in our society.

We were pleased to see that only 21% of our audience hoped that in future *Man Alive* would stay away from the subject.

I would guess that most of us, at some time in our lives, especially if we have suffered severe pain or anguish or watched a loved one suffer, have wondered about the option of suicide. The fact that most people don't deliberately end their lives even when facing desperate circumstances indicates to me an attitude of reverence for life and self. Respect for human life is so fundamental to our society that care must continually be taken to assure its preservation. When we say that someone's life is not worth saving, then we devalue everyone's life, including our own.

While we can understand and appreciate the Derek Humphreys of this world, who work tirelessly for humane and compassionate "exits", surely it is the Jean Camerons who really show us how to live and how to die with dignity.

THE QUIET INVASION
AND THE MAN WHO WAITS

The quiet invasion was the Chinese invasion and takeover of Tibet in 1950. The man who waits in exile in India is the Dalai Lama, spiritual leader of more than six million Tibetans.

In Toronto in 1980, I was able to interview the Dalai Lama. He was in the middle of an extensive trip which was to include visits to Hawaii, Japan and South Korea. The aim of the tour was to visit Tibetan communities scattered throughout the world and to discuss the various Buddhist traditions represented in the host countries. Interviewing the Dalai Lama was an extraordinary experience for me and one I faced with some trepidation. But I must begin with the background to his story.

Tibet has always been a land of mystery, the real world's Shangri-La. In James Hilton's novel *Lost Horizon*, the first glimpse of this forbidden country is striking: "The floor of the valley, hazily distant, welcomed the eye with greenness; sheltered from winds, and surveyed rather than dominated by the lamasery. It looked ... a delightfully favoured place, though ... its community must be completely isolated by the lofty and sheerly unscalable ranges on the further side." This could easily be a description of Tibet — at least before 1950.

Nestled in a green valley at the heart of the Himalayas is Lhasa, the capital and once home of the Dalai Lama. His lamasery is huge, but seems part of the topography. The stone used to build the walls was drawn from the surrounding mountains and the hues of grey and green blend into the background. The area is completely surrounded by mountains. On the other side lie China, the U.S.S.R. and India, all of which have played a large part in the history of this mysterious and strategic land, only recently made accessible to the west.

The Tibetans of the seventh and eighth centuries A.D. were among the most feared warriors in Central Asia until the arrival of Buddhism. This religion of peace brought about a complete ideological and spiritual revolution, so that by the fourteenth century, Tibetans had become supreme pacifists. In A.D. 821, China and Tibet had inscribed a stone, in both of their languages, laying out the border and guaranteeing its preservation. This was one of the few times that Tibet had become involved in international law. In the tenth century, the native religion — Bön — came back into prominence, breaking the nation into petty principalities, some faithful to Bön, some to Buddhism and some to exotic blends of the two. Bön was based on a cult of gods of the atmosphere, the earth and the underworld. Their leader/kings were considered manifestations of the god of the sky; their priests were soothsayers. Their worship included blood sacrifices and their faith was not originally based on sacred doctrine or literature. Many of these elements were transmuted into the unique form of Buddhism practised in Tibet.

One man enabled the country to unite again. Sakya Pandit, a man of great learning, persuaded the nation of the benefits of Buddhism and created, in the person of his nephew Phagpa, the first priest/ruler of the Sakya sect.

Sakya lamahood, or priesthood, is hereditary and twenty-eight successors ruled Tibet until 1358, when Changchub Gyalsten dethroned the twenty-eighth Sakya ruler and created his own line, which ruled for nearly eighty years. Internal strife and constant civil war ravaged the land. Yet China still did not involve itself with these troubles, considering that Tibet was not under its domain.

In the fourteenth century, Tsong Khapa — a lama opposed to the current leadership — established the reformation sect, the Geluk-pa. This newest Budhhist sect soon became the most popular, spreading its influence over much of Mongolia and China. The Mongol ruler, Altan Khan, named the head lama, Sonam Gyasto, the "Dalai" Lama. "Dalai" is the Mongolian word for ocean. The Geluk-pa sect continued to grow in power. In the 1640s, with Mongolian help, the fifth Dalai Lama established supremacy. Tibet had now reached internal accord and henceforth had to fight to retain independence. In 1791, the Gurkhas of Nepal invaded and were driven off by the large Chinese army and the small Tibetan force. This gave the Chinese a favored position within Tibet. The ninth, tenth, eleventh and twelfth Dalai Lamas did not reach maturity and China used the opportunity to become the power behind the throne, a power which lasted for fifty years.

The Limbus of Nepal and the Sikhs of India invaded but were unsuccessful, even though the Chinese army no longer lent support. In 1855, Nepal invaded again and won extra-territorial rights, which they maintained until the 1950s. In 1863, China invaded and annexed the territory of Gyarong. The British, wishing to establish trade relations with Tibet, went to China for permission, thinking the country was part of the Chinese Dominion. When Tibet refused the trade pact, the west learned how little power China really held. Britain successfully sent a military mission to impose the trade agreement. In 1910, China invaded and the Dalai Lama of the time fled to India. In 1912, Tibetans expelled the Chinese. The Dalai Lama returned. The present Dalai Lama has said, "With that expulsion, Tibet became completely independent and from 1912 until the Chinese invasion in 1950, neither the Chinese nor any other state had any power whatever in Tibet." The International Commission of Jurists' report to the United Nations on "The Question of Tibet and the Rule of Law" upheld this position.

The Tibetans formed their own foreign policy, taking no part in the Sino-Japanese War of 1937-1945, forbidding the transportation of war supplies during World War II, and participating as an independent country at the Asian conference in Delhi in the late 1950s. Tibetan passports were recognized the world over.

In 1947, a suspected Chinese-backed coup was thwarted. In 1949, all Chinese government agencies in Tibet were evicted due to the communist revolution in China itself. On October 7,

1950, the Chinese again invaded. They called themselves libera-
tors, supposedly freeing Tibet from its feudal system and from
American and English imperialists. Yet the Dalai Lama has
stated that there were only six westerners at that time involved
in Tibetan commerce.

By 1954, these peaceful people had begun to revolt. Their
army — pitted against one of the largest in the world — consisted of about eight thousand rifles, fifty pieces of artillery, two
hundred and fifty mortars and two hundred machine guns. All
of these weapons were purchased by the thirteenth Dalai Lama
who, although a devout Buddhist, was more of a realist than his
fellows. He faced opposition from a faithful people who thought
the gods would protect them. They performed "magdogs", war
prevention ceremonies, and believed that the danger had been
averted right up to the time when the superior Chinese weap-
onry apparently defeated the gods. The Tibetans then reached
the philosophical conclusion that their defeat was the natural
and logical outcome of collective "Karma", their word for Fate.

As has been said, the Chinese viewed themselves as libera-
tors, freeing the Tibetans from a feudal society. Exiled Tibetans
deny this vehemently, remembering a society they still cherish.
Before 1950, however, the monasteries indeed resembled feudal
estates. They owned approximately a third of all the land and
employed the neighboring population to do the manual farm
work. The monks themselves were forbidden to do this, for to
farm meant killing insects and Buddhism dictates that all followers, particularly the monks, must respect life. The monasteries themselves were full of gold and precious stones, but
these represented gifts to the gods, presented by people wishing
to ensure a safe transition from life to death. Even though the
teachings of the Buddha are rational, mystery and superstition
played a major part in the life of the Tibetans.

Bribery was a commonplace occurrence but, to the Tibetans,
bribery — with no malice attached — was simply a sign of
generosity. The social structure was strictly defined. Nobility
was attained through inheritance alone. The commoner could
climb the social ladder in four ways: being appointed an abbot;
being named the reincarnation of a high lama; being promoted
to the civil post of treasurer, a most respected position; or
through trade. By making money, a Tibetan could purchase the
outward symbols of nobility and thus command a great deal of
respect. Most of the lay population was illiterate.

Tibetan society had not advanced into the twentieth century

and the effects of western industrialization were minimal. As a people, Tibetans' lives were based on faith, and the fact that the monks' lifestyle was above their own and schooling unobtainable seemed only natural, for the monks were the keepers of the faith.

The commoners' lot, however, should not be seen in the same way we view impoverished people in the West. An entirely different attitude to life existed. Famine was virtually unknown. The produce in times of plenty was distributed so as to protect everyone in times of need. The few social amenities extant were open to all. All entertainment was free. The ministrations of a doctor or a monk were there for the asking. There was still pride in self at the lowliest level. On the one hand was a severely unequal society, on the other the protection of people on the lowest rung. At the root of this idea lay their religion. Everything in life was centred in faith. Their medicine, for example, was holistic, a mixture of psychotherapy, astrology and herbal remedies. All disease was deemed to have three roots: lack of good luck, karma, or disease-giving demons. As the Tibetan writer Dawa Norbu says, "We Tibetans have for centuries been exploring the human mind, while the so-called advanced nations have been exploring the world. Our world is internal and infinite; theirs is external and finite."

Their judicial system was unique. They attached little importance to law as such. In fact, officials did not investigate crimes other than murder, unless petitioned. When a trial actually took place, it was justice in the purest sense that was emphasized. If both sides in a dispute suffered, both would be awarded recompense in proportion to their suffering. If no clear or "just" picture emerged through testimony, the "hat tria", flogging and testifying, was used as a last resort. There were relatively few people with any knowledge of the law and there was but one major legal text, called the *Trim Yig Shelche Chusum* or the Thirteen Decrees. This book emerged in the seventh century and has remained virtually unchanged. In the early part of this century, the thirteenth Dalai Lama outlawed capital punishment, but mutilation, though no longer practised, still appears in the book out of respect for the past.

The Tibetans believe that every success must be followed by failure, every triumph by tragedy. This attitude seems to temper the extreme emotions of great joy or abject sorrow. All life is formed of these cycles and an attitude of "this too shall pass" enables them to look at life with equanimity. Consistency in self is a goal for all. Any duality in spirit or action is considered a sign of weakness. Forgiveness, for example, is not appropriate, for to forgive is to be inconsistent and infirm.

Westerners get very little exposure to Buddhism as a whole and even less to the particular form of Buddhism practised in Tibet. The present Dalai Lama, Tenzin Gyatso, has authorized a translation of the secret teachings of Tibetan Buddhism because there was so much misinformation printed, a fact which he considers dangerous. The study of the secret mantra became a source of entertainment, particularly in the West. He says, "If secret mantra is practised openly and used for commercial purposes, then accidents will befall such a practitioner, even the taking of his life and the creation of conditions unfavorable for generating spiritual experience. Instead of helping, it will harm.

"The practice of mantra requires both an accurate knowledge of Buddhist presentation and an ability to maintain vows, sustain faith and to be of strong mind. You must start slowly, recognizing suffering and developing a wish to leave cyclic existence, to stop the succession of reincarnations, to attain both liberation and omniscience. You must develop a great compassion for all living creatures and, above all, act to relieve suffering. You must conquer all coarseness, subtle demons and duality. This must be practised from lifetime to lifetime until, through prescribed stages, you can obtain Buddhahood."

The present Dalai Lama describes the aims of Buddhism in this way: "All of the world's religious systems teach a means of bringing a little peace to the mind and cleansing coarser aspects of the mental continuum. They either directly or indirectly create improvement in terms of a good mind and of altruism, but among them it seems that only Buddhism presents — by way of a vast number of reasonings, scriptures and views — the means of transforming the mind into ultimate goodness. I am not saying that Buddhism is best because I am a Buddhist. I think that, if it is considered honestly, one would think so; but, even if it *is* the best, this does not mean that everyone should be a Buddhist. All do not have the same disposition and interest. It is necessary for each person to observe a path that accords with his own disposition, interest and ability."

One statement concerning the direction and purpose of the study of Buddhism is based on the need to face up to real events in life and attain a resultant peace of mind. Chogyam Trungpa Rinpoche said, "People in all ages have been under stress and have devised and tried various means to escape from it, only to find to their dismay that the stress did not disappear but reasserted itself in other forms as threatening as before, if not worse. This shows that escape is never an answer to the basic question of how to be a human being. Escape, whether it is the mechanical uniformity and monotony of social conformity or into a fictitious world of some transcendental make-believe, is but an admission of having failed in the ever-present task of growing up."

The concepts and practices are demanding. Lama Govinda has said that Buddhism stresses "the interwovenness of things and actions, the interdependence of all that exists, the continuity in the interaction of cause and effect."

Buddhism indeed has been called the religion of reason and meditation. It emerged in India in the sixth century B.C. and is practised by between one third and one fifth of the world's population today.

Born in about 566 B.C., Buddha himself was Suddhartha Guatama, the son of a *rajah* from Northwestern India. Born a Hindu, he was a member of the aristocratic, military class. His father ruled that Siddhartha could not leave the palace compound, but he disobeyed. The legend states that outside the walls he encountered four unsettling sights, now known as the four signs. The first was an old man, the second a very sick man, the third a corpse and the fourth a wandering holy man at peace. These sights caused Siddhartha to wonder about life's meaning and, without telling his wife or son, he left on the "Great Departure", a pilgrimage that was to last for fifty years. He wandered through much of India and spoke to all the sages he encountered. He grew to believe in the possible progression of all living forms from lower to higher levels and conceptualized the ideas of karma (fate) and nirvana (release). On his travels he began to gather disciples. He declared that no disciple should be turned away because of his caste. He declared that individual behavior, not birthright, gave a person worth. This was considered heresy by the Brahmins, the spiritual arbiters of the time.

Siddhartha moved on and spent six years near the town of Uruvela. These years he passed in unbroken meditation and strict asceticism, fasting until he was at the point of death. He then realized that his body housed the only instrument through which he could reach nirvana. This, too, was against the teachings of Hinduism, which viewed the body as something to be conquered. He began to eat. His disciples left, thinking he had given up his spiritual quest. Alone, he made his way to a tree, today called the Tree of Wisdom, and worshipped near Buddh Gaya in India. There he met a girl, Sujata, who gave him rice-milk in a golden bowl. This sustained Siddhartha for forty-nine days until "The Great Enlightenment". Seated in a lotus position, he vowed, "Though my skin, my nerves and my bones should waste away and my life-blood dry, I will not leave this seat until I have attained supreme Enlightenment."

Although the dates vary, the most common one attributed to this event is the full moon of May, 544 B.C. Enlightenment, in the Buddhist view, is a spiritual experience brought about by intensive meditation and contemplation, a full realization of the universe and self as one. A major difference between the legend of Buddha and those of other religions is the absence of any divine intervention. It was a discovery made by a human being and brought about through his own efforts.

At the time of The Great Enlightenment, Siddhartha experienced details of his past life and envisioned essential points of future teaching. He had a choice between remaining in the state of nirvana or returning to the world of man to teach. He chose to return and help others attain nirvana.

One of the most complicated concepts for western man is the paradox between the ideas of selflessness and self. For example, nirvana can be achieved only through personal effort, yet Bodhisattvas (people who have achieved supreme release and remain carnate to help others) are defined as those who have freed themselves from all ideas of I, mine and yours. The eastern mind relishes this paradox.

Siddhartha taught eight steps to solving the universal ills through self-determination, often called "the eightfold path":

1. Right belief;
2. Right resolve;
3. Right speech;
4. Right conduct;
5. Right occupation;
6. Right effort;
7. Right contemplation;
8. Right meditation.

Siddhartha continued to teach both men and women until his death in c. 480 B.C., the result of eating poisonous food, believed to be inedible mushrooms or tainted pork, at the table of a well-meaning peasant.

The Tibetan form of Buddhism remains true to the basic precepts of the teachings of Siddhartha, but maintains a character all its own. Tibetan Buddhism has an intense aura of mystery around it. It has been sensationalized in many books because of its sacred icon, a copulating couple, which represents divine knowledge and enlightenment.

Paranormal experience has also added to the mythology surrounding Tibetan Buddhism. "Tum-mo", for example, is the control of body heat in order to withstand exposure to extremes in temperature. A monk studying this technique spends long periods of time partially submerged in icy water or handling hot coals. The wind men or "lung-gom-pa" are apparently able to walk at super-human speeds, observed at up to sixty miles per hour. Levitation is also a common claim. To the monks, these feats are merely the manipulation of little understood natural laws by people with exceptional spiritual development and physical stamina. But the western mind often associates these phenomena with paranormal occurrences.

The Tibetans' attitude to dying is entirely divorced from our own. They lay extreme emphasis on the last few hours of life. The dying person's mental state affects the cycle of rebirth. The attendant lamas and the individual himself try at this time to attain a higher state for his next incarnation. This ritual continues until the attendants are sure that the spirit has left the body. After the spirit leaves, no importance is attached to the body itself. It could very well be fed to hungry animals, so as to lessen their suffering. These beliefs and practices were forced underground by the Chinese invasion of 1950.

After the invasion, the Dalai Lama appealed to the United Nations. His appeal was denied. In 1951, the Chinese forced a delegation from Tibet to sign a treaty preserving their autonomy and religious freedom, but allowing China to set up civil and military headquarters on Tibetan soil. The power of the Dalai Lama was limited through the division of Tibet into three regions. This treaty was in keeping with world opinion and gave China the time to get a real hold on the country. At first the occupation forces captured the imaginations of the young, for they executed the literally miraculous tasks of building airports and roads, providing good pay and technical advancement on a scale never seen before. Then, in 1956, the upper Yangtze area rose up and began guerrilla warfare which spread to the popular uprising in Lhasa in 1959.

After this, the Tibetans were treated like slaves. The government was replaced by a military dictatorship. All privately owned land was confiscated. Two thousand, five hundred monasteries were destroyed and more than one hundred thousand monks and nuns imprisoned, killed or forced into lay life. The Dalai Lama fled, with most of his ministers and many followers, to India. A famine in 1961-62 aggravated the already unbearable conditions of strict regimentation, severe punishment and forced labor in Tibet. Guerrilla activity continued and more refugees fled to India. The Indian government granted them asylum. In retaliation, China attacked Assam, India in 1962. Until 1971, China decreed that no foreign visitor was to be allowed to enter Tibet.

In January 1982, *Man Alive* telecast a program called *Forbidden Land,* produced by Ganesh Films in the summer of 1979 and the autumn of 1980. It was the first uncensored report from Tibet in thirty years. Instead of Shangri-La, the viewers saw rubble. For example, the beautiful and ancient city of Ghanden, once a seat of learning, a trading centre and shrine revered throughout the Buddhist world, had been systematically destroyed by the Chinese.

The film crew toured Tibet for ten months with three delegations representing the Dalai Lama. The Chinese now wanted him to return as a stabilizing force and invited these delegates to see for themselves how contented the people were under Chinese rule. Before their arrival, the Chinese had sent Tibetans a warning: "Remember the delegates are like the white cranes. They come and they go, but you are like the frogs in the well. You stay. Remember that we are the ones who have fed you all these years."

The Chinese did not foresee the greeting the delegates would receive. Faithful Tibetans stormed the main square in Lhasa, trying to touch the representatives of the Dalai Lama. Children who had been born under Chinese rule joined their parents and grandparents in outward expressions of devotion. Prayers which had long since been banned were repeated with the confidence of frequent use.

The Chinese presented a row of prosperous Tibetans as typifying the new Tibet, but the real story unfolded as the delegates traveled the countryside. They saw poverty and deprivation almost everywhere they went. In the bitter cold they were greeted by dispossessed villagers, half naked and starving.

The whole country is now involved in a process of re-education. The Tibetans participate in the same gymnastic and socialist exercises that are performed throughout China every morning. Chinese children now outnumber Tibetans in Lhasa by three to one. The few native children allowed to attend school use Chinese texts and learn of their own history from the Chinese perspective. Tibetan is taught as a foreign language. But all of this was immediately forgotten as the Tibetans saw the delegates and displayed their love of their heritage. As a result, the Chinese curtailed the delegates' movements.

The sister of the Dalai Lama, Pema Gyalpo, was a member of one of the delegations and describes the suffering and oppression she witnessed while there. "I met a young girl, about twenty-two, and she introduced her mother to me. She told me that the mother had brought up the children out of the sweat of her blood. When she told me this, I thought the mother had a really difficult time but when I met them later, I discovered that the mother had literally cut herself and taken her blood to make soup so that she could feed the children."

The delegation learned of famines so terrible that the people were forced to live for months on roots, worms and insects. But even starvation has not turned the Tibetans from their faith. The Dalai Lama said, "There is a human psychological effect. When you meet strong opposition, suppression and restriction, you naturally feel more faith. I've been to Mongolia and Siberia and thousands of people came to see me, showing — just like in Tibet — a very strong faith. The faith is deeply rooted. It is very difficult to wipe out. When you face tremendous difficulties, faith gives you inner peace."

Pema Gyalpo said, "For us, religion is part of our life and to be deprived of it is one of the most terrible things. The people have suffered much from the harassment of the Chinese who come at any time of the night or day to check what you have in your house or what you were saying in your house. You were not allowed to practise your religion even in your home, you know, and all the religious objects — prayer books, scriptures, idols — everything was confiscated and the people were living with nothing. Even your bedding — everything was taken from your home. The Chinese collected from some families seven times. They've even taken cooking utensils. There are areas in Tibet we visited where the people have not even bedding for the children or for themselves. The Chinese collected everything."

One of the most vivid and powerful images seen on the program was of whole families working in a stone quarry. No modern tools were evident. The women carried huge blocks of stone on their backs. Children as young as eight toiled alongside their parents for work points which are redeemable for rations, if there is any food available. Pema Gyalpo said, "Tibetans in Tibet are very anti-Chinese. They really hate the Chinese. How can you appreciate the Chinese when they've done nothing for the last twenty years for the Tibetans? They've robbed the country clear of everything, even of the natural resources. A whole hillside would be just stumps of trees. They'd taken all the trees down to China. They've looted all the monasteries. There are hardly any monasteries left in Tibet now. They've robbed the people's homes of everything they possess."

The Chinese policy in Tibet is beginning to moderate, but how long this process will last or how widespread the reforms will be remains to be seen. A beginning toward religious freedom is visible, through displayed prayer flags and open devotions. Foreigners are now also allowed to visit. Package tours are adding to Chinese coffers. Farmers are allowed to work their own land as well as on the communal land and they have been exempted from taxation for two years.

The Dalai Lama still waits. He will not return until he is sure Tibetans are content under Chinese rule. He said, "At the moment religious freedom is just a word in Tibet. In actual practice there is no freedom. There was a slight improvement in 1979 in the main towns like Lhasa, in a few places where foreign visitors are allowed to come, but in the countryside there is still much restriction.

"From the border of Thailand up to Siberia millions of people are under the domination of communists. At the same time, the people believe in Buddhism. People do not want to forget about Buddhism and at the same time they have to remain under communist domination. Communists cannot eliminate Buddhism entirely and all the Buddhists cannot get rid of that ideology. In reality, it is better to remain side by side and find dialogue. Dialogue gives life."

In Tibet, six million people wait for the Dalai Lama's return, while the social and religious traditions they are prevented from preserving are kept alive by him in Dharmsala, India.

When the Tibetan community in Canada contacted *Man Alive* in 1980 to see if we would be interested in a program on their leader, we naturally jumped at the chance, arranged a date and began researching the subject. Along with a few firsthand reports and the information supplied by the Dalai Lama's representatives, we were fortunate to have a copy of an interview taped by Charles Collingwood during the Dalai Lama's recent visit to New York. I settled down to watch it about two weeks before my interview was scheduled but within five minutes I felt a sense of foreboding. I have long admired Collingwood's work and he was failing, in part because the Dalai Lama's English is not very good and is overshadowed by a very strong accent. On top of this, he seemed reluctant to answer many of Collingwood's questions. The questions themselves were appropriate and the Tibetan community had assured the staff of the Dalai Lama's command of the English language and his desire to speak to North Americans about Tibet's plight, but Collingwood was unable to elicit anything but monosyllabic responses. The producers therefore had to edit the interview severely and what remained was choppy in both content and pace.

We discussed the possibility of canceling the project, but felt in the end that it would be an insult to the Tibetan community. We continued the preparations with little hope.

We were given the correct greeting by the Dalai Lama's representative in Toronto. The procedure seemed straightforward. The greeting consisted of my presenting his holiness with a long, white silk prayer scarf. This he would bless and return to me by placing it over my extended arms.

The Dalai Lama and his entourage, consisting of four other Buddhist monks and members of the Tibetan community in Toronto, entered the studio a half-hour before we were to begin the interview. I'm not sure what I expected, though my mental image was larger than life. What I was actually faced with was a diminutive, bespectacled man of about forty-five, dressed in the orthodox saffron robes of a Buddhist monk and incongruous ankle socks and brown oxfords. He was beaming, obviously excited at the activity in the studio. He approached one crew member after another, greeting them warmly and questioning them about their jobs and the mechanics of the various pieces of equipment. I later learned that electronics is one of his passions.

We eventually sat down and began the process of getting to know each other. I never discuss specific questions with a guest before an interview, preferring to talk about more inconsequential things. I found the Dalai Lama's English very difficult to understand and my sense of foreboding returned. If this had been a brief interview or newsclip, an interpreter would be used, but the long translation process — between me, an interpreter, the Dalai Lama and back again for half an hour — would be confusing, boring and totally unacceptable for a feature television program.

When the crew's preparations were complete, I asked the first question: "I might never have another chance to interview a God. I would like to know how you ..." That is as far as I got. His holiness began to giggle. Not the sort of laugh which comes from embarrassment, but rather from pure amusement. I was disarmed. His charm and obvious humility swept the studio, raising everyone's spirits. But regardless of his amusement, to the Tibetans he *is* a God.

The Tibetans' fundamental belief in reincarnation is the basis of their principle of succession. *Tulkus*, children recognized as reincarnations of noted religious personages, are usually found between the ages of two and five and are subsequently placed in an appropriate monastery. The Dalai Lama is the most famous tulku. He is the fourteenth reincarnation of the God of Compassion. His brother is also a tulku and had been a monk until the Chinese takover. He escaped from Tibet and is now a teacher of Tibetan history and culture in the United States.

When circumstances indicate the existence of a tulku, the authorities are called in to test the youngster. One of the standard tests is the ability to recognize personal articles owned by the previous incarnation.

On the death of the thirteenth Dalai Lama, the Regents of Tibet consulted the State Oracle for an indication of where the tulku could be found. A guiding vision was witnessed by the Regents in a lake sacred to the Goddess Kali, who is said to protect the incarnations of the Dalai Lama. Disguised as a simple band of pilgrims, a search party set out and, when they reached the far eastern district of Amdo, were greeted as old friends by a small child. The child then accurately identified the thirteenth Dalai Lama's rosary, walking staff and prayer drum from the many similiar articles in the officials' possession. Even more astonishing was his ability to repeat the six-syllabled mantra sacred to the God of Compassion. This original meeting was followed by a long process of confirmation whereby the child was asked to perform complicated tasks in interpretation of ancient sacred texts.

I was interested to hear the Dalai Lama's own version of this incredible story. "When I was young, three or four years of age, I demonstrated or expressed clear remembrance of the past, but after that the past memory is not much. I spoke a dialect which was not used in my own place."

His humility was evident as he described the subsequent events. He was taken to the palace in Lhasa, along with two other boys who had met the same original requirements. While there, the process of selection took place and Tenzin Gyatso became installed as the verified Dalai Lama. He laughingly explained that he cried less than the other two candidates and was therefore chosen. He does not, however, see his responsibility as a joke. "As Dalai Lama, of course, I am fully committed to six million Tibetans."

As the interview progressed, the Dalai Lama's English seemed to improve. My ears, I suppose, were also becoming accustomed to his nasal, yet rather melodic voice. He went on to express thanks to Canada for accepting more than four hundred Tibetan refugees and providing an atmosphere where they could prosper. "We lost our own country. They settled here quite well. They adapted quite well. They are earning better money than in India. Also they remain as a Tibetan community. They often make the pilgrimage to India and express to me that they are satisfied and very much grateful to the people and the government of this country. In India there are still a few thousand yet to settle. There are more than eighty-five thousand Tibetans in India, so out of a few thousand they would be very grateful if a few hundred could come here. I've got hope."

I asked him if he missed Tibet and was surprised to discover that he did not. "As soon as you become a monk emotionally, you have no attachment to your own family, in order for education. That day you change your own name also. So as a monk, you see, there's not much difference between countries. So for that reason, we are physically and emotionally departed, but mentally always connected to our people."

I had read that the Dalai Lama believed that Christianity and Buddhism could learn a lot from each other. I asked him what specifics he thought the two traditions might eventually share. He first spoke of sin as a concept which we already shared. "Our concept of sin is any action which produces suffering, any action which automatically causes difficulty to yourself or which directly hurts other beings. That, generally speaking, is sin."

"So it is not that much different from the commandments given to Moses?"

"That's right. Basically there are many similarities, except on the philosophical level there are differences. I always say the whole world measures relations. We have to understand people and events which follow the teaching. That is all."

"What could Christians learn from Buddhism?"

"It seems to me they could learn certain techniques of meditation. Yoga could be practised without disturbance to the basic Christian philosophy. Certain kinds of these techniques are very beautiful."

"What could Buddhism learn from Christianity?"

"Service to society. The Christian organizations have done good jobs in mankind's history, mainly in the fields of education and health care. Also the organization of the monasteries is very practical. In the past, when we still had our own country, our Buddhist education was highly developed, but the general education and health care was quite backward. Somehow, we are not very practical. Some traditions, like in Thailand, have too many restrictions, too much isolation. The monks are isolated from the rest of society. In the scriptures, it mentions implementation of detachment, but now certain traditions have the emphasis on service to others. We always used to pray. As soon as we got up, we prayed for happiness for all. In my mind, if you're sitting on a chair, in your own room, just to pray, that's not sufficient. You must implement these things in practice. It is not necessary to give up the prayers, but you must serve in anything which gives benefit to the masses. I think we can learn from the Christian experience."

One of the major differences between our two traditions is the Buddhist concept of reincarnation. I asked the Dalai Lama to describe this belief but his English was not sufficient to deal with the abstract. I therefore returned to the business of getting to know the man. How was his day spent? What foods did he eat?

"That's quite simple. Usually 4.30 to 5.00, I get up, if I get enough sleep. If I go to sleep very late, then my sleep may not permit me to get up so early. And then prayer, some meditation. Then I usually have a heavy breakfast because, you see, last night I remain hungry. A Buddhist monk does not take any meal in the afternoon. There is no discrimination in food. You eat whatever you get. Anything available. After my breakfast, I again continue my prayer.... I enjoy gardening and the like on Sunday or a holiday.... I have a small workshop to repair small damage, like my own watch or a simple camera. It's pretty interesting."

I was again struck by his basic human qualities, his ability to converse on a colloquial level without any need for the trappings of his high office. And I told him so. "I didn't know when I was talking to you earlier that you had such a humanized picture of the Dalai Lama. I thought that it was going to be austere and difficult and uncomfortable, but you have really humanized this God."

He smiled. "That is my nature. One of my strong beliefs is, after all, we are human beings. You are Canadian. I am Tibetan. If we think about language or these things, there are differences but if I look on you deeply, you are a human being. I am a human being. The other things, the differences, are secondary and an extra barrier for meeting. I mean at a meeting face to face, you express your own feeling as a friend, that is truth. I believe we can develop a real human understanding. If you show respect or concern or share in other people's suffering, loneliness will disappear. Whether you know or not, everybody is your friend."

The interview ended. I could not think of a more revealing comment on which to finish the program. I was reminded of a typical Tibetan greeting, expressing this generosity of spirit: "Sir, and to what sublime tradition do you belong?"

A great many theologians maintain that the Christian Church was at its strongest during its first hundred years, when the Romans considered a belief in Jesus Christ a capital offence. We see this sense of conviction in the communist bloc countries today and it certainly exists within Tibet. Their faith in Buddhism and in the Dalai Lama has not merely survived the Chinese invasion, it has flourished. In Tibet, a church hierarchy does not exist but devotions continue within the people's homes and hearts. In India, their "keeper of the faith" preserves the sacred literature and, though stripped of his temporal authority, the Dalai Lama fervently maintains his spiritual leadership.

SCIENCE AND
CONSCIENCE

August 6, 1945 promised to be just another hot, humid summer day for me. I didn't have much on my mind except to enjoy the month of holidays that remained before the daily grind of high school began again. The morning news on the radio that day, however, would change not only my plans for a lazy day at the beach but the lives of everyone, forever. The atomic bomb had been dropped on Hiroshima, Japan.

On August 9, our local radio station carried the announcement by the President of the United States, Harry S. Truman: "The world will note that the first atomic bomb was dropped on Hiroshima — a military base. We won the race of discovery against the Germans. We have used it in order to shorten the agony of war, in order to save the lives of thousands and thousands of young Americans. We shall continue to use it until we completely destroy Japan's power to make war."

As with most people, my first reaction was — it's finally over; the Japanese are defeated; World War II has ended. But what *was* an atomic bomb? How could it make such a difference?

It was a long time before we knew the details of what took place that day in Hiroshima and realized the horror that had been spawned.

The bomb dropped was only 12.5 kilotons, very small indeed by today's standards, and it had been detonated 1,900 feet in the air, yet the entire city was destroyed and tens of thousands of people were blasted to death. The number of people who were killed outright or died of their injuries in the subsequent three months was estimated at 130,000.

The horror of Hiroshima stunned many around the world, but not enough to influence governments' decisions to build bigger and better nuclear weapons. When it was announced in 1949 that the U.S.S.R. had exploded a nuclear device, most Canadians were thankful that American technology was working at full speed to keep ahead in the arms race. In the meantime, we would have to learn how to protect ourselves.

When I think back to those days, I marvel at our naivety. Did we really think that hiding under desks at school would save us from a nuclear blast? And what about all those civil defence organizations that showed us what route to take out of town when the bomb hit? Backyard shelters built of concrete blocks and stocked with dried food were a popular safeguard against atomic war and just knowing where to turn our radio dial seemed to give us a sense of security.

I was working at a radio station in St. Catharines, Ontario during the cold war of the fifties and remember our control room being equipped with an emergency alarm tied in to Civil Defence that would sound when the "enemy" attacked. The operator on duty had instructions to stop all local programming immediately and to hook in to the CBC national radio network, where emergency instructions would be given to listeners. At various times the alarm would go off through some electrical malfunction. At first when this happened we would whip into action, make the appropriate announcements and plug into the network feed. But after a few times of being greeted by poetry reading or classical music, we ignored the alarm system and when it rang, merely shut it off and continued with our regular programming.

I remember doing on-the-spot live coverage of a simulated nuclear bomb attack on Niagara Falls, arranged jointly by the

Canadian and American Civil Defence organizations. They were pretending that the Russians had bombed the Niagara hydro-electric station and people in a fifty-mile area were to be evacuated. Citizens from both sides of the border volunteered to be victims and were made up with fake cuts, burns and ketchup-soaked clothing and then propped up against trees and doorways. A building was set on fire and several teams of fire fighters from the area rushed in and quickly doused it with water. Ambulances were called and passing motorists were stopped to take the survivors to local hospitals whose staffs continued the farce by applying dressings and splints to the ersatz wounds.

It was all done in deadly earnest and made an exciting broadcast, but I have often wonderd if we really thought we were learning how to survive or if we were fooling ourselves even then.

It wasn't until the 1960s, when I began producing programs for a national radio series called *Checkpoint*, that I realized the futility of the arms race and the impossibility of the world ever surviving a nuclear war. Researching material for these and other radio and television programs, plus interviewing knowledgeable people from many related fields, convinced me that continued build-up of nuclear weapons was the most dangerous threat mankind had ever known. It seemed inconceivable to me that anyone who cared about life — their own or their fellow human beings' — could approve the manufacture and stockpiling of nuclear arms. By this time I had three children and I wondered how anyone could hold a child in his arms and not desperately want it to thrive in our world.

When scientists working on the Manhattan Project informed President Truman, who was at the Potsdam Conference, that the first atom bomb test had been successful, they transmitted in code the message: "Babies satisfactorily born". I have often thought that since that test took place, *no* babies have been satisfactorily born because, through no fault of their own, they have come into this life under the threat of nuclear death. I have also wondered if those who gave birth to the nuclear "babies" and who have nourished them through the succeeding years — each generation of "babies" massively more numerous than the last — sincerely believe that their work has been for the good of mankind.

In the early summer of 1968, CBC television broadcast a symposium on science and conscience which brought together an outstanding group of concerned and articulate communicators to explore the question of responsibility in various scientific fields. I was particularly interested in what they had to say about those scientists who worked on the development of nuclear arms. Participating in one program were James Eayrs, Professor in the Department of Political Economy at the University of Toronto; Jacob Bronowski, Senior Fellow of the Salk Institute for Biological Studies, La Jolla, California; and Malcolm Muggeridge, British journalist and broadcaster. In the program, they compared their perceptions of three major contributors: Albert Einstein (German-American physicist, formulator of the theory of Relativity), J. Robert Oppenheimer (American physicist, director of the Los Alamos laboratory during the development of the atomic bomb) and Edward Teller (Hungarian-American physicist nicknamed the "father" of the hydrogen bomb).

On Albert Einstein

Bronowski: "In August 1939, Albert Einstein, who had been a life-long pacifist through the most difficult times of war and peace, was persuaded by Leo Szilard[1] and Enrico Fermi[2] to sign a letter to President Roosevelt saying, 'Experiments which have been brought to my attention make it likely that an atomic bomb could be developed. I think the United States should develop one.' But you see I have left out the part of the letter that connects the beginning with the end. What he said in between was, 'My information is that the Germans are trying to develop one; therefore I think the United States should develop one.' And what did Einstein say at the end of the war? He said, 'If I had really known how badly behind the Germans were, I would not have lifted a finger.' "

On J. Robert Oppenheimer

Muggeridge: "Take a concrete case, a man like Oppenheimer. We all know about Oppenheimer — a great scientist, I imagine. Well, he found no difficulty in harnessing his skills to the United States project to make atomic weapons."

Eayrs: "Let's not leave Oppenheimer's reputation in disarray like that, because the fascinating thing about Oppenheimer is that he was a man who had led the United States through

---

1. Hungarian-American physicist instrumental in the creation of the Manhattan Project for the development of the atomic bomb.
2. Italian-American physicist and Nobel prize winner in 1953 for the development of the neutron-induced nuclear reactor.

its atomic energy effort and had made the bomb and then developed doubts. He refused, as you know, to go ahead with the hydrogen bomb."

Muggeridge: "Yes, he refused to go further but, up to that point, he was perfectly happy to be involved."

Eayrs: "He wasn't perfectly happy; there never has been, I think, a man who was less happy and less certain."

On Edward Teller

Bronowski: "I would like to talk about a man who does not have the kind of halo that Oppenheimer or Einstein had."

Muggeridge: "Someone with a tilted halo?"

Bronowski: "That's right. Someone who, on the whole, is very much more controversial: Edward Teller. Now here's a man who has been behind the development of the hydrogen bomb, was fierce about this and, of course, many scientists, many intellectuals, think he has no conscience. But that's not so. The fact is that he has a powerful feeling that western civilization, as his adopted country — the United States — displays it, is more important than civilization as displayed in the countries he has left — eastern Europe, Hungary in particular. This is what now distorts his judgment."

Eayrs: "Dr. Edward Teller possesses a powerful capacity for rationalization. He feels the safety of civilization depends upon the further experiments which others deem to be diabolic. I think where one faults Teller is in his not pausing, in his very ruthless and very capable putting of his case, to ask himself as an intellectual — am I on the right tack? Are there other considerations? Is it possible that I could have been mistaken? And this is what makes Teller an ideologist in the pursuit of his craft."

Bronowski: "This is what Cromwell said: 'I beseech ye in the bowels of Christ, consider that ye may be mistaken.' He said this, as you know, to the churchmen of Scotland, who paid no attention because they had the 'divine sense' of what was right and what was not. You are saying to Teller, 'Do not take it for granted that the Russians are wrong and we are right.' You are saying to Einstein, 'Do not take it for granted that the Germans are wrong and we are right.'"

Muggeridge: "May I add Fuchs[1] as a third? Fuchs does

---

1. German physicist and spy, arrested and convicted in 1950 for giving British and U.S. atomic research secrets to the Soviet government.

exactly the same thing. He simply says, 'I consider that the future of mankind requires the dominance of the U.S.S.R., therefore I think it is my duty as a civilized man to give the U.S.S.R. the possibility of developing these weapons.' He is in exactly the same position as Teller."

The comments made on this program about these nuclear scientists were part of the research I studied four years later when we decided to do a *Man Alive* program with Dr. Edward Teller. Given his background and achievements, he seemed the ideal person with whom to discuss science and conscience.

He had emigrated to the United States in 1935 and by 1941 had joined Enrico Fermi's team which produced the first nuclear chain reaction. In 1943 he went to work with J. Robert Oppenheimer on the secret atomic weapons project at the Los Alamos weapons laboratory in New Mexico. It had been a year earlier, however, that Teller in a conversation with Enrico Fermi had discussed the possibility of developing thermo-nuclear weapons. Fermi suggested that the explosion of a fis-sion weapon could be used to start something similar to the natural explosions on the sun. Teller undertook to analyze the thermonuclear processes in some detail and several months later presented his findings. He concluded that a weapon based on thermonuclear fusion was indeed possible. Later studies showed that the process would be improved by the addition of tritium, an isotope of hydrogen. Because the energy came from "burning" these isotopes of hydrogen, the weapons became known as hydrogen or H-bombs.

Many scientists, politicians and even military leaders in the U.S. were against the development of this superweapon on the grounds that it would be impossible to confine its use to military targets. Edward Teller became the leading advocate for the development of the bomb, citing its absolute necessity to main-tain U.S. military superiority. When the Soviet Union exploded its first nuclear weapon in August 1949, support for Teller's position was immediate. A worried U.S. Congress and anxious Joint Chiefs of Staff convinced President Truman that a nuclear arms race had begun. In January 1950 the President gave the go-ahead. Programs for building facilities for the production of thermonuclear materials were pushed through Congress. The Los Alamos plant went on a six-day work week and in November 1952, the first hydrogen bomb test took place. It was successful, obliterating a small island in the Pacific and leaving a crater more than a mile in diameter. Throughout the cold war fifties, the Soviet scare spurred nuclear arms development in the U.S. The voice of Edward Teller was increasingly heard, warning of the threatened loss of the democratic way of life he had come to cherish in his adopted country. In the late fifties he took time from his teaching at the University of California at Berkeley to be Director of the U.S. Second Weapons Laboratory at Livermore, California. In 1962 the U.S. Atomic Commission presented him with the Enrico Fermi award. During the 1960s, however, more liberal voices were being heard and Teller found himself being attacked not only by pacifists and anti-nuclear protesters but by members of the scientific community, who felt he had compromised his principles through political involvement.

For the 1971-72 *Man Alive* series it was decided to do three programs on various aspects of science and religion. The first, dealing with science and conscience, was to be an interview with Dr. Edward Teller.

Edward Teller lived on a winding hillside street overlooking the city of San Francisco. A locked iron gate barred his driveway and a wrought-iron fence, topped by strings of barbed wire, encircled his yard. Leaving our car on the street, we walked up to the gate and pushed an electric buzzer. After a minute or two, during which we assumed somebody was checking us out, the lock clicked and the gate swung open. Two large German shepherds bounded out to us and gave us a sniffing escort up the long path to the house. Teller, short and stocky, with the bushiest eyebrows I had ever seen, was at the door and ushered us into a large, dark, book-lined room where he told us "this is where the interview will be done."

It usually takes about twenty minutes to set up the camera equipment, the sound recorder and the lights. The director and the cameraman arrange the best angles, check and re-check the light intensity, while the sound man hooks up microphones and takes voice levels. I find this a very valuable time to establish a comfortable relationship with my guests. I try to get them in a relaxed mood by chatting about the *Man Alive* series or the news of the day or anything that will establish a friendly atmosphere for the interview. Specifically I try to avoid any discussion of the actual questions that are going to be asked. This ensures natural and spontaneous replies.

I learned quickly, however, that Edward Teller was not a man for idle chatter. He wanted to know when the interview would start, how long it would take and what the questions were to be. I assured him we could start in a very few minutes and I reminded him he had promised us an hour of his time. As for the questions, I said, since he already knew we were doing a program about the role and responsibility of the scientist, I was sure a person with his vast knowledge of the subject would not need any rehearsal. Teller did not find this amusing. He glowered and his eyebrows actually flapped. I understood then why some people claimed Teller had been used by Stanley Kubrick as the model for Peter Sellers' interpretation of the title role in the movie *Dr. Strangelove: Or, How I Learned To Stop Worrying And Love The Bomb*. I could tell there would be no rapport in my interview this day. He started to get out of his chair, but the microphone had already been fastened, so he sat down again and tried a different tack.

He said it would help if he knew the questions because his English wasn't very good and that it would give him time to phrase the answers better.

I said I could appreciate that and would be happy to tell him my first question but that I wouldn't know what the following questions would be until I heard his answer to the first one.

We were interrupted by the cameraman who asked Teller if it would be possible to remove the dogs from the room, as they insisted on pacing in and out of the shot. Teller called for his wife, a pleasantly efficient woman who appeared and led the dogs away to another part of the house.

Thinking I could get his mind off the questions, I took the opportunity to observe that they were very handsome dogs and that he must get a great deal of pleasure from them.

He replied that he didn't and only had them for protection. He also explained that he had to have the gate installed and the wire put on top of his fence because student protesters from Berkeley came and threw rocks at his house. They had smashed windows and damaged his garden. He then wanted to hear the first question.

"I would like to know," I asked, "if a scientist should be primarily responsible to man or to science. That is my first question."

"That's not a good question. I don't like it. I cannot speak for all scientists. That question is too complex. Don't ask it."

At this point our set-up for the interview was complete. We were ready to start.

"Very well, Dr. Teller," I said, "I will re-word the question and ask it differently. We are now recording and my question is — Where do you think *your* responsibility lies — to science or to man?"

He obviously didn't like this version of the question any better. He scowled at me, then scowled at the camera. His eyebrows flapped a few times, then after a long pause, he answered, "There are some things only scientists can do. Their first responsibility is to be exact, because that no one else can do. Their second responsibility, insofar as they can do it, is to apply what they have found. Science, in itself, is to satisfy one of our most ancient and one of our most important urges — that of curiosity, of understanding.

"All the history of science and industry, particularly in the last century, has shown us these objectives are almost without limits. There is a third responsibility and that is to explain what has been found. It is a shame that today, more than half a century after the discovery of relativity, most people — most highly educated people — have not yet understood what relativity is. It is tragic that in applied sciences an understanding of what these applications mean is even more lacking.

"You hear again and again the idiotic statement that a nuclear war could wipe out mankind. If there is one thing we can be sure of, it is that this will not happen. Yes, a nuclear war can be more terrible than anything we personally have yet experienced, but mankind will survive. A scientist has this responsibility — to explain what he has found and to do it as honestly and as clearly and as simply as possible, but at that point his responsibility stops. He is not to make decisions about what happens to his discovery. That, in a democracy, is a responsibility that belongs to everybody."

"But everybody does not know what science has found out, so we are not really in on the decision-making process," I stated.

"You should be," he answered, "but you and many non-scientists, who lack this knowledge, substitute some very peculiar attitudes. On the one hand, you put a scientist on a pedestal and think he is some kind of high priest. On the other hand, you think he is some kind of devil. Come to think of it, the high priest and the devil are not necessarily the opposite."

"Perhaps, by not taking an active part, we have given scientists the role of playing God," I said.

"That may be the case. And unfortunately, but understandably, there are many scientists who are quite willing to play God."

"This must have been the case in the work on the development of the atomic bomb during the Second World War. Surely, the scientists knew exactly what they were doing," I said.

Teller paused. He looked at me steadily for a moment. I could see him thinking, now the questions are getting closer to home. Finally he said, "Well, perhaps we knew what we were doing — perhaps not exactly. Toward the end of the Second World War, many of us argued and some argued vigorously that nuclear explosions should be demonstrated before they were used. I personally thought that they should have been demonstrated. If they had been, it would have been clear that the power of science can stop a terrible war without killing a single person. The decision was made differently for a variety of reasons. Even now it is doubtful if we can say we knew exactly what we were doing. We certainly didn't foresee the consequences."

"Don't you think there is an urgent need for science to introduce more deeply human goals?" I asked.

"I don't believe this can be done for a very simple reason. We're not clever enough, at least I'm not and I don't think many others are. When you develop something, you never know what will become of it. We start at curiosity. We arrive at knowledge. We transform that through its applications into power, but what that power will mean we don't know until after it happens. How does one distinguish between science in the service of war or in the service of peace? Let me mention an example which I like. There was once a weapon science developed that was to be used in the battle of the sexes — nylon. As such it was classified as peaceful, but we were in the midst of the Second World War, so the girls didn't get any stockings. All the nylon went into parachutes. So what was intended for peaceful purposes went into war. Vice versa, the first application of thermonuclear explosions, hydrogen bombs, was supposed to be for war, for a deterrent. Hydrogen bombs have never been so used and I hope they never will. They are clean and powerful and cheap explosives. They can be used, and the Russians have used them, to make reservoirs for water to irrigate the land. When you work on something, you will never know where it leads. When you talk about your human goals, that's just talk — what happens is an entirely different question."

As I listened to Teller's answers, which were delivered in a gruff, almost unfeeling manner, I couldn't help but wonder if there hadn't been a time when this brilliant mind had thought to serve more humanitarian goals. I asked, "Has your attitude toward science changed from when you were young? Was there an idealism there then, that isn't now?"

"You know," he answered, "idealism is a word which I dislike. I don't think it is well defined. I certainly had the feeling, and still have, that if I could contribute understanding to anything that was not known before, this is what I would do. There was a big change in my career when it became clear to me of the terrible danger of Hitler and that science could contribute in a very practical way to the safety of the world, to freedom. That realization turned me to a great extent from a pure scientist, where my efforts used to be, into an applied scientist. I kept at it because it was more and more evident that far too few people were willing to apply their scientific knowledge."

In the 1960s and the early 1970s there was a marked decline in the number of students choosing science courses in universities throughout North America. The tenor of the times seemed to be influencing their decision to opt for the humanities. I asked Teller if this was because they felt science was in conflict with society. Did they hold science responsible for much of the violence and suffering in the world?

"It is true they are much less involved in science today than they used to be. I think this trend is exceedingly dangerous. The strength of America, which used to be overwhelming, was due to a dedication to technology. This dedication is no longer there among the young. The comfort and safety and freedom that we have known will disappear if this trend continues. I don't know why it has developed. I'm sure it has not developed because scientists contributed to cruelty in the world. Stalin — yes; Hitler — yes; Genghis Khan — yes. Science is of necessity neutral."

I suggested to him that this neutrality was often compromised in the national interest. Countries like the United States and Russia used their scientists to gain political advantage and maintain their individual power on the world scene. I mentioned the space program as an example.

"I haven't noticed it. Perhaps I have been too close to it. What I do notice is a clear-cut correlation between our ability to survive and science. What I am trying to do is as much for the safety and protection of freedom everywhere as it is for the United States. There will always be people on the right and on the left, people like President Kennedy, for example, who talk about the space program in terms of national prestige. Frankly, that leaves me, and practically every other scientist, cold. I wish to see what we do used for the world order, for ensuring peace and freedom, but not for peace under dictatorship. The tradition of science is international. The desire of science is for international co-operation. This holds for Russian scientists as well as the Americans."

"While the tradition of science might be international," I replied, "the history of science in the last fifty years has been very national indeed. Don't you think that very often scientists have become pawns in a power struggle between nations?"

Teller did not answer immediately. He stared at me darkly as if trying to make up his mind whether to answer at all. I decided to outwait him and stared back while the camera whirred. Finally he spoke. "Not really. No. There is only one point where I can even imagine I know what you are talking about. That is, we have unfortunately introduced secrecy into science. We have tried to keep to ourselves within the United States and even in more narrow circles and I think this is foolish and self-defeating. In order to build strength and safety and to establish a free world order, I would like to see science international and free of secrecy. I know the Russians will be the last to co-operate but their people will be on our side. It is only the men in the Kremlin who will not. I hope that one way or another even that can be overcome. For now, and for all time, I don't want narrow nationalism and I certainly don't want secrets."

The time allotted for the interview was over. I was hoping Teller hadn't noticed because I had decided to toss in a couple of extra questions out of left field just to get his reaction. I might as well have saved my breath.

"What has personally sustained you through your many controversies? Do you have a faith in God that keeps you going?"

"As a scientist I don't talk about things I don't completely understand. Most of us keep going because we must, or think we must. In addition, I happened to like science."

"But on the overall scale of things, do you think science has been on the side of the angels?"

"You asked me about God and I refused to answer. That goes for angels."

As I started to thank him for the interview, he stood up, removed his microphone and left the room. His wife quickly appeared, accompanied by the two dogs and a tea wagon. Over steaming mugs and plates of cookies, Mrs. Teller chatted briefly about places she had visited in Canada and how much she enjoyed having us in her home.

Later, she saw us out through the iron gate and waved us down the winding street. She seemed genuinely sorry to see us go.

I have no problem understanding the motives or dedication of a man like Edward Teller whose zeal in protecting his vision of freedom has led to his stand in the nuclear controversy. I have also interviewed politicians and military personnel who sincerely believe the nuclear arms build-up is needed as a deterrent against the aggression of foreign power. What I have difficulty in understanding are those who ignore the entire question and refuse even to think about it. Psychiatrists describe this condition as "psychic numbing". When a situation is too horrible or frightening to contemplate, some people pretend it doesn't exist.

In his book, *The Fate Of The Earth*, Jonathan Schell says, "Thoughts of the nuclear peril were largely banned from waking life, and relegated to dreams or to certain fringes of society and open, active concern about it was restricted to certain 'far out' people, whose ideas were, on the whole, not so much rejected by the supposedly sober 'realistic' people in the mainstream, as simply ignored. In this atmosphere, discussion of the nuclear peril even took on a faintly embarrassing aura, as though dwelling on it were somehow melodramatic, or a sophomoric excess that serious people outgrew with maturity."

In the last few years, however, discussions of the nuclear threat have become "respectable". More and more people from all walks of life are speaking out from their own perspective and citizens in North America and Europe are expressing their feelings through the ballot box as the question of a nuclear arms freeze becomes a referendum in an increasing number of elections.

In Europe a grass roots movement to protest the American decision to continue production of the neutron bomb and the cruise missile involved hundreds of thousands of people in the fall of 1981. They interpreted Pentagon talk of "limited nuclear warfare" as a decision by the major powers to "fight to the last European". In North America there was also a new and widespread increase in awareness of the nuclear threat.

Man Alive decided to take a look at a nuclear establishment which is currently the number one target area in North America. It is also situated right on Canada's doorstep. The Trident missile submarine base is located on seven thousand acres at Bangor, Washington, just across Puget Sound from Seattle and about sixty miles from both Vancouver and Victoria, British Columbia. CBC producer Don Cumming undertook the project as a labor of love. He is personally committed to a halt in the nuclear arms build-up and is convinced that informed and aroused individuals can make a difference in such a difficult and complex issue. The basis of the program was just that: to inform the Canadian public of the threat posed by the Trident submarine system and to show on television people who, by listening to their consciences, had actively influenced others to do the same.

The first day of our film shoot began at six a.m. at a small house tucked away in the trees a few feet from the Trident missile base. This house contained the offices of Ground Zero, an organization set up to keep track of activities on the base and to launch campaigns protesting the base's existence. One day a week, volunteers gather here before walking down the hill to the main gate of the base, where they hand out leaflets to all personnel who enter. Here we met Jim and Shelly Douglas. Jim is a Canadian from Hedley, British Columbia. Shelly, American-born, was a candidate for the United Church ministry in Vancouver. They decided in the mid-1970s that they personally would do something to halt the nuclear build-up. They chose the name Ground Zero for their operations because it is a technical term meaning the exact centre of a nuclear explosion. Many feel that is precisely what the Trident missile base could be, since the submarine-launched missile has become the most effective and accurate means of deploying nuclear warheads, posing the greatest threat to the Soviet Union.

We set up our camera at the main gate of the base in the dark pre-dawn of this cold January morning. Our television lighting system was not adequate to illuminate the scene for filming, so we turned our cars around and shone the headlights into the area. It made a strange and eerie light for the incoming workers. As each car drove up to the gate a volunteer would step forward, greet the driver and hand out a leaflet which contained a few quotes, some poetry and a suggestion to think about what the base stood for. Over 5,500 military and civilian personnel work at the base. Not all of the workers went through this particular gate that morning and some didn't stop, but many of them rolled down their windows, called a hearty good morning and took the leaflet in a friendly and even jovial manner. Just as the grey dawn started to break over Puget Sound, about a dozen Buddhist monks appeared, walking in single file to the muffled beat of a prayer drum. They gathered near the gates and stood for nearly half an hour in silent prayer. We learned later they were a sect from Japan who believe in following a scriptual request made by the Buddha to build pagodas dedicated to peace. So they were building one beside Ground Zero near the base fence.

As the sun rose and the late stragglers had finally hurried in to work, we were able to see what an awesome complex the Trident missile base is. Rows of concrete bunkers are installed here, containing enough missile warheads to destroy any nation on earth. At the centre of the base is Strategic Weapons Facility Pacific, the nuclear weapons storage area. Nearby are the missile assembly buildings and what is called the Re-fit Facility which is engaged in re-fitting Poseidon class submarines to carry missiles. Near the water is the Handling Wharf where nuclear missiles, with multiple warheads, are loaded into giant Trident submarines. The base represents the greatest single concentration of American nuclear fire power. The destructive power of the Trident system can be understood by considering that each Trident submarine will be equipped with twenty-four Trident Two missiles and each missile will have fourteen independently targeted nuclear warheads capable of striking any point on over half the earth's surface. With a typical payload of seventy-five to one hundred kilotons per warhead, one Trident submarine will be able to destroy 336 cities or military targets with a blast five times that inflicted on Hiroshima. And there's a fleet of thirty submarines. That's 10,080 nuclear warheads which, incidentally, is many times the number thought adequate for strategic deterrence. The mind cannot really grasp the significance of these figures. In his book, *Lightning East to West*, Jim Douglas tries to put the Trident into perspective by means of a meditation he wrote:

> To understand Trident say the word Hiroshima.
> Reflect on its meaning for one second.
> Say and understand Hiroshima again.
> And again,
> And again,
> 2,040 times.
> Assuming you're able to understand Hiroshima in one second
> you'll be able to understand Trident in thirty-four minutes.
> That's one Trident sub.
> To understand the destructive power of the whole

Trident fleet, it would take you seventeen hours, devoting one second to each Hiroshima.

Jim and Shelly Douglas have organized a series of demonstrations, some of which involved going over the fence and into the base. As a result of this, Jim has gone to jail half a dozen times for periods ranging from ten days to five months. Shelly has also been to jail several times along with other demonstrators from both sides of the border. I asked Shelly what her going to jail accomplished.

"How can you really tell? We know that the campaign grew. We know that when in jail we received anywhere from ten letters a day from people whom we had never met but who heard or read what we were doing. They wrote to say they supported our action, were concerned and would be taking some action themselves to try and stop the nuclear arms race. I think that when you go to jail for what's right, people begin to think more seriously because of your sacrifice and they begin to feel that they can make a sacrifice too. When you take steps, it influences others to take steps and then others. That's how it grows."

The effect the Douglases have had on others is considerable. One person who has been influenced by them is Archbishop Raymond Hunthausen. The Archbishop startled his congregation and the country when he denounced the Trident missile base from the pulpit as "The Auschwitz of Puget Sound". He told me, "What prompted me to speak out is a good example of the strong witness of people like Jim Douglas. After talking with him, I discovered he had the same convictions as myself and was willing to put himself on the line, to bring to people's attention, in a non-violent way, something we just have to be concerned about. He is willing to civilly disobey. He has spent time in jail. Some people look at that as a kooky thing to do and write him off. I think we have to get people's attention so they will become aware of the awesome nature of the weapon that, as Christians in the human family, we just cannot be part of. We've got to find a way to turn this all around or we welcome our own destruction."

"How does it compare with Auschwitz?" I asked.

"I truly feel that wherever there are such weapons of destruction, and that would apply to many locations around the world, we have to make some kind of comparison to those moments and experiences in history which were responsible for exterminating large numbers of people. It is comparable when we, who are aware of its presence, do nothing. There's a certain complicity

85

when we do nothing to challenge it. We all have a share in this. We have a responsibility and an obligation to take some type of stance."

The Archbishop took a definite stance himself. He announced, in a pastoral letter to his followers and in a subsequent speech, that he planned on withholding fifty percent of his personal income tax to protest the fact that half of the nation's income taxes were used for military purposes. This, plus his Auschwitz remark, made headline news around the country and brought a surge of support from within and outside the church. I asked him if through his action he was counseling civil disobedience.

"I suppose I am, but I've tried to point out, in my pastoral letter to my people, that it is not sufficient for them to come to any decision just because I have. I certainly acknowledge the fact that there are a good number of people who, even though they might have the depth of convictions I have, still have other values to contend with — family responsibility, for example. I'm posing a serious moral issue and I think it's the kind of moral issue that helps us grow and mature."

I asked the Archbishop what the consequences of his action in refusing to pay his income taxes might be.

"I'm sure there will be warnings. There will be advice from the Internal Revenue Service. There will be the attaching of wages or my bank account with penalties and interest. Ultimately, depending, I suppose, on the extent of my resistance in withholding, there could be the prospect of jail."

I suggested to the Archbishop that his stand might have some effect on Washington, especially if others followed his example, but that it would make no impression on Moscow.

He answered, "I have approached this whole thing from a perspective of faith. Politically my stance makes no sense at all. But I believe if one looks at this as a Christian or as a citizen of the world, and admits that these principles are right, then we should follow them now. Of course I'm for bilateral or multilateral disarmament, but that's not happening. It's moving in the other direction so I advocate unilateral disarmament on the part of the U.S. government. If that were to begin to happen, I would like to believe it would set in motion a whole new dynamic that would put pressure on the Russian government to back off. The Russian people would likely breathe a sigh of relief because what the arms race is doing to their economy, it is doing to the whole human family."

"There are people who are saying that if we have unilateral disarmament, we than become vassals or hostages to a foreign power," I said.

"Look at the alternatives," he answered. "If we continue in the present mode, the scientists, the professionals, tell us that by the turn of the century there will probably be a nuclear catastrophe. So to argue that to continue the way we're going is better than what I propose, risky as it is, is more naive than what I'm saying."

Aerospace engineer Robert Aldrich was a designer on the early stages of the Trident system. His decision to quit his well-paid job and begin writing and speaking out against the project startled and angered his former superiors and co-workers. I asked him what prompted him to quit.

"When I saw there was a shift in U.S. policy, that we were not really interested in deterrents any more, but that we were moving toward a more aggressive policy — then I just couldn't keep working for them. You see, it's their incredible accuracy; such accuracy is not needed just to threaten cities or provide a deterrent. It is to establish first strike capabilities, the ability to wipe out the other side's missiles. We may say we have no intention of ever using these missiles in a first strike, but the Soviets look at capabilities, not at intentions. In a time of crisis, our capability might prompt the Soviet Union into action to use their missiles before they lose them. Our missiles with their accuracy are not a deterrent; they are actually making nuclear war more likely."

The example set by the Douglases, Bob Aldrich and Archbishop Hunthausen had a ripple effect on people working at the Trident base. I talked to Derald Thompson, a father of six, who had been a trainer of submarine crews at a salary of $26,000 a year. He was one of the workers who had taken pamphlets handed out at the base gate.

"My first meeting with Jim Douglas from Ground Zero was at a friend's house one night. Jim likely remembers it as a very hostile meeting because I didn't like some of the things he was saying. But he made me think. Then I read an article by Bob Aldrich, a design engineer who had worked for Lougheed, about his views concerning the incredible accuracy of the Poseidon and the Trident. Knowing what I did about Trident weapons, the argument made a lot of sense to me. I was struggling with all this and then last June, when Archbishop Hunthausen made a speech at Pacific Lutheran University, he made me look at it from a moral consideration. That ended it right there. I quit."

I also talked to Chaplain David Becker who had worked on the base, ministering to the military and civilian workers until a personal re-examination of his role prompted him to leave.

"I was shocked to find that so much of the rationale for Christians serving in the military chaplaincy goes back to St. Augustine and the 'just war' theory and I just can't see that the 'just war' theory holds water anymore. So I started looking for another rationale. I searched through the gospels and the words of Jesus, trying to find some kind of platform on which I could stand as a chaplain. I finally had to conclude that there were no sufficient grounds, so I resigned my commission on pacifist grounds."

For many people in the Seattle area, the Trident missile base is an important employer. With jobs hard to get and unemployment figures rising in the state of Washington, the security of a weekly pay cheque overrides almost all other considerations.

Jim Douglas agreed. "Frankly, I think there is hardly anybody who believes in Trident anymore, including people on the base. When you scratch the surface in talking with them, it's not the Russians who are the real reason for Trident; it's economic security and the fact that here in the U.S. and in Canada to some degree, we have pretty much a warfare economy. Many people, if they had other alternatives, would find different employment. There's also a mood of despair. There's the idea that even if I quit my job in protest, it's not going to do any good. We have to break through this fixation of hopelessness. There is no excuse any longer for people not to hear the question. We can't be dismissed any longer as people who are just getting in the way when a person like Archbishop Hunthausen says that Trident is the Auschwitz of Puget Sound — that begins to get into people's hearts and it is a hard thing to deal with."

While the Trident missile base at Bangor may be the number one North American target area, there really is no "safe" place anymore. As producer Don Cumming wrote in the concluding script of our program on the Trident base — "Ground Zero is wherever you happen to be standing."

Since there is no escape from a nuclear holocaust, there is also no escape from our responsibility to try and prevent one. Each passing day increases the risk and the pressure to act. As Canadians we must stop feeling that all decisions are made south of the border and that our voice has little impact. We are literally "under the gun" in nuclear arms decision-making and as William Epstein, former Director of Disarmament in the United Nations Secretariat, says, "Canadians should argue the case for 'no incineration without representation.'"

Individuals do make a difference. Even if we can't speak from pulpits like Archbishop Hunthausen or choose not to climb over missile base fences like the Douglases, we can form or join local anti-nuclear arms organizations. We can let our elected representatives know our concern and we can vote in the municipal elections, which increasingly include this issue in referenda. It is essential that each of us make some effort on our own behalf and on our children's.

LIVING WITH
THE NUCLEAR THREAT

The knowledge that, because of the nuclear threat, we are living under a modern Damoclean sword, affects people differently. Many are determined to take action. Many shift all blame for the situation to some foreign enemy, usually the Soviet Union. By far the greatest number choose to ignore it, refuse to talk about it and generally adopt a psychic "closing off" of the whole subject. How does this refusal on the part of some adults even to acknowledge the threat of nuclear war affect young people? And what are the psychological effects of possible nuclear annihilation on children? How do they feel about the future?

To answer these questions and to pursue our interest in the growing anti-nuclear movement, *Man Alive* decided to produce another program on the subject in 1982. Once again our producer was Don Cumming. He arranged for me to interview Dr. Frank Sommers, who teaches Psychiatry at the University of

Toronto and is president of the Canadian branch of an organization called Physicians For Social Responsibility, part of the international organization called Physicians For The Prevention of Nuclear War. Dr. Sommers spends about half of his time away from his practice traveling for the organization, attending meetings world-wide and speaking out from a physician's standpoint on the nuclear threat.

I was interested in finding out from him if there was this same kind of concern on the part of physicians in Soviet bloc countries. He assured me there was.

"We have an international group of physicians with over thirty thousand members in thirty-one countries at last count, with large numbers from the Soviet Union and Eastern bloc countries. In the Soviet Union the leader of the physicians' group is Dr. Eugene Chasov who was Brezhnev's personal physician. They are publicizing the same facts to their population as we are. We have been monitoring this closely and I have material from journals like *Pravda* and *Izvestiya* that show clearly that the medical effects of these weapons, as brought out in our conferences, have been reported accurately to the public. We are not politicians. We're not strategic analysts. Our position is that as doctors we're responsible for the health of children and adults and we're telling people that nuclear weapons are not really weapons in any conventional sense of the word — they're means to genocide or even omnicide, and if we cannot offer any help, then these weapons should not be used. It's our obligation to tell people that the only method of dealing with them is prevention. So we're practising preventive medicine and there's a large contingent in the Eastern bloc who are doing the same thing.

"I feel as doctors we must say unequivocally to our political leaders, 'In the event of nuclear war, do not expect us to be able to patch the surviving populace's physical and psychological wounds, because it simply won't be possible'." This is a point he frequently makes.

Just as the interview was about to begin in his small but comfortable Bloor Street office, I noticed the picture of a newborn baby on his desk. It was the latest addition to the Sommers family, only a few weeks old. I asked him if having a baby influenced his attitude toward nuclear arms.

"Yes it does, in a very personal sense. I redouble my commitment to try and do something so that children, my own son and other sons and daughters, will have an earth to inherit."

"How can we cope with the thought that perhaps there won't be a world for this boy or my children to grow up in?" I asked.

"I would liken it to a situation where one deals with a fatally ill patient. You don't give up even if you feel your efforts will not succeed in the long run. We have to live as though our efforts matter because in truth we don't know the prognosis. Things look bad; in fact they look worse this year than last, but there are signs of hope and we have to grasp at each one of these very strongly and we have to live as if what we are doing makes a difference."

"Of course," I suggested, "we have lived with this threat of annihilation for several decades now."

"Exactly thirty-seven years," he answered, "and we've dealt with it mostly by not thinking about it. We deny its existence because our powers of imagination aren't strong enough to actually visualize what in fact would happen, say to Toronto, in the case of a one-megaton bomb being dropped. How do you conceptualize your own death and the death of your loved ones? How do you make sense of figures like six hundred and twenty-four thousand people dead and seven hundred and ninety-five thousand injured after just one megaton bomb on Toronto? It's beyond imagination. So we deal with it in other ways. We make ourselves more comfortable by saying, well you can't trust the other side. They are barbaric. They are untruthful. We've got to arm to the teeth. We intellectualize away the problem and put our faith in all kinds of rationalizations. We say that it's too difficult for us ordinary people to understand. We have to leave it to the experts who know what they're doing. Our leaders will take care of us. We assume an infantile position vis à vis a patriarchal government. We regress to old ways of thinking such as, 'well, even if there is a war, it won't be such a bad or big one.' 'Our side will likely win,' we say, 'because our forces are superior.' These are classical notions of winning and losing that people have used all through history and they don't apply in the nuclear age."

"I would guess that the largest number of people simply block the whole issue out of their minds and don't even think about it," I suggested.

"That's right," said Dr. Sommers. "That's the number one way of dealing with it. And one of the reasons is that it's too depressing and it makes us feel helpless and hopeless. These are feelings we are familiar with. Children, by definition, are power-less, so we know and remember the feeling. These feelings are behind the reasoning and the arguments of military planners and strategists when they say we need more arms. We need more than fifty thousand nuclear weapons; we need to have overkill capacity more than twenty times. It has a certain appeal because nobody wants to feel powerless ever again."

"While I agree it is somewhat like discussing your own death, surely adults should be able to do that, but children don't think about death that much, do they? How do kids cope with all the stories of nuclear holocaust?"

"The truth is that children do think about these issues underneath the surface, maybe not in the same terms that we do, but they are aware of the major issues facing us even if adults don't talk about them, which incidentally raises the children's anxiety even further. If you ask children a few leading questions, you'll get to hear about their feelings and nightmares and worries about this issue. We adults have learned to censor our imaginations. Children don't do this. They have wonderful, free imaginations and they can visualize the end of the world and all that they love coming to an end. So they ask the obvious questions — why is this necessary? How come you adults have invented these means of mass destruction and since you did invent them and used them at Hiroshima and Nagasaki, then why have you not learned from that experience and dismantled them so that we will have a life to lead? These are very difficult questions for parents to handle but we can do it by acknowledging that the fears are there, admitting to the children that we ourselves don't have the answers and are anxious about it and working with others, taking an active stance that involves the children — such as going to demonstrations together or writing letters to Members of Parliament."

"So you think parents should talk about nuclear issues at home with their children. How about school? Should teachers deal with it there?"

"Definitely. The school has an extremely important role in peace education. Just the same way as we teach mathematics and reading or writing we should have curricula in peace-making. The question of how to resolve conflicts without hitting each other over the head has applications to the schoolyard too. How do you deal with bullies? How do you handle differences of opinion? These are important basic subjects and should be incorporated in a school's curriculum. Beyond that, of course, is the question, 'How do we see the so-called enemy? — as human beings or as vermin to be exterminated?' We have seen one example within this century of the extermination philosophy being inculcated in young people. Extermination must not be seen as a way to deal with differences, particularly today when the reality is that when we exterminate them we exterminate ourselves too."

"Isn't there a line between raising consciousness and instilling deep-rooted fears? As a psychiatrist, do you feel that children can really handle all of the facts and figures and horrible information associated with nuclear war?"

"It depends on how it's done. First, the parents or teachers have to be very comfortable with the facts. They should also know what the children's limits are. It's not something one does the same with every age. The important thing is to discuss the basic points of the issue with the children, realizing there are no easy answers to the problem, but taking time to try and find solutions. I think we have to start raising children differently. They should have the consciousness and the awareness that this is one small planet hurtling along in space and that we are all interdependent but that warfare has developed to the point where we can annihilate one another. Albert Einstein said, 'the splitting of the atom has changed everything save our mode of thinking and thus we drift towards unparalleled catastrophe.' So therefore a new way of thinking has to arise and where else to begin this new way of thinking but with children?"

I had read several articles written by Dr. Sommers about the effects of the cold war on young people. He claimed it made them amoral and opportunistic. I asked him to expand on that.

"Having grown up in a communist country during the height of the cold war, the worst days of Stalin's era, and then escaping with my family when I was thirteen, accounts for my interest in this particular subject. The fact is that, even if there is no weapon ever fired, the cold war atmosphere is claiming casualties and victims all the time. In a society where there is a defined enemy and that enemy has certain ascribed characteristics, it becomes very difficult to practise tolerance or brotherly love or even a sense of curiosity or wonder about these people because they have become shut off from your realm of experience. You then project on to these people the stereotypes permitted in this society and even if you don't believe all you see and hear, you start repeating slogans that are current about the other side because you don't want to stand out in a society where the majority holds contrary views. So what I am suggesting is that in that kind of milieu, both in the East and in the West, you tend to get people who see the hypocrisy but who realize they can't honestly discuss the reality. They don't have good role models after which to pattern themselves for their growth and this is what I mean by developing opportunistic, amoral, hypocritical adults."

"Sometimes, Doctor, I have heard criticism of people like yourself who are involved in the anti-nuclear movement as just giving emotional responses to highly technical problems in areas where you really have no expertise."

"Well, that is not really a valid criticism because it's the experts who have got us to the point where we are today, where we have in excess of fifty thousand nuclear weapons in the world and where there has been so great a refinement in these weapons that we can now easily wipe all life from the face of this planet. I suggest that this is an emotional issue ultimately and anybody who claims that it isn't or that we can shut off our emotions dealing with it, is less than human. I think part of the problem may be exactly this, that the so-called experts divorce their emotions. They're totally into their left hemispheric thinking and divorce themselves from the right hemisphere and we have this kind of lopsided reality."

"I gather that you approve, then, of children who are involved today in writing poetry and plays, marching in the streets and writing letters to government leaders."

"Yes, we need more of that. It is a relatively new phenomenon and they should continue full speed ahead. I find children very sensitive and very understanding. They have an intrinsic and intuitive identification with forces that promote life and safeguard the planet."

Very little research had ever been conducted into the impact, if any, that the nuclear threat has on children until recently, when the American Psychiatric Association surveyed children in four U.S. metropolitan areas. In the foreword to this Task Force report, which analysed the survey conducted from 1978 to 1982 and was called *The Impact On Children and Adolescents of Nuclear Development*, co-authors Dr. William Beardslee and Dr. John Mack wrote, "Children are even more vulnerable because their lives are longer, they are more at risk from radiation, and they have little control or power over what may happen to them. Very little literature exists on the psychosocial impacts of nuclear developments on children, not least of all because most adults probably don't recognize that a child could indeed be concerned about nuclear developments or have opinions worth soliciting on the subject."

Don Cumming and I flew to Cambridge, Massachusetts to meet Dr. John Mack, who had worked on the project while continuing his regular duties as staff psychiatrist at Cambridge Hospital. He was delighted to talk with us about the Task Force report and to discuss, on camera, some of his views about the nuclear question.

I remembered Dr. Sommers referring to Einstein's comment about the nuclear age changing everything except the way we think, so I asked Dr. Mack if he would comment on that observation.

"You've jumped right to the centre of the whole problem," he said. "We're operating with a set of assumptions that relate to war up until this time and the idea that somehow nuclear weapons are just another form of weapon, only more powerful, is completely outmoded. These are weapons on a scale that completely transforms the nature of war. These are weapons that have the effect of destroying the user by the boomerang effect. If anyone uses them, they're committing suicide. It completely takes us into another realm and to continue to think about them in the usual terms, such as the more weapons you have, the more secure you are, is absolute madness and yet the shift to looking at it differently has not occurred yet."

I pointed out to Dr. Mack that the people who today were moving into positions of authority and responsibility were representatives of the post-war baby boom and were members of the nuclear generation — wouldn't their attitudes be different from their elders?

"You are dealing with the complicated problem of what happens to people when they get into positions of authority and become part of the group loyalty phenomenon. People in their twenties and thirties who are now entering the job pool, beginning to join corporations, getting jobs in government, may have an attitude, even belong to the peace movement outside the system. It remains to be seen if we are going to have a transformation of the way people in power think or will these people be absorbed into the homogenization of thinking that government tends to impose on us?"

I asked him to tell me about the Task Force report and its implications.

"The ages of the kids surveyed were fourteen to eighteen. There were a thousand kids receiving the questionnaires. They were from Los Angeles, Philadelphia, Baltimore and Boston

96

area high schools. We have the most detailed, intensive responses from kids in the Boston area from two high schools here because Dr. Beardslee and I were able to be present in the schools and take time with the teachers and work with the kids to encourage them to fill them out."

I asked if there was any common denominator in the young people's attitudes toward nuclear war.

"There were variations and they depend on the amount of exposure to education the kids have had on the subject. Take, for example, the question of civil defence. In the initial questioning about half the kids said, 'Gee, that would be a good idea, shelters and all that might give us some chance.' The other half said it was ridiculous. In the most recent thirty-one interviews that we did with kids, only one of the thirty-one thought there was the slightest possibility that civil defence could be of any use whatsoever. In other words, as the kids become more aware of the facts concerning nuclear war, you begin to see shifts in thinking taking place."

I asked if the young people had become more aware in the past four years.

"Absolutely. In the earlier questions about security, for instance, some would say, 'Yes, I'm glad we have these weapons; they give us security from the Russians.' Now almost without exception, they say there is no security. They say, 'the more weapons we have, the less safe I feel — we have to stop. I'm terrified someone's going to use them.' We are getting the opposite of security. You have an increasing sense of anger, helplessness and frustration as you go from 1978 to 1982."

"What does this change do to the child in terms of personality? What kind of children do they become with all these fears?" I asked.

"What one sees is an attitude among many of the kids today of 'there's not going to be a future. I can't count on living beyond possibly two, three or four years. The chances are we are going to be incinerated in a nuclear war so live for now, get everything in.' They react differently. One person said, 'I'm eighteen. I may not live to be twenty-one so I want to marry now.' But others who have been taking drugs said, 'Well, I take these in order to blot out the sense that life has no future for me.' It's not so much impulsivity, because that means you are unable to control yourself; this is an intentional 'get it now' attitude."

"Would you say that they are becoming selfish and self-centred?"

"No, I wouldn't look at it that way. A number of them express a great deal of compassion and caring. They want to love but they wonder if it's worth loving. One boy in a recent symposium in Seattle sent a question up from the audience — 'Dr. Mack, how can I love a girl when I can't be sure that we'll have any future together?' — a very touching kind of concern."

Dr. Mack said that throughout the survey there were obvious attempts to give direction to the countries' leaders. The young people had a number of ideas and suggestions for the national leadership.

"First of all, they don't distinguish between the United States and the Soviet Union. The effort to sell the notion to the American people that the problem is caused by the Soviet Union is not working in this age group. From their point of view, they're both at fault. A direct quote from the report is, 'Both of them are like children, they're immature, they want it all, nobody wants to give anything.' Some say, 'Why don't the leaders just fight it out by themselves?' On the other hand, they can be very sophisticated. They don't accept the Russian social system. They don't want to live under the lack of freedom of personal expression that they understand exists in the Soviet Union. But they make a separation between that and the nuclear arms race which they see as imperiling both countries equally and has no point at all. They point out that we have to solve this nuclear arms thing somehow and the leaders have got to get together and start talking. 'Why don't they cut this crap and start talking?' That's another direct quote from one of them."

I had read the Task Force report prior to the interview and noticed in the quotes from the young people that the words "stupid" and "incompetent" were used repeatedly when referring to adults. I mentioned this to Dr. Mack.

"Yes, this is something we noticed. One of the things that help people grow up and have ideals and values is that you look up to your parents' generation and you make what you see around you a model of who and what to be. If you feel that your parents' generation has betrayed you, that they've offered you no future but only a world which has nuclear annihilation to look forward to, then this has a disillusioning impact in terms of the relationship between the generations. Kids are always feeling that their parents disappointed them but it's very different when they see their parents' generation as creating an inevitable destruction of the world. Many of them say, 'What right do they have to play with my life? I feel cheated out of my life.' The rage is very intense and it creates a strange personality. You get this funny kind of split in many of them in which they say, 'Well, I'm going to go ahead and plan as if there were a future. I'll go to college' and at the same time they're saying, 'I don't really believe I'm going to survive.' You have this kind of living on two levels."

I asked if he noticed any "psychic numbing" on the part of the teenagers.

"That's Robert Lifton's phrase, isn't it? No, not as much as adults. To be unaware that there is no survival, in any meaningful sense, from a nuclear exchange between the United States and the Soviet Union, requires a monumental turning away from reality and kids are not doing that. Now there are these groups, the survivalist groups, that are getting their high-powered rifles and digging caves in Colorado, ignoring the fact if they were to come out of the caves there'd be nothing but a radioactive wasteland around them — no food, no electricity, nothing. That kind of mentality I have not discovered among these kids. They don't turn away from it and many are getting their parents more active. I think it would be interesting to find out how many of the active adults have been woken up from their Rip Van Winkleism by their teenage kids."

"A number of young people that we have talked to in producing this program say it is difficult to get adults to talk about the nuclear threat. They apparently keep wanting to change the subject," I commented.

"It's because it's so horrible that we have learned to hide it," Dr. Mack answered. "The world is hanging on a thread; we and the Soviets have fifty thousand nuclear weapons; each one is controlled by electronic devices, any of which could go off by mistake, turning the whole planet into a tinder-box. Adults have now had thirty or more years of learning how to deep freeze their sense of horror, whereas kids have grown up in the last few years with this constantly before them. It's a bit like when you have a wound or cut and you don't have any chance to form scar tissue, so you keep re-injuring it. Most of us have had a chance to close our wounds since Hiroshima. Those of us who were around at that time also lived through the tests of the fifties, then the quiet period after '62 when we rather slept for a few years as arms built up, but then came the failure of SALT II and the beginning of talk of limited nuclear war which the Pentagon says we can win and the wounds open for us again because we see that this is absolute madness. And the kids know that it's insane."

"Your report suggests that the young people can deal with the realities of the situation and that they should be given a voice in the national debate," I pointed out.

"Yes, their voice should be heard. They are most affected. And the realities of the situation seem to be understood by them. They pay attention to TV and newspapers and speeches and the kind of quotes that prove nuclear war is a bad thing. What really changes things around is when a person finally realizes the truth of what can happen in a nuclear exchange. What would really happen to your town if a one-megaton bomb dropped on it. For example, to give a kind of scale, Massachusetts General Hospital has one of the best burn units in the country. It can only handle two or three really serious burn cases at a time. More than that and the unit is paralysed. Boston alone would have ten thousand serious burn cases if a single weapon dropped on this country and, of course, there are thousands of such weapons prepared to be launched. When you understand that emotionally, then there is no more secret. You talk about it and hopefully translate it into action. It's frustrating when nothing happens, as the kids tell us in these reports. Perhaps attitudes will change, but the big problem is the extent to which this country is committed to war preparedness. Our industry, our political way of thinking, the whole infrastructure of our economy is warlike and related to war. To get off that, to back away, means a conversion of resources, changes in our way of thinking that has just never been contemplated in the United States. I think increasingly the kids will be heard. They will get our attention. Whether the leadership, the entrenched economic political leadership of this country actually responds in time to make a difference and bring us back from the edge, remains to be seen."

In August of 1982, as my wife and I were packing for our annual visit to Ontario's Stratford Festival, Don Cumming phoned to say he had managed to arrange an interview with one of the foremost anti-nuclear leaders of the day, Dr. Helen Caldicott. We could meet her in New York, where she would give us an hour on camera between engagements. Shakespeare would have to wait. The opportunity to have this dynamic internationally respected pediatrician on our program was too good to miss.

Dr. Helen Caldicott is the president of the American branch of Physicians For Social Responsibility, a disarmament coalition of over 16,000 medical students and health professionals, a position which takes so much of her time that she has resigned her dual pediatric posts at Children's Hospital in Boston and Harvard Medical School. Australian-born, she has been credited with stopping the French nuclear testing in the South Pacific and since moving to the United States in 1977, where she is known as the Joan of Arc of Boston, has formed the medical campaign against nuclear war and the parent-oriented Women's Party for Survival. She is the mother of three teenage children.

We decided to do the interview at the CBC's New York offices. It was a Saturday morning and the offices were quiet. We were set up and waiting before the arranged time because we knew she was on a very tight schedule. Her work keeps her on the road for over one-third of the year giving speeches, attending rallies and answering interviewers' questions on radio and television and for newspapers and magazines. She is an outspoken critic of President Reagan's nuclear defence policy. "Carter was a wolf in sheep's clothing," she proclaims. "Reagan is a wolf in wolf's clothing."

Helen Caldicott was escorted into the office-cum-studio exactly at the set time. She trots into a room, her movements quick, almost nervous. She is of medium height with dark hair and flashing eyes that become piercing when she's making an angry statement. Her sentences tend to run together or change subject before they end. She has said it all so often, it becomes a challenge for the interviewer to offer a fresh approach to what has become a litany for her.

As we began the interview, she explained to me her early fear of nuclear arms. "I read *On the Beach* by Nevil Shute when I was fourteen and living in Melbourne, Australia. It had a great effect on me. I was naturally curious and read every article I could find on nuclear weapons. To a child-like mind at the time, I never understood why they kept building more. The children still don't understand. For thirty-seven years we've been arming to blow ourselves up."

"But nothing has happened," I countered. "We're still here. We're living good productive lives."

"It's a miracle," she responded, "only a miracle. Every year several thousand men are discharged from the military who have handled nuclear weapons while on drugs or alcohol. In an eighteen-month period the computers in the Pentagon made one hundred and fifty-one errors. At one time in November, 1979, we were forty minutes from nuclear war, which incidentally made headlines in the Canadian papers but was just a little tiny piece near the obituaries in the *New York Times*."

"So you really think that things right now are out of control?"

"They nearly are. The Proton Two missiles to be deployed in Europe can reach Moscow in six minutes. That's called 'launch on warning'. The cruise missiles to be developed next year are small strategic unverifiable nuclear weapons. You can't see them by satellite. Once they're deployed that's the end of arms control possibilities because you don't have arms control by trust, you have it by adequate verification. When this happens, we'll be almost out of control."

Dr. Caldicott has visited over a dozen countries, including the U.S.S.R., describing in gruesome detail the medical effects of nuclear war. Some critics of her presentation have called it the "Helen Caldicott Horror Show." She defends her position by saying, "Why shouldn't doctors show pictures of Hiroshima? We show pictures of cancer to get people to stop smoking."

I asked Dr. Caldicott if she would give our viewers an idea of what would happen if a nuclear attack occurred.

"Well, we're in New York right now. There are probably about sixty-five nuclear weapons targeted on New York City alone, but I'll just drop one. I'll drop a twenty megaton, equivalent to twenty million tons of TNT, or four times the collective size of all the bombs dropped during the Second World War. It explodes in microseconds, with the heat of the sun, and at ground level on a clear day it would dig a hole three-quarters of a mile wide and eight hundred feet deep, converting the buildings, the people and the earth below to radioactive fallout injected into a mushroom cloud. Up to six miles from the epicentre, every person would be killed, many in fact vaporized because when our bodies are exposed to the heat of the sun, we just turn into steam and disappear. Up to a radius of twenty miles, every person would be killed or injured so that they would later die. People at home would turn into missiles, hurtling out of buildings at one hundred miles an hour. Glass is fractured into millions of flying shards which penetrate human bodies. The pressure ruptures lungs and eardrums. If you look at a flash closely, your eyes would melt. The burns would just be incredible. Hundreds of thousands of the most deadly burns. There are only about a thousand acute burn facilities in the whole of this country because it takes a long time to treat a burn. All those patients would die with no medical attention, no analgesics, no help from their relatives, no one to find them in intense agony. If you're walking twenty-six miles out from the epicentre, the heat is still so intense your clothes would spontaneously ignite and you'd become a walking torch. If you looked at the flash from thirty-five to forty miles, it is so intense you'd be instantly blinded. And there would be a fire storm of fifteen hundred to three thousand square miles where probably the fires would coalesce, sucking the air in from the periphery. If you're in a fallout shelter, the fire would suck the oxygen out and you'd become asphyxiated and the heat would convert the fallout shelters to crematoria. Now every town or city down to a population of ten thousand or so is probably targeted with at least one bomb, there's such a redundancy of weapons on both sides. We think that, in an all-out nuclear war, within thirty days up to ninety percent of Americans would be dead and that's most Canadians, too, because the whole continent would be blanketed with lethal fallout for the first few days."

"Is there any place to hide? Should we be heading for the Canadian north woods or the Australian outback — anywhere?"

"There's no place to hide because there are several things that we think may happen to the ecology of the earth. Number one is that the ozone layer which is only three-quarters of an inch thick at standard temperature and pressure would be destroyed by nitrous oxides produced by the explosion of the bombs. We think a large part could be destroyed so that the ultraviolet rays getting in from the sun could induce sunburn to exposed people so severe that you could die within half an hour. We think possibly every human being and most creatures on the planet could be blinded by this ultraviolet light, and so if creatures are blinded, for instance, the bees can't fertilize the crops, etc. That's the death of the ecosphere. The ultraviolet light could damage micro-organisms which are the base of the pyramid of life of which man is at the apex. And if they're killed the pyramid collapses and life is destroyed. There'll be millions of dead bodies, millions upon millions of trillions of insects because the birds will be killed by the fallout. The insects already are resistant. They'll transmit disease from the dead to the living — black plague, tuberculosis, typhoid, poliomyelitis, hepatitis. And not just to the targeted countries, non-targeted countries as well. There's only thirty days' supply of food in the whole world at any one time and much of the Third World depends on that food. Those people will all die of mass starvation. We think that so much debris will be shot into the stratosphere that it could radiate the heat back from the sun and it could induce another ice age. And so there are a lot of interacting factors which could in fact destroy life on the planet."

I asked her what her response was to the argument, made by proponents of nuclear arms, that we had to keep building and stockpiling them because we couldn't let a potential enemy get the advantage.

"That sort of talk is absolutely anachronistic in the nuclear age. It's OK when you had bows and arrows. It was OK even when you had conventional weapons. It's totally insane now to make that kind of statement. If Russia launches her intercontinental ballistic missiles, there's no defence. You can't stop them. If she launches one hundred, then one hundred land. So we've set up a situation of mutually assured destruction or suicide. These weapons are totally suicidal. The whole thing between the super powers will be over in half an hour."

"Sometimes we tend to think of it as a battle between the super powers — the U.S. and Russia. Canada is sort of on the sidelines," I said.

"Well, you Canadians are all going to be killed, aren't you? So will the Mexicans, because you're all part of the North American continent. If I was a Canadian, I'd be hopping mad because they're fooling around with your lives. And how dare the super powers behave like nine-year-old little boys saying, 'I've got more bombs than you've got'? That's totally inappropriate in the nuclear age. Ninety-two percent of the world's people don't live in the super powers and they should rise up and stop these two crazy giants behaving the way they do."

"But these are human beings who are making the decisions about nuclear build-up. It is possible these experts know something we don't?" I asked.

"On the whole, we know something they don't. They are not physicians. They are not biologists. They tend to practise psychic numbing. They sort of know the consequences but they've got a mental or psychological barrier to emotionally feeling the facts. When I give speeches, I say the world is run by old men in the super powers and how many of these old men have ever witnessed the explosion of a hydrogen bomb, felt the blast and the heat, understand what $E=mc^2$ means? How many of these old men ever watched the birth of a baby? How many have helped a child to die and helped the parents in their grief? That's what we're talking about. They practise power games. They confirm what Einstein said: 'the splitting of the atom changes everything save man's mode of thinking. Thus we drift to unparalleled catastrophe.' Their modes of thinking haven't changed."

Almost every opponent of the nuclear build-up refers to Einstein's famous statement and also uses the phrase 'psychic numbing'. Like any other movement, these catchwords or quotations, which sound good in speeches or broadcasts, are used over and over.

"Perhaps we need this psychic numbing, Dr. Caldicott, to protect ourselves from going crazy in this kind of world," I suggested.

"Well, the people who experienced the explosion in Hiroshima and Nagasaki experienced psychic numbing because there were so many dead bodies, there was so much horror, they just became sort of like walking dead with no feelings. For them it was a survival mechanism. For us, who haven't experienced it, to block out the reality of the world in which we live and what we're doing ourselves by paying taxes, is a form of passive suicide."

"But what about the children, what effect does all this real information have on them?" I asked.

"Well, children aren't good at psychic numbing. Children know the truth, they've got a sixth sense. Many children believe they are not going to grow up, or get jobs, or get married, or have children because there is no future. As Shakespeare said, 'out of the mouths of babes and sucklings comes the truth'. That's right. And what have we done to these children? They're desperate, frantic and parents won't listen to their fears."

I saw nothing to be gained by interrupting her flow of speech to point out that the babes and sucklings quotation was from the Psalms, not Shakespeare, and had to do with strength, not truth. Since our time was nearly up, it was more important to have her reiterate some remarks she had made in interviews earlier in the year.

"I want to read a quote of yours, Dr. Caldicott, and have you comment on it. 'Some children begin to believe it is easier not to grow up. Their angers, hostilities and fears start to motivate against living out the rest of their lives.'"

"I don't know if I said that," she answered.

"I'm reading from an article in *McCall's* magazine," I said.

"Yes, I remember reading that quote and thinking that it didn't sound like me, so I'd like to disclaim it."

"All right then. Let me try another quote. 'Other young people find it necessary to band together in a peer group and hate the enemy.' Do you remember that?" I asked.

"Yes, but not young people. Old people do that. It's a sort of tribal mentality. And the psychiatrists think that the subliminal fear we have of nuclear war, all of us, is so great that instead of taking in the fear and feelings to ourselves, we tend to project it out on to others. And at this moment, as a tribe, America is projecting it out on the Russians. A few years ago it was the Chinese. The fear is so intense that these people become inanimate objects to us. And when people become inanimate objects, then we can talk about killing hundreds of millions of human beings and it doesn't feel bad at all. When that happens, we've lost our humanity."

"So the adults see the Russians as enemies and blame them for all this. Who do the children blame?"

"They see us, as to blame," Dr. Caldicott answered. "They say, 'Mr. Reagan, you've lived your life. I haven't even finished playing yet.' They say, 'Why do you keep making bombs when we've got enough to overkill the Russians forty times?' Obvious questions."

"Some say children should be shielded from this information, that they shouldn't be told."

"You can't shield them. They're too smart. They watch television every day and know what's going on. These children have enough knowledge now, because they play these Atari games, which are nuclear war games, to know what nuclear war means. They know it's all over in a couple of hours and everyone's dead. They're not silly enough to believe it when the administration talks about fighting a prolonged winnable war over the course of six months."

"You have given up your job to devote yourself full time to the anti-nuclear movement. More and more people are becoming concerned and want to get involved. What can the average Canadian or American citizen do?" I asked.

"Citizens should be informing themselves. You know, doctors once were very arrogant and used to tell the patient that we'd just look after everything, and we'd use a language that they didn't understand. We've learned now, because of patient pressure, really, to boil the language down so that they can understand what's wrong with their bodies. Similarly we have to start doing that with the Pentagon jargon. Boil the language down so people know what a cruise missile is, what its flight characteristics are, how it flies under radar undetected, how it homes in accurately on its target, which means it's unverifiable.

It's really an extension of the art of medicine. Because now people know that nuclear war's bad for their health but they don't really understand the pathology behind the arms race, which are the weapons systems, and who's doing what with what, like the STAR talks and the SALT talks. They can't use their democracy unless they're adequately informed. They should read my book, *Nuclear Madness: What You Can Do.* They should contact Physicians For Social Responsibility in Toronto and other cities in Canada. And we have a very graphic film called *The Last Epidemic.* People cry after they see it, even hard-bitten cynical journalists. And you can show that film to clubs, to Rotary Clubs, to churches, to businessmen's luncheons, and women's groups. And then start organizing. And we have to stop saying they ought to do this, Reagan ought to do that, the Russians should do this. *I* have to do it, because I'm an adult and I've got children and I'm a parent and I want them to survive."

Her eyes were intent and piercing now and I could see her anger. I knew she had to leave in a few minutes. She was scheduled for an interview at NBC — fortunately only a block away. I had time to squeeze in just a couple more questions.

"Sometimes, when you work so hard, then go home at night and turn on the news, only to hear that more money has been appropriated for nuclear arms, you must think 'what's the use?'"

"It just makes me madder. It makes me more determined. I could easily have become cynical and said, 'what the hell, I'll become a hedonist, go back to Australia, lie in the sun, drink Australian beer and wine.' I mean, why not? Just wait till the end comes. But I don't believe that is morally correct. I don't believe it's correct because I'm a parent and my ultimate responsibility is to make sure my children grow up and live a normal life. It's not correct because I'm a pediatrician and I took the Hippocratic Oath. And my responsibility really is to all the children of the planet. And what are we here for? Surely not to destroy God's creation."

So many people I have met and interviewed admitted that their concern about nuclear arms began when their own children were born. Somehow the build-up became more frightening, and the pressure of time more desperate when you looked into the trusting eyes of your child. I asked Dr. Caldicott if she was motivated mainly by fear for the future of her own children.

"Yes, the most creative and wonderful thing I ever did was

107

give birth to those babies. And I think the strongest physiological instinct is the instinct a woman has to protect those babies — even before protecting her own life. And I think if we can mobilize that instinct in all women and some men we can save the planet."

We said goodbye to Dr. Caldicott and watched her trot out and down the street to NBC — more interviews, more spreading her gospel attacking nuclear weapons. She certainly has an effect. Her dedication, commitment and logic have won thousands to her cause. So have Dr. Frank Sommers and Bishop Hunthausen and Jim and Shelly Douglas — but sometimes I wonder if there is any stopping this nuclear juggernaut that appears to have a life of its own. Will all the protest meetings, election referenda, letters to parliament and television interviews slow down the obsession to build more and more nuclear warheads? Who really is at the controls of the nuclear machines? We tend to think our leaders are, but I find very revealing an excerpt from the memoirs of Soviet leader Nikita Khrushchev. He tells of a conversation he had at Camp David with U.S. President Dwight D. Eisenhower.

"Tell me, Mr. Khrushchev," the President asked, "how do you decide on funds for military expenditures?" Then, before I had a chance to say anything, he continued, "Perhaps first I should tell you how it is with us. ... It's like this. My military leaders come to me and say, 'Mr. President, we need such and such a sum for such and such a program. If we don't get the funds we need, we'll fall behind the Soviet Union.' So I invariably give in. That's how they wring money out of me. They keep grabbing for more, and I keep giving it to them. Now tell me. How is it with you?"

Khrushchev replied, "It's just the same. Some people from our military department come and say, 'Comrade Khrushchev, look at this. The Americans are developing such and such a system. We could develop the same system, but it would cost such and such.' I tell them there's no money; it's all been allotted already. So they say, 'If we don't get the money we need and if there's a war, then the enemy will have superiority over us'. ... Then I put the matter to the government and we take the steps which our military people have recommended."

So, who is in charge? Ultimately, in a democracy, the people are. The onus then seems to be on us, because it is unlikely the voice of the Soviet citizen makes much impression on its government, even though Russian mothers and fathers want a future for their children as much as we do. At this dangerous stage of our nuclear development, ideological differences mean very little. As John Kenneth Galbraith said in a recent Toronto speech, "None should doubt it. The ashes of Capitalism will be indistinguishable even by the most accomplished surviving ideologue from the ashes of Communism."

The grass roots movement seems to be the only hope. If enough Canadians and Americans let their views be known at the ballot box there may still be time to turn the war machine around. I think the words of Edmund Burke are as true today as ever: "The only thing necessary for the triumph of evil is for good men to do nothing."

LIVING LONGER

Our attitudes to those who have grown old, as well as their attitudes toward themselves, are both complex and illuminating. A perfect illustration was my father's Aunt Et.

She came to live with us when I was six years old. She was ninety. For the next six years she was part of my daily life. Not until many years after her death did I fully appreciate the legacy of virtues she bequeathed.

In her prime she had been a tall, buxom, large-boned woman of considerable strength and stern demeanor. A firm believer in careers for women, she started a grocery store and stage-coach depot on the historic "front" of Sydney township at Bayside, on the shore of the Bay of Quinte. She soon added a livery stable to provide a change of horses for the coach line and finally a post office for the convenience of travelers between Toronto and Kingston. As the Bayside postmistress she achieved a status far higher than her easygoing husband, Wes, who practised his carpentry craft in a small workshop behind the store. The only element missing in this ambitious lady's life was a child and when both of them were in their forties, Et and Wes were overjoyed with the birth of Raymond. Et decided she should close or at least limit the business to devote herself to child-rearing but when Wes died suddenly, three years later, she was forced to keep the operation going as her sole source of income.

After the turn of the century, changes took place over which Aunt Et had no control. Motor buses began to replace the horses for the Toronto to Kingston trip and passenger terminals were located in the larger centres of Trenton and Belleville. Rural route mail delivery service began and bypassed Bayside as a postal station. Only the store remained, which she continued to run as a service to the community. Young Raymond remodeled his father's old carpentry shop and by the time of World War I achieved such a reputation for quality work that he was attracting customers from as far as Oswego, New York. It was there, on a business trip, that he met, courted and later married Miss Winifred Ramsay, and in 1917 the young couple presented baby Marie to aging Grandma Et.

Two years later, the influenza epidemic swept through the nation and one of its victims was Raymond, only twenty-seven. Now seventy-five, Aunt Et once again took over the reins of business. She expanded the grocery store to include a dry goods section with bolts of material, yarn and sewing supplies. She added a toy section featuring rocking-horse chairs manufactured according to Raymond's old blueprints and a patent medicine corner where she dispensed such popular items as Dodd's Kidney Pills, Fletcher's Worm Powder, Lydia Pinkham's Pink Pills for Pale People and home-made cough syrup.

Alone and homesick after Raymond's death, his young widow returned to Oswego with little Marie. She remarried a few years later but would not visit Canada. Aunt Et never saw her grand-daughter again.

For the next fifteen years this remarkable woman carried on by herself but time was slowly wearing her down. Her hearing failed first, then her memory. Some days she would forget to open the doors of the store and since she couldn't hear the customers' knocking, would wonder why no one came shopping that day. Her large body was becoming bent and her walk slow. Increasing senility divided her mind between awareness and memories. Sometimes she would prepare supper and set the table for three, pulling up the handmade high chair for little Raymond, then return to reality as she stood calling them in the deserted carpentry shop.

Although my father had asked her many times to move to our farm a few miles north of Bayside, it wasn't until a small fire — the result of an overturned oil lamp — burned a part of her storage room that he firmly insisted. With great reluctance she agreed, on the condition that she be allowed to pay room and board and share in the household chores.

I still remember the day we brought her home. She had stayed to supervise the moving of her furniture and personal belongings. With a young boy's curiosity, I had been scurrying through the nearly bare rooms, poking into boxes of books and pictures and leftover toys. As the last load was ready to go, I found her in the middle of the empty store gazing around at the walls and counters. Where was her mind now? Was it in September 1936 or was it many years and hopes and heartaches ago, in the days when the worn, scarred counter had handled so much merchandise? The curved glass now reflected bare shelves. The pigeon-holes, alphabetically arranged for letters and parcels, were empty. Did she see them full again?

She was so tall that I had to reach up to put my hand into hers. She never looked down. She gripped my hand hard to steady herself as we started for the door and said, in that loud voice the hard-of-hearing use, "Come on, Raymond. It's time to go."

And Raymond I became as far as she was concerned. At first it bothered me and I would shout angrily, "My name is Roy, Aunt Et." She would smile and tell me not to be rude. My mother said just to ignore it. "It certainly won't do you any harm if Aunt Et wants to call you Raymond."

Since I was the youngest in the family and she couldn't be left alone, I spent a lot of time with Aunt Et while my parents and brothers and sisters were out in the fields or barn. She spent most days sitting in her old Boston rocker by the kitchen window, humming softly while she rocked and stared out over our fields, watching the seasons change. Sometimes she would call me to look out of the window. "Isn't that Wes coming up the lane?"

"No, Aunt Et," I would answer. "That's just a fence post. No one is coming."

At other times, with absolute clarity of mind, she would oversee my homework and quiz me on current events. When her eyesight began to fail, she would ask me to read her Bible to her. She knew each chapter and verse so well that I was never able to avoid what I considered the dull parts. "Now Raymond, you're skipping again. God meant us to read every word or he wouldn't have put them all in there."

Of an evening, we would turn the radio up louder than normal so that she could hear Jack Benny and Fred Allen and Amos 'n' Andy. I'm not sure she understood what we were all laughing at but she enjoyed being in the family circle around the radio.

She did understand the news. With the outbreak of World War II and two of my brothers donning uniforms, Aunt Et listened solemnly as the newscasts and bulletins from Europe became darker and more frightening. Many times, however, she would confuse reports of action at Dunkirk or Dieppe with Ypres and the Somme and we knew she was talking about another war. Then there was the day when we were discussing the relative merits of Britain's General Montgomery and Germany's Field-Marshal Rommel and she ventured the suggestion that William T. Sherman would show them both! With a shock, we realized she was talking about the American Civil War. Indeed, her memories of Abraham Lincoln were very clear. She was nineteen the year he was assassinated and could remember the details of that night at Ford's Theater as reported in the press of the day. Like many elderly people, she could recall in detail what happened many years ago, but fail to remember what happened the day before.

In terms of Canadian politics, she had been twenty-one when Confederation came along and would support the Tories all her life. She was quick to complain to any visitor that the country would be in much better hands if we could get rid of that Grit rascal, William Lyon Mackenzie King, who had been in office, she insisted, far too long.

She enjoyed family discussions on any topic and would argue firmly for her point of view — even with my father. And although she claimed it was "a lot of fuss about nothing", she was really very pleased when each year, around her birthday, local reporters would drive out to the farm and do little features on her. To the perennial question, "And to what do you attribute your longevity?", she would give a different answer every year, very often to the same reporter.

When I think back now, what I remember most is just her presence. She was a solid rock of assurance and understanding when the world didn't go right for a young boy. When parents and brothers and sisters and playmates all conspired to make life miserable, Aunt Et's ample lap and soothing voice afforded comfort and kept the ogres at bay.

My mother was a small, gentle, hard-working farmer's wife who raised ten children and worked in the fields as well. In many ways, Aunt Et was another burden she didn't need. It took all Mother's strength and mine to move Aunt Et from room to room, to the toilet, to her bed or to the sink where she insisted on helping with the dishes. Many times I'd see Mom re-wash or re-dry dishes Aunt Et's failing eyes had missed or take out stitches when her stiffened fingers botched the mending. Though Mom could have done these chores more efficiently herself, she maintained it was important that Aunt Et continue to feel useful. Long after Aunt Et died, Mom would say that, by being with us, she had taught us all lessons in living and had given us far more than we had ever given her.

When I was twelve, I left home to live with an older sister and go to a new school. Excited and eager to start this new adventure, I scarcely listened when Aunt Et said her goodbyes to me. "Be sure and help with the chores, Raymond, and work hard at your times tables. Your reading is very good but your arithmetic needs a lot of improvement or you won't be able to work in the store."

A few days after I left, as the neighbors gathered at our farm for the annual silo-filling bee, Aunt Et asked my mother if she would help her lie down on the parlor couch for a little nap before supper. One of the farmers, who had stopped by the house to replenish the water bucket for the men in the fields, lent his arm in the way I had always done. A half hour later, when my mother went to wake her for the evening meal, she found Aunt Et had died peacefully in her sleep.

I think I grew up the day Aunt Et died. I don't remember ever being a child after that. And that was all right, because Aunt Et had helped me make the transition. Her "Raymond" could go into the world now. Aunt Et's work was finally done.

It was normal when I was growing up for the younger families to give their elderly relatives a home, quite typical to see three or even four generations under the same roof. The gulf between the generations was often bridged by the old. Our lives are more complex and hurried now and in our rush to keep pace we sometimes ignore the needs of the elderly.

Statistics Canada tells us that by the year 2000 about three to

114

three and a half million Canadians will be sixty-five and over. They are the fastest growing group in our population because Canadians are living longer and the chance of surviving to old age has increased for everyone. Nine out of every ten of us will reach sixty-five. Two-thirds of these will reach seventy and forty percent will reach seventy-five. Of all the massive societal changes in the last half of the twentieth century, this is undoubtedly the most profound.

Aware of these facts and determined to make a corporate contribution to the study of the issue, General Foods Limited organized two conferences in Toronto and Ottawa in 1979 and 1980. They invited to these events experts in gerontology, nutrition and geriatric support services to help focus public, professional and governmental attention on the needs of Canada's senior citizens. Since I was asked to take part in these conferences, I was able to meet and listen to people who had devoted their lives to the concerns of the aged.

One such person is John Brocklehurst, a professor of geriatric medicine at the University of Manchester in England. A warm, humorous man of great compassion, Dr. Brocklehurst impressed me with his insights and attitudes. "In the past, great age was so unusual that it was honored and in pre-industrial society old people had much to give. There were no communications media to allow all people to be instantly informed on all things and the old were the repositories of wisdom and knowledge. They had the accumulated experience. They were the historians. The move from a rural to an industrial society occurred gradually over the last two hundred years but in the past seventy-five years we have moved through stages of mass production and automation to computerization — to the day of the mini-circuit and the micro-circuit. More and more we depend on machines and on rapidly developing technology. Today, even at the age of fifty, a person is likely to be profoundly obsolete. So although the old are a highly significant group in society, their expertise, their life's training and knowledge may no longer be relevant to the times."

Dr. Brocklehurst agrees with many experts in the field that this obsolescence, or feeling of lack of worth, is one of the biggest problems the old person faces. Compulsory retirement at sixty-five adds to this feeling. Suddenly you are turned out of a very meaningful part of your life. You are no longer needed and your value as a contributing human being is reduced.

One of the ways to avoid this is to prepare well in advance for

115

retirement. "It may be educationalists' greatest challenge over the next quarter century to prepare people for their marvellous bonus years," he says. "You cannot prepare for retirement the week before you retire."

Dr. Brocklehurst feels that, for many, a second career would be the answer — not in paid employment, necessarily, but in creative, exciting or service-giving activities. "How many people have spent their working lives in activity that is dull, often dreary and monotonous?" he asked. "How many have dreamed of the things they would really like to be doing but couldn't? How often do we lament the passing away of craftsmanship, loss of individually made furniture, ornaments, rugs and tapestries? How often do we regret the shortage of volunteers to help other people in need — handicapped children, young people in difficulty and the old themselves? The setting up of voluntary visiting schemes, good neighbor schemes, drop-in day centres — all of these can be immensely helpful to the old. These things, I believe, are the purposes of the bonus years: to use our skills as craftsmen, artists and creators; to absorb ourselves in history, biography and music; to grow prize chrysanthemums or breed prize rabbits; to work for others as volunteers."

One of the founders of modern gerontology is Dr. Alex Comfort. While he is perhaps best known for his controversial book *The Joy of Sex*, his 1976 book *A Good Age* is considered by many to be one of the best and certainly one of the first modern approaches to successful aging.

At the conference in Ottawa, Dr. Comfort expressed a concern that we tend to lump all old people together as if they were clones. He stressed that old people are still people and differ as widely as any others and that this fact must be understood by all of us.

"We should remember," he said, "that there are two kinds of aging. There is the physical process with which we are familiar, the greying of the hair and the weakening of the muscles which really isn't very important for most of us. In the absence of illness or adverse social circumstances, most of us do not find that our intelligence, our interest in work or our enjoyment of life declines with age."

Dr. Comfort also discussed another kind of aging, called sociogenic aging, meaning the role which our folklore imposes on the old. He attacked society's stereotypes of the old and how this attitude affects their self image. He sees society dubbing the elderly as "unintelligent, ineducable, asexual and unemployable" and maintains that this puts great pressure on them to fulfill these expectations.

Comfort said that a lot of people reach old age enormously relieved to find that the stereotype is not in fact true and that although it "applies to all other old people," it doesn't apply to them.

He also had criticism for the physicians who believe in the old age stereotype. "The embryo physician believes that geriatrics is a branch of embalming, that the only thing which you need to do for old people is to jolly them with benign neglect and that any symptomatology which you may see is a result of a passage of time. Then when old people do in fact get in a confused state through over-medication or through infection or through electrolyte imbalance, or when they develop the dementias which we impolitely term senile, but which are only senile in the way that measles is infantile, we say, 'Well, poor old chap, what do you expect at his age?' We treat the whole thing in a fatalistic manner."

Comfort joined Brocklehurst in decrying early retirement. "Work is probably the best of all preservatives and most people would rather remain at work. I will be happy to argue with any economist the enormous fiscal advantages of retaining skilled people in the labor force."

The fact is, of course, that as people get older they leave their jobs either through personal choice or forced retirement. For many, not only does a feeling of uselessness set in, but they find themselves in economic straits. Rapidly rising inflation makes a mockery out of government subsidies. Food, heat, rent and clothing take increasing bites out of the monthly pension cheque so that the elderly are no longer able to meet their financial obligations and must rely completely on government organizations for assistance. Rather than setting up support systems in the home, Canada seems to favor institutionalization, taking away the independence that is so cherished by us all.

Dr. Cope Schwenger, Professor of Community Health with the Faculty of Medicine at the University of Toronto, says that only two countries in the world have a higher rate of institutionalization than Canada — Sweden and the Netherlands. Schwenger developed statistics having to do with institutional care over a period of fifteen years and found that between eight and nine percent of Canada's elderly are in some kind of institution, including hospitals. Alberta, the survey suggests, has the greatest proportion of institutionalized elderly at well over ten percent. Ontario's is around seven percent.

"Why is this?" asks Dr. Schwenger. "Is it climate, geography, mobility, affluence or too many hospitals? Britain, where the rate is between five and five and a half percent, didn't have the money to build institutions, so they went into a home-care plan under the National Health Service from its inception, and are very glad they did."

Seventy-five percent of people in Canada over the age of sixty-five will die in an institution. Fifty percent of these will die in hospital. A peaceful death at home, surrounded by loved ones, seems a thing of the past.

The attempt to keep old people in their homes and still provide a degree of professional care has been achieved in some areas of Canada. One of the most noteworthy is in the Niagara region of Ontario. It was there, while filming the *Man Alive* program *All our Tomorrows*, that I met Doug Rappleje, Director of the Niagara Senior Citizens Department.

Doug is a tall, bespectacled man with an air of efficiency that reminds you of your friendly accountant — which is what he was until asked to manage a local home for the aged. He found that he really liked old people and began setting up programs designed to meet their needs and use their abilities, not just deal with them as society's rejects.

Throughout the Niagara district, under Doug's guidance, a vast network of support programs is combined with long-term care to give old people a choice of lifestyle and to satisfy the needs of each person.

The Day-Care Program is one of the most popular, with seniors being picked up by a special bus in the morning, brought to the local centre for the day, then taken home in the evening. It's a chance to get out, make friends and have a good meal. At the centre they can shoot pool, go bowling, have a hairdo or just visit. All the facilities of the centre are available and the cost to the elderly is about two dollars a day. In many cases, where the old person is living with sons or daughters, this represents a break for the family, too. Typical was the reaction of one young woman I interviewed: "My mother-in-law lives with us and I don't think I could cope with her twenty-four hours a day. Having her come into day-care, being with people her own age and getting interested in crafts, enables us to carry on as a family. We can enjoy her when she comes home and hear her talk about the day she has had."

Doug says the Day-Care Program provides an alternative for the elderly between struggling to live in their own homes or being in an institution. "I think it's wrong when elderly persons have to come in permanently to a long-term facility simply because they're lonely or they need a good meal or they can't get proper foot care — which, incidentally, is very important to the aged."

Eating alone all the time is a miserable business for anyone. Many old people suffer from malnutrition. Shopping may be difficult and it is hard to buy small portions, harder still to make the pension cheque stretch. Yet nobody wants charity. That's just another blow to one's dignity. At the day-care centre, the seniors pay for their day, have a hot meal and someone to enjoy it with, but have no dishes to do afterward.

For those who cannot get out to visit the centre, other services are provided. "Meals on Wheels" is a very popular program, with volunteers driving their own cars to deliver hot, nutritious meals at noon and very often becoming friends and confidantes of the elderly. This visit also provides a welcome break in a lonely day and enables the volunteer to check on health conditions or other needs while there. The cost to the recipient is one dollar per day.

Many elderly people living at home can cook their own meals and take care of themselves but are unable to cope with the numerous chores necessary to maintain a home. For these people, Doug came up with the Senior Citizens' Assistance Program.

"This is really to provide home maintenance assistance. For minimum cost we provide people to rake the lawn, put up storm windows, do repair jobs. We also provide transportation for doctors' appointments or visits to friends. We also have people come in to teach nutrition and safety in the home. There is no question that this program is going to become our most important."

When I talked to Doug, the assistance program had been in operation only a year and a half and he already had 700 clients. I asked one of the clients how important it was to have this kind of help. "Well, we would have to sell our house if we didn't have it. We just couldn't keep up with the outside work. My wife has a heart condition and I get out of breath easily and if I had to cut this backyard myself it would take forever. Also shopping for groceries. They will drop us off at the store, then come back and pick us up again. I just can't express in words how important it

119

is to a lot of us people. It's just wonderful."

Another fascinating alternative in the Niagara area is the Foster Home Care Program, where old people are invited into private homes to live in a family setting.

I visited one home where the young husband and wife had decided it would be good for their two children to be exposed to older people so, through the Foster Home Care Program, they "adopted" four grandmothers. The wife told me why they did it. "My grandparents lived with me when I was a child and my husband's grandparents lived with him until they died, so we know how valuable it is to grow up in that atmosphere. You might think it would cause problems but it has been just the opposite. We've become closer, more of a family unit. My husband works quite a bit of shift work and it used to become lonely sometimes. Now I've got four ladies to keep me company. The kids call them all grandmother. My youngest one thinks it's just wonderful. In school the other day she announced that she had more grandmothers than anyone. Of course she was counting her real ones too."

I talked with one of the grandmothers about the program. "Don't you find the kids get noisy at times?" I asked.

"Well, when we first came here, it took a bit of getting used to but they've taken to us marvellously. They get a bit noisy at times, but on the other hand, so do we. We just put up with each other."

"What does this Foster Home Care Plan mean to you?"

"Well, I can't walk like I used to but I do get out. I like to go to church and go shopping and I go down to Sunset Haven to visit, but I'm eighty-five years old and I can't do everything for myself. Now, a plan like this is for those of us who don't have a home of our own but still don't want to move in with a crowd. You see, there's three or four hundred people down there at Sunset Haven. Here it's more like home. Even the food tastes better. Now, don't get me wrong; the food is fine down at the centre, too, but you can't cook a meal for four hundred people the way you can here for eight."

The feeling of being part of a family is very important to most of us but it seemed even more essential to the elderly I interviewed. There appeared a need and a remarkable ability to communicate with the young.

Recognizing this, Doug Rappelje started day nurseries in some of the old-age homes. Working mothers could drop off their children in the morning and pick them up in the evening, secure in the knowledge that they had spent a most interesting day with the attentive residents.

Another group I met were the Volunteens, hundreds of teen-age boys and girls who volunteer to come into the old age centres after school and on weekends to help serve meals, write letters or read to the blind. Often the residents were more comfortable asking these young people to do things for them than bothering a nurse.

There may be organizations similar to the Niagara Senior Citizens Department in other parts of Canada, but I had never before seen such a comprehensive network of programs for the elderly. Doug Rappelje told me, "We must all work very hard at changing attitudes toward older people who are suffering from society's stereotype of them. There is some improvement but we still have a long way to go. We must look at the potential of the elderly instead of their limitations, otherwise we are wasting one of our greatest human resources."

These programs in the Niagara region meet the social and physical needs of the elderly. But what of their intellectual needs? Many universities throughout the world are discovering that there are many old people who wish to engage their brains at an advanced level of thought and whose major concern is to be challenged. These universities are currently developing exten-sive programs to meet this need.

One stereotype society has of the elderly is that they are a passive lot. But some are beginning to realize the political wallop they have. One group in Toronto's Borough of York made head-lines and history when they decided to take on City Hall, which was planning to move them from their beloved Beech Hall to new facilities. The *Man Alive* program, *The Battle for Beech Hall*, went on the air on December 13, 1981 but the controversy had been raging since February 1979. That was when the one hundred and fifty senior citizens, some of whom had been living at Beech Hall for twenty-seven years, read in the *Toronto Star* that the building was to be demolished and they had to leave by that September.

The decision had been made, at a closed council meeting, to use the land for other developments more profitable to the borough. The excuse given was that Beech Hall needed renova-tion at a cost of $655,000 and that since Metropolitan Toronto had constructed a new building called Outlook Manor not too far away, it would make good sense to move the Beech Hall residents. The one alderman who voted against the motion leaked the story to the press. The residents were unbelieving, then shocked, then furious. Several were eager to express their opinions in front of the *Man Alive* cameras.

As they spoke, it seemed to me that their struggle against the system, their being taken for granted, their eventual arousal into a political force, all represented a microcosm of the state of the elderly throughout Canada.

One man asked, "How would you like to have somebody come and knock on your door and say because part of the foundation was giving way, you'd have to move? Well, you say, it's not. There's nothing wrong with that house. I'll stand by it."

At the heart of the struggle were four very intelligent, active members of the community who, while saddened by the Borough's attitude, were ready for the fight. All in their seventies or eighties, these three women and one man described their affection for Beech Hall. We were fortunate to find them at an informal meeting in one of their apartments. I was struck by the comfortable, homey atmosphere there, so unusual in the average housing development for the elderly.

"It's just the grandest place to live. I've been happy here from the first day I put my foot inside my apartment. I felt at peace. I felt happiness. I lived in my own place for over thirty-five years. I raised three children. They're all married, with homes of their own. I could go live with them but I don't want to. I prefer to be on my own. I'm independent. Coming here was just like coming home. I can leave my door open and my neighbor across the hall leaves her door open. We sit and chat to each other there or we go out and sit under the trees in the park."

"It's an ideal setting for senior citizens. There is grass around, and trees. We each had our own garden we could work. If you wanted flowers, OK. If you wanted to stick in a tomato plant, all right."

"There's nothing like it. Have you seen other senior citizens' arrangements in the city with this much grass and ground around it? There's not another home like this in Metro. You might find something like this in Grande Prairie, but that's about it."

Under the Borough's plan, the old people were to be moved into the brand new high-rise apartment, Outlook Manor. The seniors told us in no uncertain terms what they thought of that.

The man leaned forward in his chair, obviously livid at their proposal. "You know they've given us the idea that they're moving us to a lovely, clean building where there are no stairs. Well, people my age are just not used to elevators and heights. They're afraid of them. The worst thing is they don't give us a bedroom. We've had our own bedroom all our lives. Suddenly you're put into one room and it's demeaning. It's degrading to all senior citizens, no matter where you go, all over the world, to be pushed into a box."

The women joined in, leaving no doubt as to the depth of their conviction. One said, "I call it a jailhouse and I figure that's all it is. I told the lady when I went down to city hall that if I wanted to live in a jailhouse, I'd go steal something; then they could put me in and I'd live there for free. I don't feel like paying money to live in one room. She wasn't too happy about that. She thought I was disgusting. I didn't think I was disgusting."

A quiet voice from the end of the couch surprised us all. Fighting for control, this angry woman added, "I sort of got nipped under the collar about it. I was sitting on my chesterfield one day and this lady came in and told me I had to move. She said if I didn't get out and move into that new building, I'd never get another place in the area. She was telling me what to do about my own place and I pretty nearly threw her through my window. I didn't like that."

Tempers did indeed flare. Residents started getting support from neighbors who enjoyed having them on their street. Together they attended a council meeting to state their case. A tough, eighty-nine-year-old Scotswoman spoke for the group: "We're fighting for a way of life. We're fighting for the freedom to say we like things the way they are. Leave us alone. Raise our rents if you have to, but leave us alone."

They asked council for a delay of thirty days to give them time to come up with alternative proposals. Council refused. The closing would proceed as scheduled.

At this point, Beech Hall found an ally. An organization involved in co-operative housing heard about the fight and suggested a plan.

Spokesman for the co-op, Alexander Wilson, told us, "They were beginning to see they were fighting a losing battle with the Borough. The place was going to be closed. The only possibility for saving the property was in buying it. That's where a co-op could help. If they formed a co-op they could go to Central Mortgage and Housing to get financing enabling them to buy the project."

The residents pondered the possibility of owning their own

building. "At first," said one, "I wasn't sure. I didn't know very much about co-ops. But as I got a little more knowledge, I figured this is what we needed."

Another added his experience. "I thought basically it was a good idea because you have more personal interest in your apartment and the building and the grounds because you'd be part owner."

The general attitude was summed up by a third woman. "I was like the other ladies, I didn't understand too much about it, but it sounded a lot better than having to move some place you didn't want to and away from where you had lived for most of your life."

With help from the co-op group, the seniors organized their own co-operative. With federal government support, they would qualify for grants and loans to repair Beech Hall completely and keep it open. The federal government agreed to put up the financing and, shortly before the deadline, the Seniors' Co-op offered to buy Beech Hall from the Borough for $415,000, which would pay off the Borough's mortgage on the project. Everyone expected council to approve the sale at its next meeting. Some members of council, however, took the position that paying off the mortgage was not enough. Money could be made by selling Beech Hall to developers at a profit to the Borough. The co-op couldn't pay more. Council rejected the proposed sale to the co-op by one vote.

It was a bitter blow to the seniors and their neighbors. The effort, the excitement and the disappointment affected the health of some. Several began to pack and say their goodbyes. Fortunately, a large number decided they would at least go down fighting.

They launched a door-to-door campaign and collected six thousand signatures on a petition calling for the Borough to reconsider the co-op's offer. At the next council meeting, three hundred Beech Hall residents and supporters filled the council chambers to plead their case.

An alderman presented his position. "No politician in his right mind would take on forty-five percent of the population of this Borough, so when somebody does, maybe you had better start asking why. I believe that the issue that's before us with Beech Hall is not whether we're kicking the senior citizens around, because I'm satisfied we're not. I think it's the fear of change. I think it's the fear of the unknown. What we've tried to do is to assure those in the community that we're going to develop that site. We're going to put up a really nifty, top-notch development."

This assurance meant nothing to the seniors, who pointed out that as citizens of the area they had built the Borough over the years. "We've paid our dues. Why should we be kicked out now like a bunch of old horses that you don't need any more. We've been faithful to you, now it's your turn."

As a compromise of sorts, the co-op asked if council would lease Beech Hall to the seniors for thirty or forty years. The Borough would still own the land but without the expense of maintaining the project. The compromise was rejected. Council still insisted on selling Beech Hall at a profit.

For most of the seniors the battle was now over. Within four weeks after that council meeting, half the residents had moved out. In another month only four residents remained. The long battle had made this group even more adamant during the months since we first met them. Their quiet arguments had turned to outright condemnation of the Borough and an even stronger determination was evident. Amid the other residents' packing crates, we asked how they were feeling and what they intended to do. Here are their comments:

"I don't care. I don't give a damn. I'm not going to let them push me around. Just wait 'til the next election. I pray that God forgives them for what they've done."

"I'm not moving. No. I'm staying here to the bitter end. Nobody is going to push me out."

"Nobody has given me a good reason why I should move."

"I stuck it out before when things were hopeless-looking. It's getting pretty lonely but I get thinking — God damn it, if I just stay here, we'll win. We're going to have Beech Hall back again."

The Borough put Beech Hall up for sale or lease to the highest bidder. At the last moment the Central Mortgage and Housing Corporation authorized an increase in the co-op's offer to $750,000. A co-op representative told us, "We were very worried because we thought that the money we were offering was not going to be the highest bid in cold, hard cash. But what we had going for us was that there were still people living there and in order for the Borough to accept someone else's offer they would have to evict them and those people were determined to stay. They had neighbors behind them too. Things were very tense."

The co-op's offer arrived, just minutes before the tenders were opened. To everyone's surprise, theirs was the best offer.

Finally the Borough gave in. They would lease the project to

125

the co-op for forty-five years. Beech Hall had been saved. It had taken eight long months.

In the end, only fifteen of the original one hundred and fifty residents returned. Some were too ill to come back. Others just couldn't bear to pack up again. But within a year, new seniors had filled the apartments.

After it was all over, one of the four residents who had remained through the entire battle commented, "We seniors have a lot of fight in us, regardless of our age. We've all got years of experience and we've got a lot of knowledge that gets put to the test when something like this comes along. I think with the help and support of others, we could do almost anything."

From my own family experiences and from working on programs such as *All Our Tomorrows* and *The Battle for Beech Hall* and on conventions with gerontologists, I have come to the conclusion that the key issue is society's attitude to aging.

Anthropologists have suggested that societies may be classified into four categories based on their attitude toward the aged:

1. Societies that degrade and abuse their aged;
2. Societies that simply ignore human beings once they are seen as old or obsolete;
3. Societies that view their aged as vulnerable and needing assistance and that help their aged and expect them in return to be "properly grateful";
4. Societies that accord respect to their aged, treat them as equals or even with special honor.

Which category are we in?

Dr. Robert Butler, Director of the National Institute of Aging in the United States, has coined the term "agism" to describe our prevalent attitude. He says age discrimination in our society is as violent as racism or sexism. Compulsory retirement and age discrimination in employment are some of the manifestations of agism. Disregard for the special interests of aged voters by politicians and of aged consumers by business and advertising are additional examples.

Although agism is cited as a major social problem along with sexism and racism, it is considerably different. Those who are racist or sexist have the luxury of knowing that they will never become members of the groups they downgrade. This is not true with agism. As a matter of fact, we all aspire to become members of the aged group.

The mass media have played a role in our attitudes toward

the aged. Most of our advertising is youth-oriented. Intergenerational relations are often portrayed as tenuous and hostile.

It is felt that a de-emphasis of tradition and religion worsens the condition but, whatever the reason, stereotypes and common misconceptions about the aged are held as truth in our society.

An age bias has even been shown by members of various helping professions such as counsellors, psychologists and even parish priests and ministers. Most prefer to work with the young. Even medical students and nurses consider geriatrics to be one of the least desirable areas of specialization — again reflecting negative attitudes toward working with the aged.

Since stereotypes are learned early in life, and even young children can hold negative stereotypes about the old, perhaps that is where we must begin. Positive stereotypes are also formed early and genuine appreciation of the old by the young comes only with close contact and shared experience.

I believe attitudes towards the aged in Canada are improving but we still have a long way to go. With growing public concern and anxiety regarding economic issues, support programs that would assist the aged have been questioned and increasing concern has been expressed regarding the "greying" of the budget.

We can at least say with satisfaction that as a society we have moved from mistreating and ignoring the elderly to a point where we show concern with their needs and attempt to assist them. We face major challenges now, however, in being able to maintain these gains in the face of harder times and an increasingly older population.

Ultimately we also face the challenge of moving beyond any kind of patronising attitude to regarding the aged as our equals.

For our own sake, as well as theirs, we must rise to that challenge.

CHILDREN IN CRISIS

There is something special about a child. There is a deep-seated emotional response triggered in us by the sight or sound of a young person. A gurgling infant in a stroller will bring smiles to the faces of nearly every passerby and it takes a concerted effort not to playfully tousle the hair of a wide-eyed youngster in a shopping cart. When we hold or hug or just wink at a child we are touching once again our own youth, remembering and cherishing a time of life that was carefree and full of wonder. Those of us with children of our own can well remember when we wished the fever or the scraped knee could be somehow transferred to us to spare the suffering or tears of our son or daughter. This is one of the reasons why we are filled with such deep revulsion when we hear or read of brutal physical damage done to children.

In the course of preparing several programs for *Man Alive*

about the way we treat children in our society, we compiled a vast amount of shocking information, later confirmed by interviews with child-care professionals and the children themselves. Reported cases of children being beaten, chained up, starved, sexually assaulted or killed have become all too commonplace, with about 120,000 cases of child abuse reported in Canada alone each year. It is felt that only 25% of the total incidents are reported.

How can this strange paradox be explained? On the one hand we, as a society, may lavish on our children the tender love that spontaneously springs from the heart, or on the other, smash their bodies and psyche with an anger and hatred that defies belief. Most parents will maintain that they want only the best for their children. There is a conscious effort to provide a better life for their offspring than they themselves had. If this were truly the case, our history would show a constant improvement in the state of children's rights and a steady progression in their overall well-being. And many would, indeed, argue that this *is* the case.

We read of ancient philosophers beating their pupils. Children were killed and offered as ritual sacrifices to the gods. During the Industrial Revolution, many children were treated as slaves. Historians point to the turn of the century as the first realization of the need for child welfare concern. Even then, children's rights were simply lumped in with other humanitarian endeavors. In Canada, for example, in 1897, a man named J.J. Kelso prepared a paper and solicited support for "The necessity of a Society for the Prevention of Cruelty in Toronto". It was to "stop cruelty to children; rescue them from vicious influences and remedy their condition; to halt the beating of animals, overloading street cars, overloading wagons, working old horses, driving galled and disabled animals; to introduce drinking fountains, better methods of horseshoeing, humane literature in schools and homes; to introduce children to be humane and teach everybody to practise and teach kindness to animals and others".

Because of his efforts, the Humane Society was organized and became the first organization to have the welfare of children as part of its mandate. Later this became our Children's Aid Society.

While positive steps have been taken and laws enacted that deal with individual cases, our overall attitude toward children seems to have changed very little. Throughout history, children

— like women — were never considered the equals of men and both were assigned a separate and inferior role. Now the rights of women are being recognized. The bonds of "ownership" by the husband are being broken and equal status under the law, at least in Canada, has been achieved. This has not happened with children who are still treated as the chattels they have always been in law, deprived of virtually all civil rights and liberties.

The language we use in describing children in or out of court is revealing. In terms of the law, if individuals or institutions take a child away from parents, they are regarded as "depriving them of a possession". One who takes a child into care without parental permission is said to be "harboring another's property". In a divorce proceeding, a parent is "awarded custody" of the child along with other "properties of the union". In everyday life, parents refer to "disowning" a rebellious son or daughter. When they leave home because of problems with parents, they are referred to as "runaways" as were slaves of old. When they assert their independence they are criticized for being "willful". Even in the most loving homes we still refer to them as "my boy" and "my girl". This is why, even though we become enraged when we encounter verbal or physical abuse of a young person by parents or guardians, we are as inhibited from intervening as we would be from trespassing on their lawns or walking uninvited into their homes.

In the early 1960s, Professor Henry Kempe of Denver, Colorado identified the "battered child syndrome". At that time he was referring to physical abuse alone. Since then, emotional and nutritional neglect have been added to that phenomenon. Authorities now believe that 10% of all injuries in children under five are non-accidental and that between 10 and 15% of all children who fail to thrive are nutritionally deprived. Emotional abuse is very hard to chart and equally difficult to treat. Sexual abuse is common, but most victims conceal the fact because they fear further physical harm or social rejection. Sometimes the abuse takes the form of medical neglect or the willful, improper administration of drugs.

The Child Abuse Unit at the Hospital for Sick Children in Toronto was established in January of 1973 and is seeing an ever-increasing number of patients. When a young patient is a suspected victim of abuse, the team swings into action. The Departments of Radiology and Haematology are called in to assist. Radiographs often support the diagnosis of child abuse and speak for the child who is unwilling or unable to tell his own story. An X-ray survey of the entire skeleton is done on every suspected abused child under three years of age and in older children when ordered. Color photographs are taken to assure an accurate record of the location, size and age of the injury.

A few years ago, I was asked to narrate a special slide presentation for the unit, to be used in training sessions. They showed me many of these color photographs. I couldn't hold back the tears as I saw the emaciated body of a six-month-old baby who had been starved and physically hurt. Rage came when I was informed that, two months earlier, he had been seen by another medical centre, where new and old fractures had been identified, but no one had contacted the Children's Aid Society on his behalf. I saw pictures of a young boy with extensive bruises and abrasions causing severe swelling to his back and thighs. He had been punished for a very minor reason with a belt. The imprint of the buckle still showed. Another revealed a fifteen-year-old boy who was severely beaten with a whip. The outlines of the lash were clearly evident in the lacerated skin. Another child was a mass of purple bruises and swollen almost beyond recognition. A babysitter had admitted to this act of violence.

I was shown X-rays of children with multiple fractures and swelling along bone shafts — evidence of torsion force, or twisting. I was so repulsed by the pictures that I suggested anyone who beats children should be forced to see all this very graphic evidence of the consequences. I was told it would likely have no effect on the overall problem because of the nature of child abusers. Neither would putting them in jail for their actions. Through interviews, the unit had compiled fairly accurate profiles of child-battering parents and guardians. Several characteristics emerged, primary among them, a lack of mothering. Their own unhappy childhoods had not been imprinted with the "mothering" instinct. They often came from broken homes, treatment institutions or foster homes and most had experienced some form of abuse in their own young lives. They had feelings of isolation, were unable to turn to others for help, and so had no way to handle the problems their children presented.

Often child-abusers marry someone just like themselves — insecure, distrustful, needy. They have low self-esteem and a lack of confidence that has persisted since childhood. They often exhibit what psychologists call "role-reversal". They imply that they expect their child to care for *them*. This contributes to unrealistically high expectations for their child's performance and lack of appreciation of the child's needs.

With very few exceptions these parents are not sadists and take no cruel delight in mistreating their children. They have a low tolerance level with hair-trigger tempers. Any minor irritant, such as a child crying, can develop into a violent reaction. With no one to turn to and no positive mothering experience to fall back on, they neglect or abuse the child. Some of these children do not survive and the ones that do are left with a horrible legacy.

A typical example is a teenage girl named Diane. I interviewed her for a *Man Alive* program we called *Listen To The Children*. She looked old beyond her years and her thin, sad face reflected the pain of trying to survive in what for her had been a confusing and uncaring world.

"I left home when I was fourteen. I kept threatening my mom I'd take off some day because she kept hitting me all the time — every time she could get her hands on me. It didn't matter to her whether she killed me or not. She always said that I was ... that I should be put in a hospital. So I left home. She tried to put me in some. She succeeded in a few."

"What kind of hospital?" I asked.

"Psychiatric," answered Diane.

She revealed that throughout her young life she had been shuffled between foster homes, social agencies, psychiatric institutions and finally ended up in the courts, where she had been charged with a series of offences including arson and assault.

My on-camera interview with her was held in a small, modest, but neat apartment that had been secured for Diane by social workers and welfare officials following her release from jail. We sat sipping coffee at a fold-up kitchen table. She was pale and unsmiling, but very open and eager to communicate.

"In court I never got to say what was on my mind. I can't come out with stuff like that in a strange place, not even to a lawyer. I just wish people could sit down and try and find out what the world is really all about — and the kind of problems people are in. At times I want to give up and go back to prison."

"Why?"

"I guess because of all the hassles I've got now. But if I went back I'd fight to get out here again, because I'm not one to be confined. In the Don Jail I put a rope around my neck and I hung it from the ceiling and I thought, well, this is it. If they had come in five minutes later I would have been gone. I've slashed my wrists. The last time was just before Christmas. I thought I don't really want to live in this world if that's the way it's got to be. I've tried to get jobs, you know. I've tried to make friends, but even in prison they'd all say, 'get away from me'. They don't understand."

"Why do you think you try to commit suicide?"

"I keep thinking about my past. It's a nightmare right now. Every night I try to fall asleep and the first thing that comes into my mind is my mother. I feel sorry for her. She can't communicate or try to understand her kids."

"Would you say you love your mother?"

"Yeah. Somewhere in my heart it says you have to love her. What would I get if I hated her? It's not gonna accomplish anything. It's not going to satisfy nothing. I mean I've had a lot of arguments with people about my mother, saying that she should be dead. They say she shouldn't be around my life, but I don't look at it that way. I really don't."

"Do you see your parents at all?"

"No, I don't."

"Would you like to?"

"I would love to."

"Why?"

"I guess it's because they're my parents. I want to have a chance to say . . . I love you."

Diane could go no further. She began to sob softly. I reached out and took her hand and held it for a long time. The interview was over.

In my interviews with young people who have been mistreated there was always a recurring statement which surprised me. Inevitably, in answer to my question about their own plans for raising children, they said they intended to follow methods similar to their parents'. Statements such as, "Kids have to be made to obey," or, "I likely deserved what I got" reflected the only method of child-rearing they knew. Almost without exception, the children wanted to be returned to the homes in which they were battered. I naively thought that people who had suffered so much at the hands of their parents would not want to return and certainly would not wish to inflict the same hurt on their young. This is not the way it works; hence the horrible saga of battered children continues from generation to generation. When I thought about my own life I could see that the opposite was also true. Despite the hardships and frustrations of raising a family of ten children, my parents never struck me. In turn it never occurred to me to hit my three children.

I have also talked to numerous child-care professionals about some parents' attitudes toward their children. They have told me the problems stem from a general attitude that society as a whole seems to share: that there are different rights for adults and children.

Barbara Chisholm, noted authority on children, told me, "We are in a crisis situation with our children. We want to believe that, if we just leave the family alone, somehow everyone is going to grow up to become good Canadian citizens. There's been a major problem of resistance to reporting child abuse. I think we are in a situation in our society right now in which a lot of hostility toward children is becoming visible at the surface. Child abuse is merely one expression of it. Parenthood cannot be done by prayer, by wish, by exhortation or by punishment. It can only be done by sharing, on the part of a lot of people. It's a complicated, mixed-up, confused world out there and parents get no added wisdom along with their biology. They just get added responsibilities and problems.

"We haven't really believed in the family. We preach about it and talk about it as our basic institution, but as a society we don't believe in it. If we really did we'd put our money where our mouth is and really make sure that the institutions we build, such as children's aid societies and their programs, have standards behind them which are not minimum, but maximum. We would really see that qualified personnel dealt with troubled families. We would really make sure that when a young mother has a child, with or without benefit of wedlock, that we are in there saying, 'OK, this is a tough time. Now, how can we help?' We must recognize that the rights of children are equal to the rights of parents. The community at large, society at large, is responsible for all their children."

At a Family Court office in Toronto I asked lawyer and children's rights advocate Jeffery Wilson if we needed a Bill of Rights for children.

He replied, "Most definitely. We need some statement and it should be enshrined with the 'religion' of the law. We cannot rely any more on 'best interest' laws. I'm quite frankly fed up with the notion that I can give you a hit on the head if you're a child because it's in your best interest. In our Criminal Code in Canada, we have a provision which sanctions the use of force as a means of discipline. Using force should be the exception, not the rule. I want it written that children have a right to play and recreate, and children have a right to equal opportunities in education, that children have a right to nutrition — so that if I see a family which is not providing those kinds of things, I can go to the court and say, 'I'm not just talking about best interests, I'm talking about rights.' "

Perhaps the most shameful example of complete disregard for the human rights of our children is in the commercialization of their bodies. A dangerous trend has developed in the 1970s and '80s as our movies, books, advertising and fashions move more and more into presenting children as sex objects. The more accustomed we become to seeing this, the less impact it has. There have always been fringe groups of paedophiles but never before, in modern history, has this attitude to children even approached social acceptability. Never before have groups advocating sexual involvement with minors presented their cause so openly. Groups with names like *Paedophile Liberation Organization, Childhood Sexuality Circle* and *The Renée Guyon Society* (which recommends the age of consent be lowered to four) are springing up everywhere. These groups are not referring to the natural experimentation between children, but the active participation of adults, often including incest.

The professionals have differing attitudes toward the dangers of this stance. Dutch psychologist Frits Bernard says adult/child sex is basically harmless. Others remain generally opposed to the act, especially incest, but feel society makes the situation worse by imposing guilt on the child. Most child workers, however, condemn adult/child sex, but worry about our attitudes to children as sexual beings. They advocate their right to experiment and express themselves. Mary Calderone, Director of the U.S. Sex and Information Council, says children have a fundamental right to know about sex and be sexual. Toronto psychiatrist Frank Sommers expresses a change in attitude within his own profession. "We used to think that kids went through a latency period between six and eleven, but there's enough evidence around now that shows this latency is a learned suppression, not a real dormancy."

It is difficult to see the harm in normal sexual growth and experimentation but what happens when emotional readiness has not caught up with physical maturity, when adults are eager to exploit that maturity or when the children have had little more than a cursory introduction to sex, leaving them intellectually unprepared?

We are faced with that situation now. We have child/adult stars in our movies: Brooke Shields, Jodie Foster, Kristy McNichol and Linda Blair. Our advertising is often centred around young children looking and behaving in a provocative manner. We see the numbers of teenage pregnancies and young male and female prostitutes rise alarmingly. Police departments have set up task forces to combat child pornography in which more than 30,000 children participated in the Los Angeles area alone in 1981. Worst of all, we see an enormous increase in crimes against children, who become more than sexual objects through this attitude. They become, in fact, sexual targets.

In 1981 Azza El Sissi produced a program for *Man Alive* called "Pretty Babies" in which these trends were examined in the Toronto area. I asked Dr. Frank Sommers to describe why our society accepts this change in attitude. He described society as "turning to the novel. They look at what hasn't been explored, what hasn't been tried. There are always forces in society pushing against limits. I suspect a lot of people are afraid of sexuality ultimately, afraid of the work that goes into good peer sexuality and there is no fear of that kind of pressure coming from an unequal partner. Children cannot be expected to make sense of these powerful emotions in their limited world. It's taking advantage of an unequal relationship which I don't think is psychologically healthy."

I asked his opinion of sex education, whether it helped children to be more discriminating later on or whether it laid too great an emphasis on sex itself.

"There is a great deal of evidence which supports sex education. When children grow up in homes where they can talk with their parents about sexuality and when they go to schools with good sex education classes, they generally are found not to act out sexually. Rather than emphasizing sex too much, it changes the emphasis. The sexuality which has been emphasized — in television, for example — is teasing sexuality. It's not tenderness-oriented sexuality."

New York psychiatrist Stephen Levenkron says, "Society is learning to respond sexually to little girls. Children are the last sexual frontier and the barriers are coming down."

I asked family counsellor Dr. Mario Bartoletti if he worried about these barriers coming down. He said he would fight it with everything in his power. "We have struggled and fought for legislation and protection, through Children's Aid, in order to give them a chance to grow and be children and move into the adult world gradually. These were hard-fought battles and I would not like to see them lost.... The legislation is strong enough, but a big issue is how we interpret the law. We can say that an action is against the law and you've been convicted, but now by social understanding it's OK, so you get off with a warning.... We are now beginning to understand how unequally the female rape victim has been treated. Can you imagine how much more dramatic the situation is when it involves children? A woman, as an adult, has the equality of rights given to all adults, but a child does not, because a child, in effect, is still the property of the parents and now we're going to lower the taboos? I think we're marching backwards. Literally with flags flying and banners waving, we're marching backwards."

The most obvious result of society's trend toward viewing children as sex objects is in the advertising industry. The "youth culture" has taken an unusual turn. Where once women strove to look younger, we now see eleven- and twelve-year-old girls dressed like the archetypes of waterfront prostitutes. The popularity of this type of advertising is attributed to the idea that little girls offer men emotional security because they are vulnerable and non-challenging. Ad agencies pursue this mode because of the high financial rewards. Some agencies, however, refuse to get involved and openly condemn the participation of their fellows. One such is the Jerry Goodis Agency, whose president, Jerry Goodis, has spoken out on many occasions about the misuse of child models.

In an address to the Toronto Ad & Sales Club in September, 1981, Jerry stressed this aspect of modern advertising.

" ... Advertising as it is practised in Canada today faces two problems. The first is that too much of our advertising is stale.... The second is an outgrowth of the first. It's caused by advertisers and their agencies who grab onto any new idea, no matter how puerile or socially objectionable, just to be reflecting what they perceive to be the newest wrinkle in mass behavior.

"This indiscriminate, unthinking exploitation of just any new social phenomenon, no matter how worthless, betrays lack of both common sense and common decency. It also fails to meet the test of what I believe to be good advertising — communication that reflects the positive motivators that are always at work in society, so as to mobilize them on behalf of the ideas, the products and the services of our clients.

"Currently, the worst manifestation of the misuse of new

ideas can be found in the sexual exploitation in advertising of very young females. The readiness of advertisers, modeling agencies, and film makers to adopt this new and, in my opinion, distasteful strategy is more prevalent in Europe and in the United States than in Canada, but we are being affected by it.

"We're in a world of instant communication. We live in a phenomena-prone society. Fads, cults, and cultural mutations travel quickly.... When magazines, like *Vogue* and *Cosmopolitan*, offer covers of little girls made up as sex objects, and when U.S. advertisers hire twelve- and thirteen-year-olds as seductive merchandisers, it is time for Canadian agencies to draw a line along the border and to say, 'we won't make that kind of advertising in Canada.'

"Sexual exploitation is a phenomenon which did not originate with advertising. It has infiltrated advertising only because advertising is a creature of the society in which we live, and young children are made available for this kind of advertising only because their parents permit and, in fact, pursue the commercial exploitation of their daughters and sons.

"The impact of the commercial and the extent to which it is already being copied is evidence of the awful vulnerability of advertising to reflect bad ideas....

"Now, at a time when our industry is finally overcoming the sexual stereotyping to which women have often been consigned, we are confronted by advertising that delivers a new dimension in unreality: the sexually-precocious female child....

"Frankly, if it were only advertising that was guilty, I would be much less concerned than I am. The real problem is that advertising, after all, mirrors the values and the standards of the society it serves. It is the other sectors of the community ... people in the intelligentsia, the arts, the universities, who are primarily responsible for creating the new social attitudes that are later accepted by the rest of us.... Much of the most irresponsible talk about children and sexuality is coming from professional psychologists — people to whom we have entrusted the emotional and mental well-being of our society."

I spoke to Jerry for *Man Alive* in his Toronto office. He described a problem he faced when redecorating his office. "I was looking through a book of wallpaper samples the other day and the whole theme of the book is seduction and the model that they're using, dressed in high heels and a low-cut gown, with lipstick and with all kinds of cosmetic stuff all over her face was, without exaggeration, eight years old at the most. I asked myself why on earth would they do that? I put the book away. It upset me. It says to society there is no age limit to anything. If you want to do it — do it. That really frightens me. The responsibility goes back into our acceptance of anything that will sell. As long as we have the free enterprise system, everything is kosher, everything is just fine."

The unprecedented popularity of the child/model/sex symbol is epitomized by Brooke Shields, whose provocative movies and advertisements have caused a ripple effect throughout the teenage world. This effect is now popularly known as the "Brooke Shields Syndrome". You don't have to look far to see girls made up to the hilt, wearing heavy make-up and skin-tight blue jeans. They're everywhere and unlike Miss Shields, or other professionals, they are without the protection of an agent, stage mother or studio.

Gordon Wolf, a Toronto welfare counsellor, described the effect that this advertising has. "The naive twelve-, thirteen- or fourteen-year-old girl who dresses herself up with tight clothes and a lot of make-up because that's what she sees, that's what appeals, and then goes out on the street, isn't aware of the effect that that can have on a lot of men who are watching her. Then she all of a sudden discovers that she's over her head and in a situation for which she doesn't have other kinds of skills and knowledge in order to cope."

Along with the growth of sexy child advertising is the growth of "kiddie" pornography. Magazines such as *Naked Kids*, *Joyboy*, *Lollipop* and *Canadian Moppets and Teens* are now more and more in evidence. The police are trying to find ways to stop children from being caught up in it, but are finding it harder and harder to decide what is legally obscene. We went to the Toronto headquarters of Project "P" (pornography), a joint task force of the Metropolitan Police and the Ontario Provincial Police.

I expected to be shown examples of the seedier side of pornography, but neither I nor my film crew were prepared for the display of hideous materials and paraphernalia that had been confiscated by the police during raids on the sex shops in Toronto. Bins were full of equipment used in bondage and torture acts. Machines used for mechanical coitus lined the walls. Inflated rubber nudes were piled in the corner. Shelves and filing cabinets were stuffed with posters, photographs, magazines, video cassettes and films containing graphic displays of every sexual perversion imaginable. But the most depressing and stomach-turning material contained "kiddie porn".

There I spoke with Mace Armstrong, a member of this special unit. He described kiddie porn as much more expensive than other materials. "A kiddie porn book can sell for anywhere from $15. a book — that's the minimum for a twenty- or thirty-page book — to $40. for one magazine. It's profitable, it's black market and it's risky."

I showed him a poster we had obtained of a very young girl. I asked him if his department would judge it obscene. "This is a poster of a partially nude female. The genitalia are not showing. A partial breast is showing. I would say this is not obscene."

"Is it anything in your view?" I asked.

"It probably does exploit sex, but not unduly. I would place the young girl at probably thirteen or fourteen years old. Again, not in good taste, but not in good taste does not make it a violation of the criminal code."

I then showed him the cover of a rock album. "This again appears to be a young child in what you might call a sexy position," he replied. "Her age could be anywhere from eight to twelve years. She's fully clothed. This is common in today's marketing business. You see it everywhere you go."

"But your unit basically has no interest in this?"

"Not in that, for sure. It certainly is exploiting the child. There's no doubt about it, but not unduly. I don't think you'd get to first base in court with that."

A correlation between this type of material and child prostitution has been put forward. I asked if this was backed up by Project P's experience, and Mace Armstrong assured me this was the case. "We have an area in Toronto, off of Yonge Street, where both male and female prostitutes become involved in the making and manufacturing of this material and this is one of our concerns."

For many youngsters the streets are home. Approximately 130,000 children, between twelve and nineteen, are living on Canadian streets right now. Most of them are runaways or have been thrown out of their homes without skills, training or discipline. Neither innocent nor wise, they quickly find out that there is a market for their bodies. Police report that some who practise prostitution do not realize they are breaking the law. They merely associate their actions with pocket money. The more worldly-wise deal with the situation pragmatically. They must survive.

We spoke to a group of these children at a drop-in centre. One girl described how many of them end up on the streets. "A lot of people, when they get kicked out of their homes, don't know what to do 'cause they're not trained and they end up down on Yonge Street being a hooker or something like this and even guys are out there turning tricks and they get in a whole mess and some of them even go out and kill themselves because of this 'cause they don't know what's going on."

The boy sitting beside her described why he began prostituting himself. "I done it for money. I made a lot of money out of it. Like, you know, it's not worth it 'cause your pride is down the drain. You don't feel like the same person. When I came here I had high hopes, dreams you know. It's shit. That's what it is. It's a lot of garbage." When asked if he was homosexual, he vehemently denied it. "I don't even consider myself bisexual. I don't 'cause I don't enjoy what they do. I mean, they have fun, they get their rocks off, but I don't get off at all. My place is with a woman, not a guy, right?" This boy had been on the streets for six years, since he was thirteen years old.

Another boy of nineteen described his experience. "I used to hustle, right, but then I got sick of it because they're gross. Like, I've got two boys, right, and if my boys grow up and I seen them on the street hustling I'd probably kill the guy who tried to pick them up. I think they're gross. They're jerks, man. I'd rather rip 'em off than go with them. I don't agree with people going out and taking advantage of young people because they have no money. I don't agree with that. All they want is sex, right. They're just after your body, man, and to me that's a one-way street. . . ."

A girl of seventeen, on the street since she was twelve, pointed out some of the dangers involved. "I don't like doing it, right, but you have to. You have to live and you're taking chances, right, 'cause some guy — like I've had it happen — some guy'll take you to some parking lot somewhere in the back seat and pull a knife on you and there's nothing you can do 'cause there's nobody around. All you can do is stay calm, you know, and hope for the best. Like, I was just lucky 'cause a cop comes in the parking lot, right."

Asked if they thought prostitution should be legalized, the group all agreed that it should not. The girl spoke for the group. "No, I'm totally against it, but I have to do it because how else are you going to get food, clothes, a roof over your head? Like, this is wintertime, now, you know."

We were able to talk to another girl in a little more detail about life on the street. Her name was Sheri and she was seventeen years old. She told us of her introduction to sex. "I was about four or five years old. This guy was babysitting me. He was really big and chubby. My mom left him babysitting us — me and my three sisters — and he just started coming on to all of us. We didn't know what to do. We were too young. My mother just kicked him out of the house. That's all she done."

Her only other involvement with adults was on the street. "I used to trick with guys about sixty, fifty and forty. It bothered me a lot 'cause they weren't my age and I wasn't actually into it at the time. Like, I didn't know if I was doing something right or doing something wrong. I didn't know if it was legal or illegal. I found out a while ago when I was working on the street. I got charged with soliciting."

We asked her how she became involved in prostitution. "People I used to call my friends were doing it, so I started. I didn't get into it that much, but when I needed the money, I had to do that 'cause like, when I was on the street, I went three or four days without something to eat and I was very sick. I didn't enjoy working on the streets at all."

This life had apparently affected her overall sexuality. "I'm gay. I like guys once in a while. I've been hurt by a lot of guys. That's why I'm not into it right now."

We asked her what she would like to happen in the future. "I would like to find people who are into adopting somebody and are not like my parents, because if I had to go through that again, I'd just die, 'cause I just got out of the hospital not too long ago, 'cause I tried to commit suicide and everything because of my parents."

Sheri's past was disastrous and unfortunately her future looks equally bleak. The attitude of her parents initially, then society, created a person with few hopes for the future. If our attitude toward children does not change, we will be faced with many more Sheris.

When parents, courts and society in general have failed, some young people are rescued by institutions run by compassionate and caring individuals, who have devoted their lives to picking up the pieces. Two of the most popular *Man Alive* programs in the 1981 season featured Bosco Homes in Regina, run by Father Lucien Larré. The homes are a last resort for boys and girls ranging in age from ten to eighteen.

I first met Father Larré at a teachers' convention in Saskatchewan, where we were both featured speakers. I was immediately impressed by his warmth and his obvious dedication to children. When on the platform, talking about his work, his sense of humor and his graphic descriptions of his charges keep an audience alternating between rollicking laughter and tears. Our paths have crossed several times since then and on one warm summer afternoon, seated at a picnic table in Toronto's Edwards Gardens, we had a long, leisurely conversation in front of the *Man Alive* cameras.

"I was working as a guidance counsellor in Miller High School in Regina," he explained, "and I became aware that a lot of students had tremendous needs that we couldn't fulfil. I often felt, in fact, that we were expelling youngsters who needed us most. I tried to keep them at the rectory or at the school, but it didn't work out, so finally I realized I had to start a home, so I bought our first house. I didn't have any money and, belonging to a religious congregation, didn't realize that such things were illegal, but I actually wrote an N.S.F. cheque when I bought the first house."

Bosco Homes now comprise seven houses in Regina. They appear to be ordinary suburban homes, no different from their neighbors. Psychologists, house parents and trained counsellors make up the staff. The young people come from all over Western Canada and as far north as Inuvik. Some are runaways with no place to run. Some have learning disabilities. Some are schizophrenic or otherwise severely disturbed. Some are orphans in need of a home. And some are delinquents, whose offences range all the way from petty crimes to homicide.

"These youngsters have sometimes been through from twelve to fifteen foster homes. They've been into psychiatric wards and other institutions. Very often Bosco Homes is looked upon as a sort of last ditch stand. When nothing else works, we say, 'Well, let's try Bosco and see what happens there'."

"What does happen there?" I asked. Statistics show that 60 to 80% of all young people who come out of state-run institutions end up back in again. My research into Bosco Homes indicated a reversal of those figures. Some 80% who left were able to build new, productive lives in society.

"I think the key to our success is definitely the relationships," Larré answered. "We work very hard to foster home relationships with them which is something they've never had with a mom and dad. They seem to absorb a sense of conscience along the way and they change and grow. Sometimes we educators make the mistake of believing that if a child's head is well stuffed, that's all we have to do. I took a little lad who was sniffing a lot of stuff and I sat him down and explained the facts to him. I said, 'You've got to stop all this sniffing because it's going to damage your brain.' Two weeks later on Easter Sunday, a half-hour after supper, he took a high-powered rifle which he smuggled into the house and he blew his head off. I thought, 'What's going on here? This kid knows the facts, but he doesn't care.' There's more to education than just stuffing a head. You can have all the information there and do nothing with it."

"How do you create this family environment in an institution?" I asked.

"We have volunteers, of course, but we also have hired staff. We have teachers and psychiatrists who work there, but I find in every home you need dedicated persons who live there on a twenty-four hour basis and this gives the youngsters the security and the continuity they need. These are the house parents. In some places — psychiatric wards, for example — people work eight-hour shifts. The child tries to attach himself to someone, then in eight hours they're gone. He tries on the next shift, then finally gives up. But in our situation, where we actually live with them, they can and do get involved. It takes a lot of time, but it works."

Larré told me that when the young people arrived at Bosco, they had a very low self-image. They had learned to be losers. They had lost at school, at home and sometimes in the courts. Their feelings of being rejected and unwanted had resulted in giving up on themselves and everyone else.

"The first thing we have to do is care for them. We have to believe in them. Then gradually they get some confidence and start believing in themselves. They have been rejected so often that many of them will set themselves up to be rejected again. Some of the little boys will come up to you and hit you or punch you, then wait for you to hit or punch them back. Or they'll do some damage, break something, then they'll say, 'OK kick me out.' We say, 'No, we don't kick people out. We've never kicked people out,' and they look at you as if you're some kind of kook and say, 'What do you mean you don't kick people out?' and we say, 'No, we don't kick people out, but what are you going to do about your behavior?' That's really startling to them, when they find they finally have to face up to their behavior."

"What have the backgrounds of these children been?" I asked.

"I find that most of the problems go back to poor relationships within the family, as a matter of fact; in many, there have been no relationships at all. The youngster has never bonded or had a symbiotic relationship with a mother, for instance. They don't grow their own feelings. They are feelingless. Some have no conscience and it's hard to grow on that. It's like trying to build a house on sand. We have ones who have been in a sick relationship with a parent. The parent has been very needy and has fed emotionally off the child. The child gets hooked into this sick relationship and can't get out of it. Later, they tend to become schizophrenic. They become very helpless, confused and can't make decisions. The big stress in our society now is towards the head and the body. If we can stuff the child's head, we're in business. If we can take care of the body, give it lots of exercise and get it in good shape, we're happy. But we're missing out big dimensions in human growth — the emotional or social development and the spiritual development. Now, the head and the body could likely be handled by machines. I suppose it would be technically possible to exercise and feed a body with machines, or feed the mind with computers or television, but the other two dimensions can only be fostered with human relationships. And that's where, as a society, we fall down."

I wondered how much stress was put on the spiritual at Bosco House. As a Roman Catholic priest, did Father Larré try to indoctrinate the children with his beliefs? Were they made to attend religious exercises?

"I guess we'd have to say we were non-denominational. I don't find it important to say that an institution is run by the Catholic Church or the United Church or the Salvation Army. I find, in Christianity, we do too much of that. We seem to be too worried about who's going to get the credit for the good work. I think it is much more important that the good work is done and done for the love of God and nobody should worry about who gets the credit for it. At Bosco House we have never tried to parade as a Catholic institution or that we're doing nice Catholic things. We have tried to serve these little ones, foster good relations and bring them to good health, but we have never tried to indoctrinate them. We invite them to go to church, some will come, but the vast majority will refuse. You see, when they first come to us they don't even believe in people. They'll relate to the dogs in our house before they relate to us. They'll trust the dog, because they've never been hurt that way. Then perhaps six to eight months later they'll start believing in people, then they can get interested in religion, but we don't start there.

"I remember one little lad who certainly had no interest in

religion. His father was a problem alcoholic and used to kick him around the floor. One day he kicked him so badly he broke his ribs and he had to have a lung removed because it was punctured. Now, can you imagine this little fellow kneeling by his bed at night and saying, 'Our Father, which art in heaven?' How can he believe in a pie-in-the-sky-God that he can't see, when he can't even believe in his own dad? I find at our setup at Bosco House we try not to indoctrinate them or preach to them. We try to show them Christianity by letting them see and trust people. Religion can come later."

Some churches and individuals do support the work of Bosco Homes. At the beginning, Father Larré said he received no support from anyone because it appeared to be some "fly-by-night operation". They operated on borrowed money for some time. Now it is supported by up to 75% from government sources and 25% from charitable donations. These include service clubs and church groups. They receive as much money from Protestant churches as from Roman Catholic. He felt, though, that his kind of work is not high on the list of church-supported work.

"I guess it depends on how we look at religion. Generally we use church money to print bibles, to preach the word — spend it on the general apostolate of the church. What do you get when you look after emotionally-disturbed youngsters? You get no vocations to priesthood from there. There's not much chance you're going to get strong converts to any church. I think we have a somewhat warped view of Christianity at times."

Father Larré is a large, portly man and the first thing you notice about him is his walk. As he comes closer you notice his built-up boot and shortened right leg, the result of polio in childhood.

"I sometimes say I was blessed with polio," he told me. "You wouldn't think anyone could prosper from polio, but I did. I had to learn to overcome it. It took me two and a half years and a number of operations and I had to learn to walk all over again, but it gave me a different perspective on life. I had to learn that I could be happy without jogging and exercise. They aren't that important. I think it has helped me to have more empathy with people who are suffering. I talked to an alcoholic just the other day and he asked, 'When will I ever stop drinking?' and I said, 'When you listen to your suffering. It will tell you.' Suffering is a great university."

I asked Father Larré to talk about failure. It seems to me that failure is a feeling common to every parent at one time or another and it needs to be kept in a healthy perspective.

"We've had our failures. We've had suicides. We've had a number who died after they left us and it looked like suicide. Some choose to run, and we lose them. I would say we lose about twenty per cent that way, but the vast majority will eventually get into a relationship and begin to grow and change."

"How do you handle this failure with children?" I asked.

"I'll never forget the first suicide. The whole anguish of that event as I kept asking, 'What could I have done? What could I have said? What did we do wrong?' You stay awake nights worrying and finally you have to accept that you've done your best and that's it. You have to leave it in the hands of God. Now, that's easy to say with your head, but with your heart it's quite another story. When I fail with a youngster I still have a good cry. It happens when one will decide to leave or run away. I'll talk to them, try and convince them to stay, urge them to work on the problems, but you can't force them. It's the old saying, 'You can lead a horse to water, but you can't make it drink.'

"I remember one lad who said he was leaving. He was determined to leave us and go to Edmonton. So I offered to drive him out to the highway and drop him off. When I saw him sitting there, I couldn't help it — I just had to cry. I just kept thinking, 'Oh, you poor little kid.' I drove over to McDonalds and bought him a hamburger and a milkshake, I knew the kind he liked, and I brought it back to him. He was grateful for that, but it was all I could do. You can't help them sometimes. You get to love them like your own children and when you fail with them it's pretty heavy. I think the thing to watch in my work is not to become thick-skinned and say, 'Well, so what? It's just another case. Why should I worry about it?' When you get that way, you can't help anyone. So you still have to get involved, even though it's painful at times."

Knowing the frustration that parents face, even in a small family, I wondered how Father Larré handled his anger when dealing with fifty or more problem-laden young people.

"When I started in this work, I believed that I should never show my temper. I should always be well controlled and have a nice clean clerical look about me. When things went wrong, I had to turn the other cheek and so on. You can't do that. You can't bury your feelings all the time. I had to learn to be honest with the kids. I had to be able to say, 'There are limits and I won't put up with this, so stop it. Cut it out!' It sort of shocked me at first, but I had to learn to be honest with myself too. I think, in raising children, we have to admit we can't be perfect and, if we pretend we are, we discourage them. They say, 'Well, it's easy for him. He's perfect, but what chance have I got?' When we are able to be honest and say, 'I have my faults. I have my imperfections,' they can identify with that. They can say, 'Aha, he's not perfect and he made it, so why can't I?'

"I remember one young lad who made me so frustrated. He was so lazy he wouldn't do his homework. He wouldn't do anything. I got angry with him and said, 'If you ever pass your Grade Twelve, I'll eat my shirt — buttons and all.' Well, I've learned not to say things like that anymore, because about eight years later he came back to see me. He had a B.A. and a B.Ed. and he's teaching in Ottawa, and he said, 'OK, where's your shirt, Father?' I've learned not to make wild bets about what people will do in life."

"When do you consider the job is done?" I asked.

"We don't discharge people, as you would from a hospital, just because they can function and hold a job. We often have them out of our program as far as the government is concerned, in that we get no funding for them, but we try to stay with them like normal parents would. After they leave us, we see that they get a job and often get them set up in a room or apartment. If they get fired, we help them get another job. We help them go to university. Some have been out of our actual program for six or seven years and they might be in British Columbia or Texas, but they'll phone us, often collect, like children do, and keep in touch. I feel the job is done when this little person is in tune with his feelings, in tune with other people and with God. Most of them leave us before we get *that* far, but for me the job isn't finished until they are fully alive in that way. We don't look at them in terms of just functioning on the job or getting off welfare. We would like to see them as happy, independent persons."

In the course of my interview, Father Larré told me several anecdotes, some humorous, some shocking, about many of the young people who over the years had passed through Bosco Homes. One example was a young teenager, Mary Ellen.

"Mary Ellen is a very special girl. She taught us a great deal. When she came to us, Roy, she couldn't count change for a dollar. She couldn't read a clock. She was on heavy medication. She foamed at the mouth. She couldn't keep herself clean or comb her hair properly. When we took her in, we *said* all the right things to her, of course, we said we loved her and would try

148

to make a home for her and so on. But, with our feelings, we were giving her quite another story. She was picking up our feelings, that we were frightened of her, that we wanted to get rid of her, that because of her violence she might burn the house down. It took a great deal of effort to work things out, but we learned from our experience with Mary Ellen that you always seem to communicate on two channels simultaneously. With our mouth we tell young people what's in our head, but with our feelings we tell them what's in our heart and they are quick to pick these up. That Mary Ellen grew to be a well-balanced, happy, loving person was a minor miracle."

We met Mary Ellen at a Bosco Homes reunion in Regina and listened in on a conversation between her and Sister Mary McGuire, a co-founder of Bosco Homes, currently studying psychology in Chicago. Sister Mary had been Mary Ellen's house mother.

Mary Ellen: I remember when I arrived. I had to come and sit by you and you told me that you loved me.
Sister: How did you feel when I said that?
Mary Ellen: Sad.
Sister: Sad?
Mary Ellen: Yeah. It hit me kind of funny. It was the first time I had every heard that word in my whole life. I didn't know quite what to do with it.
Sister: You had a hard time believing me, didn't you?
Mary Ellen: It took me a couple of years, but you stayed with me.
Sister: How did you feel when you came to Bosco House?
Mary Ellen: Scared. I was so used to foster homes. I didn't know what Bosco was all about. I didn't know if I would be staying, or just for overnight and leave the next day. I was really scared.
Sister: Later on you were afraid we would kick you out?
Mary Ellen: Yeah, I was very much afraid of that. You know it happened to me so many times before and so, what's one more place?
Sister: Do you remember what the turning point was?
Mary Ellen: It was the day I smashed the window. I was testing you.
Sister: To see if we really loved you?
Mary Ellen: Yes, and you guys stuck by me even though I smashed the window. You came down hard at the time. You were mad at me for what I did but you still loved me as a person. I realized that you guys did love me. That was the big turning

point.

Mary Ellen has left Bosco House and is living and coping on her own. Her story at Bosco taught Father Larré, Sister McGuire and the staff a great deal about the fragility of relationships and the subtleties of trust. They taught Mary Ellen there was such a thing as love.

Mary Ellen: I feel good that I can go out and make friends. Even if I'm still shy, I am aware of that and can conquer it. I had a lot of fears of people because of what I went through, but now I can live on my own and not depend on Bosco. When you leave, I'm going to miss you, but it's not the end of the world. I know you'll come back to see me. In the meantime I may have problems, I may get angry and all that stuff, but it's not going to keep me from what I should be doing — making friends, working and living a normal life. It feels good when I think like that.

Mary Ellen found Bosco House in time. It, and similar caring group homes across Canada, are like safety nets for children who have been thrown away by society. But the nets are too small and too few. They cannot possibly answer the needs of the thousands of children who have become victims of our carelessness, our ignorance, our selfishness and our greed.

In 1979 we celebrated the International Year of the Child. At that time seminars were held, speeches made and articles written on every aspect of children's welfare. It was a heady exercise of good intentions, but very little progress has been made. Some new legislation has been passed to strengthen our child service agencies, but we are still far too timid in our child abuse investigations and in our handling of kiddie porn. I'm not suggesting that everyone rush out and adopt an abandoned child and I find bumper stickers that ask cutely, "Have you hugged your child today?" insulting. But an expression of simple decency toward a fellow human being is surely not too much to expect.

On December 21, 1976, when the General Assembly of the United Nations proclaimed the forthcoming Year of the Child, it emphasized the need to adopt the following rights:

- The right to affection, love and understanding.
- The right to adequate nutrition and medical care.
- The right to protection against all forms of neglect, cruelty and exploitation.
- The right to free education and to full opportunity for play and recreation.
- The right to a name and nationality.

- The right to special care, if handicapped.
- The right to be among the first to receive relief in time of disaster.
- The right to learn to be a useful member of society and to develop individual abilities.
- The right to be brought up in a spirit of peace and universal brotherhood.
- The right to enjoy these rights, regardless of race, color, sex, religion, national or social origin.

To adopt these rights as a universal declaration is one thing; to practise them in our own homes is more difficult. In the daily emotional stress of family life, everyone makes errors of judgment. There could not possibly be a standard recipe for raising children, but it seems to me our modern lifestyle has put selfish concerns ahead of caring for others, including children.

We often demand obedience to *our* rules whether fair or not. We exert pressure to live up to *our* expectations, no matter how unattainable. We want *ourselves* to be reflected favorably in our childrens' behavior and achievements.

In our attitudes to our children here in Canada and to the millions of unseen children around the globe there is something basic and very important that we as individuals can do. We must take a long look at ourselves and ask if it is not our own selfishness at the root of our mistreatment, exploitation and neglect of children.

THE DOWRY OF CONSTANTINE

*"The root of all the trouble besetting the
Throne of Peter today is our temporal
power together with our wealth and our
international prestige."*
POPE ALEXANDER VI

*". . . the dowry of Constantine is too much
to carry in today's world."*
POPE PAUL VI

*"You can't run the church on
Hail Marys."*
ARCHBISHOP PAUL MARCINKUS

There was certainly no shortage of research material when
Man Alive began to put together a program on the Vatican Bank
scandal in the summer of 1982. Thousands of words had been
written in leading world journals describing a financial adventure that sent shock waves through the banking community
and cast dark shadows of suspicion and doubt on one of the most
revered institutions in the world.

The difficult task was to sift through the mass of information, trace the labyrinth of corporate deceit and emerge with a
half-hour program that not only presented the story fairly, but
made it understandable.

The crux of the whole affair was that between one and a half and two billion dollars had disappeared; banking firms had collapsed; a government had toppled; many people had been jailed; a secret lodge had been uncovered and the man who could provide the link to the whole affair, Roberto Calvi, was found hanging by his neck under Blackfriars Bridge in London, England. This discovery turned world attention to the Vatican because, as "God's Banker", Calvi had been responsible for handling a large portion of the church's funds.

Many Roman Catholics were surprised to hear that their church had any money to invest. Real estate — perhaps; art treasures — certainly; but constant requests for financial support and pressure for increases in "Peter's Pence" (a voluntary contribution to the Pope) had indicated a lack of funds necessary to carry out the church's world-wide humanitarian activities.

To trace the source of the Vatican Bank's wealth, one has to go back to February 11, 1929 and the signing of the Lateran Treaty. Prior to this the Vatican was not only penniless, but in debt. It had had to borrow $100,000 from a Roman bank seven years earlier for the funeral expenses of Pope Benedict XV. But the treaty, signed by Benito Mussolini, established Vatican City as an independent and sovereign state, enhancing the dictator's prestige considerably, as it enabled him to use the church hierarchy at times to support his regime. It also brought the equivalent of some 80 million dollars into the Vatican treasury.

Realizing that neither he nor his curia knew much about high finance, Pope Pius XI then set up APSA (Administration of the Patrimony of St. Peter) and appointed to it a number of lay bankers who, along with church officials, would invest this new-found wealth. They, in turn, were advised by such accomplished money men as J.P. Morgan of the United States, the Hambrose Brothers of the United Kingdom and the Rothschilds of France. In 1942, Pius XII created the IOR (*Instituto per Opere de Religione* — Institute for Religious Works), commonly known as the Vatican Bank, which was set up to transfer money to various Catholic orders and organizations all over the world.

During the 1950s and '60s APSA and IOR did well with their investment portfolios, steering money into almost every sector of Italian industry. Their biggest investment was in SGI (*Societa Generale Immobiliare*), a real estate and construction company. The president of the company was Count Galleazzi, a former governor of Vatican City, and four board members were Vatican men. SGI's holdings were vast and included such properties as the Monte Mario region of Rome, where the Rome Hilton is located, the Pan Am building on the Champs Elysées in Paris, the Watergate Complex in Washington and the Stock Exchange building in Montreal. Investment money was also traced to drug firms that made contraceptive pills and companies that manufactured munitions.

Pope Paul VI's deep concern about Vatican financial ventures led him to take some action. In 1954, when he was still Giovanni Battista Montini and pro-secretary to Pius XII, he asked for reform in the Vatican's administration of finances. Instead, he was promptly transferred to Milan.

Returning some years later as Pope, he brought his own staff with him, critically referred to as the "Milan Mafia". One of these men was Cardinal Egidio Vagnozzi, an arch conservative, who became the Vatican representative in Washington and a close friend of Cardinal Cody of Chicago. According to author Malachi Martin, Paul once said of Vagnozzi, "He has said 'Good Morning' to the Devil and got away with it."

Paul was dismayed to discover the far-reaching involvement of the Vatican Bank. It provided financial support for Italy's Christian Democrat government. It was the largest investor in the government-run IRI (Institute for Industrial Reconstruction) which had 300,000 employees and accounted for 40% of all Italian investment. It owned 102 million square feet of real estate in Rome alone. For the most part these investments went unnoticed because of the Vatican's tax exempt status within Italy and because its financial records were a closely guarded secret. Throughout the 1960s and '70s successive Italian governments asked the Vatican to forego their tax exempt status at least on Italian stock earnings.

Paul's feelings about big money were evident in his 1967 encyclical *Populorum Progressio* where he castigated the "international imperialism of money" and deplored a system where the "poor always remain poor, and the rich become even richer."

In response to this encyclical, the *Wall Street Journal* said, "The Pope's words could easily be turned on the church itself. If indeed 'the superfluous wealth of the rich countries should be placed at the service of poor nations', what then of the superfluous wealth of the church?"

It appears that Paul was embarrassed, not so much by the church having money, but by where it had invested it, because in 1968 he set up PECA (Prefecture of Economic Affairs) to co-ordinate investments and prepare balance sheets for Vatican perusal. He selected Cardinal Vagnozzi as its head.

PECA's first aim was to get Vatican finances out of Italian holdings, such as its controlling interest in the real estate company SGI, and invest the funds in the more appropriate and lucrative international arena. The Vatican chose a Sicilian financial wizard, Michele Sindona, to handle these large and intricate dealings.

In 1969 and 1970 Sindona sold the Vatican's SGI stock for 350 million dollars, leaving only a 5% interest, then completely removed all shares in other Italian companies, such as Condotte d'Acqua, Pantonella and Serondo, the contraceptive factory. He then re-invested in a Luxembourg bank (40 million dollars), Gulf and Western (15 million dollars) and those other traditional moneymakers: General Motors, General Electric, Shell and IBM.

If the Vatican had stopped Sindona at this point, thanked him for his services and carried on with its blue chip investments, the story would end here instead of continuing along the road to criminal charges, prison and death.

Unfortunately, somebody got greedy.

In 1971 the Vatican put a new man in charge of the IOR, Archbishop Paul Marcinkus, a six-foot-three-inch American priest from Cicero, Illinois, with a reputation for slicing through red tape and getting things done. Marcinkus is a man of nicknames. The Italians call him "il gorilla" because of his size and his role as bodyguard to the Pope. His close friends on the golf course, where he plays with a five stroke handicap, call him "chink", a play on his name. The bankers of Zurich refer to him as the "gnome of Rome" because of the veil of secrecy behind which he operates. One thing I have never heard him called is a knowledgeable banker. An American priest who knows him well said, "He's a great golfer and a fine linguist, but I know a couple of teenagers who know more about finances than he does."

With the American Archbishop minding the bank in Rome, Michele Sindona, still the Vatican's financial advisor, headed for the United States in 1972. He set up a permanent address at the Pierre Hotel in New York and promptly bought a controlling interest in the Franklin National Bank. He had already arranged large investments in the Swiss Finabank, BPI (*Banco Privata Italiano*) and others. The following year, 1973, brought the first trouble for Marcinkus and the IOR. The American

Securities and Exchange Commission discovered that 454,000 shares of a company called Vetco Offshore Trading Industries had been purchased illegally on behalf of the Vatican Bank. The Vatican Bank was required to pay 320 thousand dollars in penalties for its involvement. This was enough to start the authorities investigating all of Sindona's dealings. In 1974 everything fell apart. BPI claimed losses of 150 million dollars, Franklin Bank 43 million dollars. An Italian arrest warrant was issued in Rome for Sindona on charges of falsifying accounts at Banco Unione where the Vatican had 15% holdings. On October 9th of that year Michele Sindona disappeared. The same month the Franklin Bank collapsed. The following January the Swiss ordered the closing of Finabank with losses of 82 million dollars. All of these bank failures represented financial loss to the Vatican.

Sindona finally resurfaced in Geneva and for the next five years successfully fought extradition. When he was finally brought to trial in 1980, an American court convicted him of 65 counts of fraud and perjury, sentencing him to 25 years in the federal correction institute in Otisville, New York.

Malachi Martin, a writer and Vatican critic, noted, "... American investigations into the Sindona affair never cleared up its central mystery. How much money had disappeared and where it had gone. But many thought the answers involved the Vatican Bank and its president, Archbishop Marcinkus. For the bank, perhaps unknowingly, was associated with Mr. Sindona's Machiavellian scheme of fiduciary trusts, phoney deposits and phantom holding companies. Near the end, Mr. Sindona was left with only one major backer: The Vatican Bank and Archbishop Marcinkus."

In Italy the event was named "Il Crack Sindona" and the government appointed a commission to study the whole affair. A member of the commission was Massimo Teodori, a professor of political science and an independent Member of Parliament.

In Rome for *Man Alive*, I had the opportunity to interview him about the Sindona affair. I asked him where he thought the money had gone.

"It's quite difficult to know where the money stolen by Sindona has gone because of the intricacy of his operation. He had a system of empty boxes throughout the world — South America, Central America, London, Liechtenstein. It's difficult to see the final distribution of the money. Certainly a lot went to individuals. Sindona himself, his family, his associates and others bene-

156

fited. Certainly it went to political people and others in power. Certainly both the Vatican and the Mafia have their money back — the money they gave Sindona to do financial operations."

"So Sindona was involved with the Mafia?" I asked.

"Well, one does not have a membership in the Mafia, but certainly there are many links between Sindona and important people in the Mafia. We know that in the fake kidnapping of Sindona in the fall of '79 the people who organized his traveling to Sicily from the States were Mafia people. Charles Gambino, a boss of organized crime, was with Sindona in Sicily those three months. There were also financial links with Mafia people."

Sindona claimed he had been kidnapped to explain part of his absence prior to his 1980 American trial. The claim is generally believed to be false.

I asked Teodori if Sindona had belonged to any other organization. I had heard of a connection between Sindona and a sinister lodge called P2 (*Propoganda Duê*), an offshoot of the Italian Masonic Lodge, which had infiltrated almost every area of Italian business and political life.

"He was affiliated with the P2, a strange lodge of masonry involved in a number of crimes and very obscure affairs. It is clear that the chief of P2, Licio Gelli, had been for five years — from '74 to '79 — the main manager of the Sindona affairs and provided the Italian power link."

In 1979 Giorgio Ambrosoli, a prominent lawyer, was assigned to liquidate the remains of Sindona's crumbled banking empire. He stated publicly that in order to facilitate a couple of large deals, Sindona had paid a commission of 5.6 million dollars to "an American bishop and a Milanese banker." A few days after making the charge, Ambrosoli was gunned down by a professional assassin. Sindona was later indicted for having arranged the killing, though he denied having had anything to do with it.

In an interview, Sindona said he had been cheated by the Vatican. I asked Teodori if he thought this was true.

"Sindona now is a sort of victim. He is a victim of the left and he's a victim of the Vatican, but no, I don't think they cheated him. The SGI affair, for example, went through different steps. It's difficult to say who gypped whom. At the beginning, as you know, Sindona and the Vatican were partners."

"You don't believe Sindona very much anyway, do you?" I asked.

"No. He is a big liar. He tries to put together some things that are true and other things that are complete fantasy."

"Was it fantasy when he said at his (1980 U.S.) trial that the Vatican was going to give him a character reference?" I asked.

"Certainly the Vatican supported Sindona until 1979, until the killing of Mr. Ambrosoli. Ambrosoli was the public lawyer in charge of Sindona's bank affairs after the bankruptcy. He was assassinated. After that period, we have documents in which it is clearly said that certain important persons of the financial affairs of the Vatican didn't support Sindona anymore. And Sindona said in an interview that one of the causes of his hardship was this change in attitude of the Vatican."

"Do you know who these important persons were?"

"Yes, Cardinal Caprio and Cardinal Guerri, who were the cardinals in charge of financial affairs with Sindona from the beginning."

It was announced in 1980 that the Vatican would present video tape of former APSA head, Guerri, and former IOR chief, Caprio, as character witnesses for Sindona. This never happened. The Vatican changed its mind, saying it didn't want to set a precedent for future cases.

Vatican losses through "Il Crack Sindona" were large. One member of the Vatican "family" stated that 10% of its total worth had been lost. Swiss banking sources put the figure in the region of 240 million dollars. Cardinal Vagnozzi publicly stated that losses were minimal, but reports persist that the total figure may well be over one billion dollars.

The IOR itself appears to have lost some 30 million through investment in Sindona's banking stocks, but its head, Archbishop Marcinkus, privately told journalists that the loss was more than compensated for by profits made on earlier Sindona dealings.

From prison, Sindona agrees: "Marcinkus earned at least 200 million dollars from me. The Vatican did not lose one dollar on deals with me!"

One would have thought that the Sindona affair would mark the end to the scandal and intrigue which swirled around the Vatican, but the worst was yet to come. It came in the form of a man named Roberto Calvi who, it turned out, was not only a friend and protégé of Sindona, but a confidant and business associate of Archbishop Marcinkus.

Calvi began his career in 1947 as a clerk in Banco Ambrosiano, then a medium-sized provincial bank with heavy religious orientation: until 1972, depositors had to show a Roman Catholic baptismal certificate to use its services. By 1971 he had worked his way up to director general and in 1975 was made president. By moving the bank into foreign investments, insurance and other financial services, he had built it into a financial empire with assets by 1981 of 20 billion dollars. Along the way he was coached by Michele Sindona who also introduced him to Licio Gelli of the P2 Lodge. Calvi became a member. Gelli had helped install Juan Peron in Argentina and was well known in South American fascist circles. The IOR had signficant holdings in Banco Ambrosiano and Archbishop Marcinkus became closely involved with Calvi's ambitious expansion schemes. Calvi set up a holding company, Cisalpine, in Luxembourg and then, through it, set up an offshore bank in Nassau, Bahamas of which Marcinkus became a director. An offshore bank is one that comes under no country's taxation system or central bank.

Sindona says both he and the IOR helped Calvi with the transactions and that Marcinkus's name and Vatican influence was used to attract depositors. "Marcinkus was made a director of L'Ambro (Banco Ambrosiano) in Nassau for two reasons," Sindona recalls. "Calvi and I thought that the name of Marcinkus on the board would help us create good prestige in the international community and Marcinkus wanted to show himself involved in international banking."

What they developed was a conglomeration of real and spurious holdings, including many "shell" or "nameplate" companies used to transfer large sums of money and give the appearance of respectability to questionable schemes.

Sorting out the complicated design of Calvi's empire is mind-boggling, but it appears to have been set up in this way:

The head office of Banco Ambrosiano was in Milan, Italy with branches throughout the country. Calvi set up Banco Ambrosiano Holdings (originally called Cisalpine) in Luxembourg, which allowed him to move money outside Italian jurisdiction. Then came his Bank Ongourtello in Switzerland which spawned the Banco Ambrosiano Overseas Ltd. in Nassau and the Banco Commerciale in Nicaragua, Banco Andino in Peru and its counterpart in Buenos Aires. He then set up twelve "shell" companies in Panama, including the World Wide Trading Company, which borrowed several hundreds of millions of dollars from Calvi's banks. When these loans came due, Calvi would stall with letters of patronage signed by Archbishop Marcinkus of the Vatican Bank. At the same time he gave a letter to Marcinkus releasing the Vatican from any responsibility for the loans. Approximately one half of the money borrowed by his Panamanian companies was used to buy shares in his original Banco Ambrosiano in Milan, an illegal maneuver. By law you cannot buy stock in your own bank using resources controlled by that bank or its affiliates.

As we talked with more and more people in Rome about Calvi's illegal machinations, it became increasingly difficult to understand how the Vatican could maintain business relations with such an unscrupulous character, especially after its experience with Sindona. A Milanese journalist and author, Leo Sisti, has followed the story from its very beginning and told us that the IOR had simply continued with Calvi where Sindona had left off.

"You see, the relationship between Sindona and Marcinkus was the most important thing in the Italian story in the early '70s. Sindona was given the task of finding money for the Vatican because it needed money for its expenses. Calvi is a heritage of Sindona. Sindona introduced Calvi to Marcinkus. Sindona became a sort of credit card to Calvi, allowing him to make his business deals with Marcinkus."

Massimo Teodori agrees: "All the methods of Sindona became the methods of Calvi, like setting up empty boxes throughout the world in order to do financial operations. The Vatican was involved as partners with Sindona and became partners with Calvi. More than that, Calvi represented in Italy what we call Catholic finance. He was the major banker for the Catholic side of the economy. That's another reason that the Vatican was involved. I would also add that the morality of the financial operation of the Vatican is the same as the morality of the worst bankers. They don't seem to morally judge the partners they have."

I was interested to know what Calvi was like personally. Several people I talked to described him as a cold, emotionless man who had a passion for secrecy. He lived in a villa in the hills of Lombardy, surrounded by barbed wire and protected by guard dogs. Sisti met him several times in Milan.

"He looked like a typical banker, who you would meet in Italy or in England. He wore grey or blue suits and jackets that matched, but he was a timid man who never looked into your eyes when he talked. He was a cold man with cold blue eyes. He was known to the world as 'God's Banker'. Italian journalists used to call Mr. Calvi the banker 'with the blue eyes'."

It is quite likely that the gigantic financial structure designed by Calvi with the help of the IOR would have collapsed eventually anyway, but its initial undermining came from his old mentor, Sindona.

In the fall of 1973 posters began to appear on the streets of Milan headed "Calvi in Jail". They accused God's Banker of fraud, falsifying accounts, misappropriation of funds, illegally exporting currency out of Italy and tax evasion. The attack was orchestrated by Sindona, who, awaiting his own trial on fraud, felt he had been abandoned by both Calvi and the IOR and decided that if he was going down, others would go with him.

In an attempt to call off these attacks, Calvi deposited $500,000 in a Swiss bank account, payable to Sindona. The blackmail payment came too late. The accusations made the Bank of Italy suspicious and its official investigator, Mario Sarcinelli, began to investigate Calvi. Suddenly Sarcinelli was arrested and jailed on flimsy charges by a Roman magistrate. Though the charges would not hold and Sarcinelli was released, he was forbidden by the magistrate to return to his investigative duties for a full year.

It was correctly suspected that only one person could have exerted that kind of pressure on the courts — Licio Gelli, head of the powerful P2 lodge.

Italian police, in a raid on Gelli's villa, turned up a complete card index system listing the members of the P2 organization, including Roberto Calvi. There was also information about some of Calvi's illegal transactions. This led to further investigations of Calvi and his associates. In February of 1981, Luigi Mennini, Managing Director of the IOR, was arrested on fraud charges, but released on parole. Although a layman, he sought and was granted refuge in the Vatican.

On May 20 that year, the list of members of the P2 Masonic Lodge was published. There were 962 names, including many prominent Italian political businessmen and jurists.

On May 22 the arrest of Licio Gelli was ordered. He was variously reported to be in Argentina, Uruguay and Switzerland.

On May 26, as a direct result of hundreds of important government officials being revealed as members of the P2, the Italian government of Premier Arnaldo Forlani collapsed.

In July, two months after the exposure, Calvi was arrested and convicted on charges of illegal currency transfers. This investigation stretched back three years to the discovery of a "hole" in Banco Ambrosiano accounts amounting to 790 million dollars and 1.4 billion dollars in unsecured loans made to their foreign subsidiaries, mostly in Latin America. This news caused the government to close the Italian Stock Exchange for the first time in 64 years, because they feared a financial collapse.

Calvi was fined 13.5 million dollars and sentenced to four years in prison. In a bout of depression while in jail he cut his wrists and took an overdose of tranquilizers in an unsuccessful attempt to kill himself. Calvi was released on bail pending appeal and, just twelve days later, asked for and received a vote of confidence from his Banco Ambrosiano's Italian directors. Despite pressure from the Bank of Italy to step down until after the inquiry was concluded, he refused.

Banco Ambrosiano's affiliates in Latin America, worried about their increasing indebtedness because of skyrocketing interest rates and the rapidly falling lira, now demanded written proof that Calvi had backing from the Vatican for his lending operations.

In September, the Vatican bank supplied Calvi with "letters of patronage" which are not formal loan guarantees, but are often used to affirm a borrower's reputation. Calvi showed these letters to Banco Ambrosiano's directors and their affiliates, but what he did not show them was the letter he had written to Marcinkus absolving the Vatican of any financial responsibility. Later, this exchange of letters was to figure prominently in assessing liability. Investigators felt that, while the Vatican might be legally free of restitution, the letters did show a conspiracy to "induce people, especially Ambrosiano directors, into error". One of these directors, Roberto Rosone, was asked by the Bank of Italy to reveal the names of the bank's foreign shareholders. Before he could comply, he was shot in the legs in what an Italian magistrate called "a typical mafia warning". Then one of the investigating judges, Emilio Allessandrini, was assassinated.

In the spring of 1982 Calvi, still out on bail, became increasingly nervous and began fearing for his life. His family trace these fears back to his exposure as a member of the P2 and of the documents linking him in business deals with Licio Gelli.

His son Carlo has described his father as "really nervous whenever Mr. Gelli's name was mentioned." He says Calvi refused to talk to Gelli because he was so frightened.

Calvi's wife, Clara, also describes the security that became part of their lives. She was protected by ten bodyguards and, when in Rome, traveled in armored cars.

In May, Calvi sent his wife away because he feared for her safety. She says he was extremely frightened the night before she left, that he had been crying. Calvi said to her that "they might kill me and then I will not see you anymore."

On June 7, the board of Banco Ambrosiano met to deal with a demand from the Bank of Italy to account for their foreign lending of some 1.4 billion dollars. No one seemed to know where this money had gone, except Calvi, and he refused to say. He urged his directors to ignore the investigators' requests. This time the board would not go along with Calvi and, by a vote of eleven to three, insisted that he tell the authorities what he knew.

Calvi left the meeting seemingly quite calm and met with a friend, wealthy Sardinian property developer Flavio Carboni. They dined together that night in Calvi's Milan apartment.

For the next few days, Italian authorities say that Calvi tried, without success, to find fresh funds. They claim he made a new approach to Marcinkus to ask the Vatican bank to buy 150 million dollars in Banco Ambrosiano stock at prices well above the market rate. He was turned down.

On Thursday June 10, Calvi vanished from his apartment in Milan. With a forged passport and a newly hired bodyguard, Silvano Vittor, he traveled to Klagenfurt, Austria.

According to Vittor, Calvi really opened up when they got to Austria. He says Calvi seemed quite happy, that he told jokes, was relaxed and really quite funny.

On Friday, a director of Banco Ambrosiano in Rome received a call from Calvi. "It was around lunchtime. I told him the Rome office was worried because we hadn't been able to contact him. They didn't know where he was. He told me to tell them to stay calm and not to worry because he was heavily involved in secret negotiations."

On Saturday, Flavio Carboni flew to Klagenfurt in his private airplane.

On Sunday, Clara Calvi received a phone call from her husband. "He said the job he was doing had some troubles, but they were going to blow over. Some crazy wonderful thing would happen for us that would change our lives."

Vittor drove Calvi to Bregenz, Austria on Tuesday, June 15. He told Vittor he had gone there for a meeting with Flavio Carboni and Hans Kuntz, a Swiss businessman from Zurich. They spent the night in Bregenz and Calvi told Vittor that, because of a change in plans, they were flying to London. Kuntz arranged for a private jet from Innsbruk airport and they landed at Gatwick about dusk on Wednesday.

In London, Calvi usually stayed at the prestigious Claridges Hotel or at an exclusive private club. This time Kuntz booked him into the Chelsea Cloisters, a shabby apartment complex used mainly as a student hostel. The cost per week was what Calvi normally paid per day. Vittor registered for both himself and Calvi. He said that Calvi became very nervous, called his room squalid and instructed him to phone every twenty minutes if he went out. Calvi stayed locked in his room.

Thursday June 17, Flavio Carboni arrived in London. Though a multimillionaire he stayed in a public housing compound near Heathrow.

In Zurich, Calvi's daughter, who was preparing to fly to Washington for a planned family meeting, received a telephone call from her father. He told her to be absolutely sure to catch her flight and that he would phone again. She was then approached at her hotel by a woman who introduced herself as Mrs. Kuntz and handed her $50,000 in Swiss francs with no explanation.

On Friday the 18th, back in Milan, a crisis meeting was held by the directors of Banco Ambrosiano. They were told by their auditors that the 1.4 billion dollars was missing. The board voted for Calvi's dismissal. Following the meeting, Calvi's personal secretary Graziella Corrocher fell to her death from a fourth-storey window. Police found a "suicide" note which read, "curse him for all the wrong he is doing to all of us from the bank and the group of whose image we were once so proud."

Early Saturday morning, a clerk was walking across Blackfriars Bridge, over the Thames, on his way to work at London's *Daily Express* newspaper when he noticed what appeared to be a man's head showing through some workmen's scaffolding. He looked closer and saw the limp body of a man hanging from a rope. The astonishment of the clerk was nothing compared to the reaction in Italy, in the Vatican, and in financial circles around the world when the police announced that the body was that of Roberto Calvi, "God's Banker". Police found about 12 pounds of stones and bricks in his trouser legs, a forged Italian passport, two watches, three pairs of spectacles and $14,000 in various currencies.

Was it suicide or murder?

That question still had not been answered when we went to

Rome in October, 1982, to film our *Man Alive* program. I believe it will never be answered to the satisfaction of all interested parties. Neither will the question of the Vatican's involvement or culpability, nor the whereabouts of the 1.4 billion dollars.

Our biggest disappointment in preparing the program was that no Vatican official or church authority would grant us an interview. Even though the church undertook its own investigation into the matter, only the most general statements emerged.

Though co-operation from the church was denied us — they even refused to allow our cameras inside the Vatican boundary — we were able to line up an impressive list of government officials, members of the banking community and journalists, in order to shed some light on the affair for Canadian viewers. While it had been headline news around the world for several months, in Rome the story had become an obsession. People were lining up at newsstands to read the latest revelations and even a non-Italian-speaking visitor knew what was being discussed at the next table in restaurants and coffee bars as the words "Calvi", "Marcinkus", "Ambrosiano" and even "Sindona" leaped out of conversations.

Seven weeks after Calvi's death, Italian authorities had ordered the liquidation of Banco Ambrosiano; this in turn affected some two hundred other international banks, which would lose several millions of dollars. Then came the public revelation of the 1.4 billion dollars which had been loaned to the Panamanian "shell" companies. This was followed by the news of the Vatican Bank's endorsement of those questionable loans. Calvi's mysterious death and his membership in the sinister P2 lodge combined with all this to form what an Italian journalist described to me as "the biggest story in Italy since the Second World War."

To develop this story for *Man Alive*, we selected people who could speak from firsthand knowledge of the investigation:

Stefano Rodota, professor of civil law, Independent Member of Parliament and a member of the commission investigating the P2;

Massimo Teodori, professor of political science, Independent Member of Parliament and a member of the commission investigating "Il Crack Sindona";

Luigi Spaventa, Oxford-educated Italian economist and Member of Parliament;

Nerio Nesi, Chairman of Banco Nationale, Italy's largest bank with worldwide affiliates;

Leo Sisti, the Milanese author and journalist who has written extensively on all aspects of the case.

The thing we naturally hoped to discover was where the missing money had gone. The confusion and speculation that resulted from that question gave us a good indication of the mystery which still surrounded the entire case.

Leo Sisti: "All the money was raised in Euromarkets, especially London, and we think it was channeled to foreign subsidiaries of Ambrosiano in Nassau, Lima and in Managua. There are indications that some of the money was used for the traffic of arms in the Falklands war."

Luigi Spaventa: "There is a lot of talk, but no evidence, that some of it went to Solidarity in Poland."

Stefano Rodota: "I think that Calvi was obliged to support Solidarity because of the help he had in the form of endorsement from the Vatican Bank."

Sisti: "It is still only speculation, but if you look at the list of Ambrosiano creditors you will find a German bank that is the one used by German trade unions that made many loans to the Polish people. There are also statements of Calvi recorded without his permission by Mr. Carboni, mentioning loans to Solidarity. I don't think that the Pope or Marcinkus knew exactly where the money went, but everyone knows that a lot of it was used to buy shares in Ambrosiano by its foreign subsidiaries and this is illegal. We also know that fifteen per cent of Ambrosiano stock was owned by the Vatican bank. Officially, it was only and a half percent, but through the "front" companies based in Panama and other countries, it owned fifteen percent."

Nesi: "Something that all Italians and others interested in these matters are wondering is: where did the money go? It's almost impossible to say exactly what was done with such a staggering figure. Certainly, some ended up in bad speculation in South America. It may also be that some ended up in genuine religious work. We do know that some was used to buy back shares in Ambrosiano, which is clearly illegal because the president of a bank cannot strengthen his power by using means that come from the bank itself. Part of it also, we know, ended up in Swiss banks."

In mid-September of 1982, Swiss authorities surrounded the Union de Banques Suisses in Geneva and arrested a man with a Chilean passport in the name of Luciano Gori. He had tried to withdraw sixty million dollars from a numbered account. Police believe all the money came from the Ambrosiano Bank. The man was soon identified as Licio Gelli, Grand Master of the P2.

We tried to find out more about this strange and fearful organization which apparently held such power over governments and influential people.

Rodota: At the beginning the P2 was a branch of the ordinary Italian Masonic Lodge. Around 1975 or 1976 it began, step by step, to realize its true objective, which we know now was to build a relationship between the political milieu, the economic milieu and the public administration. If you look through the list of the P2 lodge members, you will find there the top people in public administration, the top of the secret service, the top of the army, etc. As you know, in Italy the political top changes rapidly, but continuity is maintained by the heads of public administration. You have in the P2 a good representation of continuous power."

Rodota also described a belief commonly held in Italy — that the P2 was likely involved in the murder of Prime Minister Aldo Moro, whose body was found in a car parked in the centre of Rome in May 1978, after being kidnapped over three months earlier. A Christian Democrat, Moro had tried to co-operate with the leftist factions of the government, a move which the fascist P2 would want to prevent.

I asked Rodota about the P2's involvement outside of Italy.

Rodota: "Gelli, Grand Master of the P2, had an official role. He was honorary consul to Argentina and a member of the diplomatic community with a personal relationship to the top people in Argentina's government. He was involved in important economic affairs there and, through Ambrosiano and specifically its branch in Buenos Aires, he had continuous financial transactions with the regimes in South America. Gelli needed Calvi as a member of the P2, because he wanted a good point of reference in the economic network. Ambrosiano was a private bank with a good tradition. The majority of banks in Italy are publicly owned and are controlled by public authorities. As a private bank, with less control, Ambrosiano was better for the secret activity of the P2 lodge."

"Was the Vatican aware of Calvi's P2 connections?" I asked.

Rodota: "Oh yes, of course. Because the list of the P2 was published in the Italian newspapers and the connection between Ambrosiano and the Vatican bank was continuous during and after that. I think it was impossible for people having so close an economic relationship not to know what Calvi and Ambrosiano were doing, also the relationship between Ambrosiano and the P2. Even before the explosion of the P2 scandal, it was well discussed in the newspapers, in police investigations and in the parliament. I have no evidence of the degree of knowledge by the Vatican Bank, but I do not think they can be so naive."

In banking circles, both in and outside of Italy, there is great pressure for the Vatican Bank to offer reimbursement of funds lost through the collapse of Banco Ambrosiano. Up until now the Vatican, primarily on the basis of the letter Calvi gave Marcinkus, has refused to accept any liability.

"What has been the effect of the actions of Banco Ambrosiano?"

Nesi: "Very negative effects. When an important bank like this one goes bankrupt, the whole banking system feels it. In this case, not only the Italian banks, but the whole international banking system as well, had an interest in it. This has increased the seriousness of the whole phenomenon."

Spaventa: "We now know a few figures. The minister of the treasury declared that the Vatican Bank alone owed Ambrosiano in the order of 13 hundred million dollars, which is a very substantial sum and that is only part of the story. In the end, I think we may see something around two billion that will somehow have to be paid out of the taxpayers' money, either directly or indirectly."

"What are the chances of the Vatican reimbursing this

money?"

Spaventa: "So far, very slim, apparently. Again, the minister has said that they should be morally obliged to pay it back, but that's merely moral obligation. It seems, so far, that the kind of morality on the other side of the Tiber does not quite coincide with the kind of morality we think they should adhere to. So, what will the Vatican do? Publish their financial reports? Unlikely! Pay back the whole sum which our government says they owe? Unlikely! Find an agreement for part of the sum which they owe? Possible!"

Nesi: "It's a difficult question. Personally, I think they should pay it back because the Vatican has taken upon itself, through the IOR, to guarantee large sums that some companies had contracted with the Banco Ambrosiano and with its affiliates. The Treasurer of Italy has announced in the House of Commons that their debt is 1,287 million dollars — a staggering figure. Of this, 128 million dollars is with Banco Ambrosiano here and 1,159 million dollars with foreign affiliates of the Banco Ambrosiano. I think the moral concern of many Catholics is troubled. I believe the prestige of, not only the IOR, but also of the Vatican has been lowered a great deal. I hope that after the debate that has gone on in the Italian parliament, which has created a situation of deep discomfort, the Vatican will find some system, even gradually, to meet its obligation. The Vatican is very interested, I think, in ending this affair as quickly as possible and coming out of it as best it can. The only way to come out of it with dignity is to recognize its own debt and to ask for a rate for a long-term repayment."

Another element in the case, where almost total agreement is reached, is the cause of Calvi's death. It is difficult to find anyone in Italy who believes it was suicide. An official inquest was held in July of 1982 in London, at which a pathologist testified that the body showed no signs of "being bound or manhandled ... no marks of fingers or fingernails ... no trace of drugs or injections." The verdict was suicide or "self-suspension", as the English court called it. Calvi's family immediately appealed the verdict. In interviews since, all members of his family describe him as being in good spirits in their last telephone conversations and eagerly awaiting a family reunion.

I asked Stefano Rodota if he thought Calvi committed suicide.

Rodota: "I think that he was murdered. He tried once to kill himself, when he was in prison in Italy, and he used a more traditional way — cutting his wrists. His family spoke to him several times before he died and there was nothing to show he was depressed. There are three hypotheses. One, the connection with the sale of arms to Argentina. Two, money owned by Ambrosiano bank was given to Gelli who is now being investigated by the Swiss police and three, Calvi knew too much about Ambrosiano's political/economic transactions. It is possible Calvi was murdered to block his making revelations about these to the police."

Leo Sisti said that it was unlikely Calvi had committed suicide using the method imparted to him.

Sisti: "Calvi suffered from vertigo. It is not believable that he would climb under Blackfriars Bridge and hang himself. He also had many appointments pending in London and Zurich. Also, he is known to have had a bag with him on his trip filled with many papers. This bag has disappeared."

"How about Calvi's secretary, Graziella Corrocher? Did she commit suicide?" I asked.

Sisti: "I think so. We now know there were people who tried to convince her to take pills and some drugs because she felt very depressed in the last months, so some people may speculate, but personally I'm convinced that she committed suicide."

Rodota: "The whole affair makes it look to me like another murder. She was with Calvi from the beginning. She was the person collaborating with Calvi day by day. She knew too much!"

In the spring of 1983, Britain's High Court quashed the coroner's verdict of suicide and ordered a new inquest into the death of Roberto Calvi.

After a two-week hearing the jury returned an "open verdict", meaning it could not determine how Calvi came to his death.

The jury did not accept charges by Calvi's family that he had been murdered. It also rejected the finding of the earlier inquest that he had committed suicide.

Both his wife and daughter testified that he telephoned them from London just before he died to say he was closing a huge financial deal with a right-wing Vatican lay group to repay the 1.4 billion dollars owed to Banco Ambrosiano. Mrs. Calvi, who campaigned for the second inquest to prove her husband was murdered, acknowledged at the hearing that his life insurance of 4.5 million dollars would not be paid out if the suicide verdict were upheld.

Chief Superintendent Barry Tarbun, head of the British investigation into the hanging, said his inquiries would continue.

It is possible that time will clear up some of the mystery that surrounds this strange and complex case. But one question will possibly always remain unanswered. How could the Vatican and the IOR become involved with Calvi and his illegal and shadowy schemes, especially after their experience with Calvi's criminal predecessor, Michele Sindona?

Teodori: "I would certainly say that in the last ten years the Vatican bank, which stood for religious works, has been involved in all the most adventurous financial enterprises around Italy. The Vatican has a very realistic kind of management, so it has nothing to do with the bank at the Vatican, the IOR. The IOR has nothing to do with religion; it is just business. And business at the Vatican Bank, as demonstrated by Calvi and Sindona, is a most adventurous and most hard kind of business. I think it is impossible to be stupid for a number of years. You can make a mistake once, but when you make a series of the same kind, it becomes a policy. I don't know if it's the policy of the full Vatican or the policy of some person who is in charge of the Vatican finances, like Marcinkus, or others."

Spaventa: "Perhaps the Vatican did not know what was going on. Certainly the Vatican Bank, IOR, and, more exactly, the man still in charge, Archbishop Marcinkus, knew he was dealing with rather unsavory characters, Mr. Calvi and his associates, in very strange ventures — offshore banks, nameplates on doors and dealing with billions of dollars which could find little justification in normal banking practices. Moreover, Marcinkus was even sitting on the board of one of these offshore organizations, so he certainly knew what he was doing."

"How could the IOR get away with all this?" I asked.

Spaventa: "Because the IOR is a foreign bank which is in the State of the Vatican. Because this is a foreign state, there is not much we can do about it. We cannot send the police there. We cannot raid the place. We cannot legally do anything. There has been considerable tolerance on the part of the Italian authorities to let the IOR lead a double life, have the best of both worlds, operating in Italy and at the same time being treated as a foreign bank. The net result of course is that there have been plenty of capital exports through this bank. Capital exports are forbidden here. We have very strict exchange regulations, but of course people could always say they were giving a gift to the Vatican or to the Catholic Church, deposit money with the IOR and then, where did the money go? It was not subject to the control of the Bank of Italy, or to the Treasurer, or any Italian body."

"After Sindona, one would have thought they would avoid Calvi," I said.

Nesi: "I don't want to involve the Vatican in such a case. The interlocutor was and is the IOR. It is the bank belonging to the Vatican, but it is not the *Vatican*. While in some of these cases it might be a matter of naivety, one must keep in mind that the IOR and the Banco Ambrosiano of Mr. Calvi were in reality partners. They had done many business deals together, most of them bad."

Rodota: "I think the relationship to Calvi can be explained quite simply: the Vatican Bank had the opportunity to make some investments outside of Italy through Ambrosiano. It was seen as very profitable even though some were not legal, because we have some very, very severe rules about the transfer of Italian money abroad. It was done for money and profit."

Following Licio Gelli's arrest by Swiss police in September 1982, the P2 head was jailed pending extradition to Italy at Champ Dollon, a maximum security prison close to the French border.

On the morning of August 10, 1983, a prison official discovered Gelli's cell empty, except for a dummy clothed in pyjamas, a hypodermic needle, the smell of chloroform and traces of blood. News flashed around the world that Italy's most wanted man had been kidnapped. Within hours it was reported that the kidnapping was a sham and that a guard, Edouard Ceresa, had been bribed to help smuggle Gelli out of the prison grounds and across the border into France. Gelli has since been reported, in undocumented press accounts, to be living underground in Monte Carlo; riding anonymously through France on tour buses; hiding in an island monastery in the Mediterranean; to have slipped into Uruguay with a false passport and to have been hidden away by powerful P2 lodge brothers in Argentina. It has been suggested that the resources required for his escape from Switzerland mean there are substantial funds available to him. When Roberto Calvi was president of Banco Ambrosiano he once estimated the mysterious grand master's personal assets to be in excess of 500 million dollars.

The hearing into Calvi's death and Gelli's escape from prison have continued to keep this bizarre story of money, murder and political intrigue on the front pages of the world's press. Each new episode revives the tales of curious links with the church of Rome.

To this time, church officials have declined comment on many aspects of the Calvi/Ambrosiano/Vatican Bank affair, except to maintain that the IOR is in no way obligated to cover any loans that led to the collapse of Italy's largest private bank.

A commission of fifteen Cardinals met in Rome for three days in November of 1982 to look into the charges and reported that they found the Vatican Bank and its president, Archbishop Paul Marcinkus, clear of any wrongdoing.

Legally, the Vatican Bank is no doubt in the clear; however, many feel there is a moral obligation to investors in Banco Ambrosiano and to the Italian taxpayer. Everyone would like to believe that the Vatican had no knowledge of the unsavory deals in which the IOR figures so prominently. This is possible. It is also possible that the IOR was simply being used by Calvi and his associates who took advantage of the church's naivety in banking matters. To believe this, one also has to believe Archbishop Marcinkus, the president of the IOR, to be gullible to the point of incompetence.

From his jail cell in Otisville, New York, Michele Sindona described Marcinkus as a "nobody who had pretentions to become a financier. I would never have believed he would become president of IOR. He thought that because he had a position as a banker he *was* a banker. Two weeks at Harvard University attending lectures and he thought he had become a banker. You can consider him honest or not honest, it's up to you. In my opinion he did all those things at IOR because he wanted to become a Cardinal. He wanted to give the Pope a lot of money and he found all the systems to make money."

Very often we hear people say 'money is the root of all evil'. The correct biblical quotation is 'the *love* of money is the root of all evil'. There is a great difference.

No one will deny that the church, any church, needs money to carry on its work. It needs a great deal of money to operate its spiritual and humanitarian programs all over the world. The problems arise when the church coffers show a surplus. Investment portfolios are the obvious answer, but what sort of investments? I have been present at councils of several denominations as they agonized over what kinds of stocks or bonds were appropriate for their investment. I know of churches that have canceled investments in corporations when there was the slightest hint that the money might be used for questionable purposes or to help support repressive regimes. The greatest safeguard that can be employed by the financial board of any church is to open the books and provide a complete and honest accounting of its investment transactions to its members. This the Vatican has never done, and shows no sign of doing.

While I agree with Archbishop Marcinkus on his oft-quoted remark, "You can't run the church on Hail Marys", I believe the average Roman Catholic would like to know that the gift accompanying that prayer is used in a legitimate and considered way.

THREE MEN OF FAITH

Ralph Waldo Emerson once said, "An institution is the length-ened shadow of one man." For nearly 2,000 years the institu-tions that have borne the lengthened shadow of Christ have done so with uneven grace. At its best the church provides a structural community within which its servants, the priests and ministers, assist people of faith to transform their lives and hence society. In many cases, however, the structure itself has stifled the creative expression of that faith so necessary for its own survival.

It has been my privilege, in the course of my broadcasting career, to meet and talk with three exceptional men of the church whose quest for the expression of their own deep individ-ual faith took them on very different journeys.

All three, Paul-Émile, Cardinal Léger, Bishop James Pike and Archbishop Ted Scott, have received their institutions'

175

tribute of high office. One, Cardinal Léger, chose to leave the pomp and splendor of that office to express his devotion to God in the simple role of missionary to the lepers of Africa. Another, Bishop Pike, could find no peace or comfort inside the ecclesiastical framework, so embarked on his own sad, but faithful odyssey. The third, Archbishop Ted Scott, has made the system work and used the machinery of the institution to carry his own personal faith across his beloved Canada and out to the world church community.

Widely different in many ways, all three can teach us much about the power of faith.

CARDINAL LÉGER

There is no disguising the poverty and deprivation that characterizes daily life in the villages and rural areas of Cameroon, on the west coast of Africa. Its economy is based almost entirely on agriculture and a relatively prosperous farmer might earn $250 in a good year. Almost every child in Cameroon has some form of intestinal infection. Their water, in short supply for most of the year, is polluted. Of the five million population, some 1.2 million suffer from leprosy. The desperate problems of Cameroon and its neighboring countries have stirred the hearts of many people in the West but few have reacted as directly or as deliberately as Canada's Paul-Émile, Cardinal Léger.

A prince of the Church, accustomed to the privilege and wealth of high office, Léger now hangs his magnificent red robe in the closet of his small room at the Canadian mission in Cameroon. Its two small houses, scarcely more than shacks, make a stark contrast to any Cardinal's palace. A secondhand car that Léger drives himself has replaced his limousine and chauffeur and instead of ten secretaries to assist him, he now takes care of his own correspondence by hand.

Cardinal Léger is a symbol of loving sacrifice, the sacrifice of a man of faith who has put his beliefs into action outside the institution of the Roman Catholic Church and its next-to-highest office.

I first met Paul-Émile, Cardinal Léger in the fall of 1969. He had returned to Canada after two years in Africa to receive the $50,000 Royal Bank Award for humanitarian works and to embark on a three-month Canadian tour to raise money for his leprosy clinics. Because of his demanding schedule and concern over his physical condition, it was no easy task for the *Man*

Alive producer to arrange a filming session with Léger. Reports of the Cardinal's near-exhaustion and generally frail condition had started the minute he disembarked at Dorval airport to be met by hundreds of admirers led by Montreal mayor Jean Drapeau. The two years had taken their toll.

Léger planned to spend two weeks resting at the home of his brother Jules before starting his fund-raising tour, but he agreed to give up a morning for the *Man Alive* interview. I was surprised to learn that he had heard of our show, as it began on the CBC at about the same time that he had made his dramatic move to Africa. I would learn later that Canadian visitors to his new home had described the series to him in great detail.

On our way to Montreal by plane the morning of the interview, my producer Louise Lore and I discussed the correct protocol to observe when meeting a Cardinal. We were to be introduced to him in the lobby of the Queen Elizabeth Hotel before the actual filming. A room had been set aside there for the interview.

"Does one curtsy to a Cardinal or kiss his ring?" asked Louise.

"I don't know," I replied. "I once met Cardinal Flahiff of Winnipeg but that was at a party and I didn't know he was a Cardinal until someone told me later."

The situation resolved itself in the most informal way possible. As we entered the lobby we spotted Léger chatting with a few people, one of whom, after glancing in our direction, leaned over and whispered in his ear. He immediately turned and strode toward us. Before we had a chance to do anything he threw his arms around Louise in a brief hug, thrust his hand out to me and beamed, "Welcome to Montreal. I'm Léger."

He had one of those faces that, with one smile, change from weary and sad to warm and beautiful. As with many people you've only seen in photographs, he was smaller than expected. He wore a plain black suit with Roman collar. Except for those famous bushy eyebrows and deep-set black eyes, he could easily have passed for a simple missionary priest.

"I have only two requests," he told us, after we had settled in the comfortable chairs provided for the interview. "I will not answer questions about the political situation in Quebec or about the attitudes of the church toward married priests."

"I hadn't intended to ask you about Quebec," I assured him. "That wouldn't be fair, would it? After all, you haven't lived here for two years."

Louise and I had discussed bringing up the married priests

issue, which was very much in the news at that time, so I didn't offer any guarantees concerning that request. This omission went unnoticed as Léger smilingly launched into expressions of happiness at being once again in his beloved city.

Léger's intense feelings for Montreal cannot be overstated. Once, as Archbishop, he returned from a trip and upon arrival stretched out his arms to well-wishers, proclaiming, "Montreal! Oh, my city! I give you my life ... all my life."

He was born only a few miles west of Montreal, in Valleyfield, and grew up in nearby St-Anicet on the St. Lawrence River, where his father ran a general store. Early friends recall him as an "ailing, sensitive boy who was afraid of his own shadow" and given to "inexplicable bouts of weeping".

From childhood he was devout, attending mass every day. He entered a seminary at fifteen, but ill health kept him at home, where a doctor forbade him to open a book for two years. He smuggled his Latin text into his room, however, and when he returned to the seminary, caught up with his class rapidly.

Léger was attracted to the Jesuits, but spent only a month in one of their colleges, where his emotional personality was judged unsuitable. A Quebec City Jesuit once stated, "He was so emotional, he used to cry during spiritual exercises. Our life demands men of different fibre."

He then joined the Sulpician Fathers and, in 1929, entered the priesthood. During the next four years at La Solitude, the Sulpician mother house near Paris, France, he rose to be assistant to the Superior, the only Canadian to attain that post.

In 1933, Léger was transferred to Japan where, in his words, he became a "missionary priest". He founded the Canadian Sulpician Seminary in Fukuoka on the southern island of Kyushu and soon began studying the Japanese language fourteen hours a day. In six months he could say the catechism in Japanese. In twelve months he could conduct retreats in that language and after four years was giving philosophy lectures in Japanese at the seminary. When he learned that Japanese students have more respect for professors with beards, he grew a heavy black one.

In 1939, Léger returned to Canada, where he was appointed Vicar General for his native diocese of Salaberry de Valleyfield. He went to Rome in 1947 to become Rector of the Pontifical Canadian College where forty Canadian priests were studying.

In 1950, Monsignor Joseph Charbonneau, Archbishop of Montreal, resigned for reasons of ill health. Some say his resignation was actually forced because his support of labor unions conflicted with the policies of the Duplessis government. The labor situation in Quebec at the time was a severe test of the Church's tact. The need for diplomacy and discretion in the office of Archbishop was thought to be a major reason for Pius XII's appointing Paul-Émile Léger to that post.

The elevation was so unexpected in the lay community that only one Montreal newspaper could come up with a picture of Léger when the appointment was announced. In his new role, Archbishop Léger at first sounded like a rigid defender of those stances adopted by the Roman Catholic Church in connection with divorce, contraception and euthanasia. He also denounced comic books and movies dealing with sex and crime and got Montreal City Council to order the closing of all stores on religious holidays.

Later, he seemed to break with tradition and began to speak out against the pomp and splendor of the Church. He urged nuns who administered hospitals to spend more money and not amass capital. He broke down barriers between religions and set up liaison committees between the major religions in Montreal. When asked about this period in his life, Léger recalls, "I had no desire to play at being a prophet or to transform political and social institutions. But the gospel by itself can do so. From the start I attempted to establish myself in a free zone as far as all temporal power is concerned and I shouldered my responsibilities as spiritual leader. My predecessors were of their day and age, with personalities that were occasionally scintillating, but I refused to reap the harvest that had been sown by others before me."

One of his major achievements while Archbishop was to begin the secularization of the Quebec educational system. Though some critics maintained that this move resulted in a marked weakening of faith among the people, Léger insisted it was necessary. "When I was elected bishop, seventy-five establishments in the province were under the direction of the clergy. I realized that the church, which since 1760 had been a kind of Noah's Ark preserving the remnants of the French Catholic presence, simply had to abandon certain areas where she exercised a monopoly. She had to accept a new situation."

Then, in January 1953, he became Cardinal of the largest Roman Catholic diocese in the British Commonwealth. At forty-eight, Léger was the second youngest man to achieve that rank. From the ceremony in Rome he wrote to a friend in Canada,

"How can one help but praise the power of God, who made a boy from St-Anicet a prince of the Church?"

When Pope John XXIII opened the Second Vatican Council in October 1962, Cardinal Léger was one of the more prominent leaders of a fresh and progressive thrust in church policy. He spoke out repeatedly on such topics as liturgy, birth control, conjugal relations and religious freedom.

Léger remembers the Council as a "long and painful experience" and goes on, "It was a terrible ordeal for a spiritual leader — that lucid look at the Church and the world. Every time I spoke, and I suppose it must have happened more than twenty times, I tried to make positive judgments and to avoid being negative. But when I took up a position dictated by my own conscience as a pastor and a Christian, I came under the sentence of the Council itself. It is not easy for a man, whether he be a Cardinal or not, to stand before 2,300 judges. The bishops in council were undoubtedly our judges. When I spoke on the liturgy, for example, and insisted on the necessity for the vernacular so that it could be understood by all, the next day other bishops put forward the opposite viewpoint and I wondered whether I was right. Could I be right? We were breaking entirely new ground whether as instruments of the Holy Ghost or as individual human beings."

Talking to reporters at the time, Léger expressed his impatience with the slow-moving deliberations of the schemata that had been prepared by the curia before the Council started. One in particular called "The Divine Constitution" or "Divine Revelation" caused "anger and torment" in Léger. The schema attempted to relate the role of scripture and tradition to their common origin in the "word of God". The document affirmed the value of scripture for the salvation of men while maintaining an open attitude toward the scholarly study of the Bible.

"I remember, in the early stages of the Council, the tragic vote on *Revelation* when the fathers formed two opposing factions. That very evening, during an audience with Pope John, I unburdened my heart to him. I told him I felt that piercing thorns were tormenting my soul, but he replied, 'Go forward. Do what your heart tells you. Go on!'"

Canadian theologian Gregory Baum described Léger's efforts at the Council as "the most consistently progressive of any". Some observers felt that the turmoil of Vatican II and Léger's admitted frustration with the hierarchy was the reason for his decision to walk away from the pomp and power of high office.

Immediately after the Council, he traveled to Africa, visiting three of the leper colonies that he had helped establish through a fund he had set up called *Fame Pereo* (Latin for "I am starving to death"). As early as November 1963, reports that Léger was contemplating giving up his rank of Cardinal to work among the lepers in Africa were rejected by the Vatican as "stupid". Many pointed out at this time that he was being considered a candidate for the papacy. When he returned to Montreal in January 1964, he himself denied a report that he planned to resign.

Then, on November 9, 1967, the news was announced by the Vatican. Léger had resigned as Archbishop of Montreal. It was headline news in most papers and the lead item on every radio and television newscast that day. Reporters swarmed to a press conference called by Léger's staff in the baroque throne room of his palace. The luxurious decor — deep plush carpets and crystal chandeliers — presented a vivid contrast to the surroundings he would shortly face in the leper colonies of Africa.

He read a statement first in French, then in English, saying in part, "Faith is before everything else the witness of a life. Those who may not understand my words may be touched by my decision. Youth loves sincerity and genuineness. So I ask you all to set out on the narrow highroad of faith, and to answer the call of God by a devotion to poverty which, from a purely human point of view, may often seem useless. The glass of water freely given is still today the most convincing proof for the existence of God, who is present in the fevered face of the poor man ... In making my decision, I have thought not only of Africa. It is for the greater good of the church of Montreal that I have become a simple missionary in the midst of the poorest of the citizens of the Third World. The time has come to go from words to actions. I wish to dedicate the few years allotted to me to giving spiritual and material assistance to the lepers, and so I am leaving for Africa."

In answer to reporters' queries about his decision, Léger said, "I have reached the age where a certain sclerosis of soul and body might set in. The spur must be used to get out of a rut."

Replying to the question of how a Cardinal could become a simple missionary, he smiled and said, "Being a Cardinal does not mean you cannot do any good."

The announcement by the Vatican caused surprise in church circles. Léger was twelve years below the retirement age for diocesan prelates and his post was considered an extremely important one.

Tributes and regrets immediately poured in. Mayor Jean Drapeau said, "We will long remember him for his supreme skills which he abundantly demonstrated, and for his numerous good works."

The Right Reverend R. Kenneth Maguire, Anglican Bishop of Montreal, declared, "His departure is a matter of real regret; he will be missed very much."

Rabbi Dr. Harry Stern of Montreal called Léger "one of the most courageous leaders of interfaith relations both here and in the Vatican."

United Church minister Roy Ashford of Montreal described him as "a real liberal", and added "the warm ecumenical climate here in Montreal exists because of the Cardinal's efforts."

Maurice, Cardinal Roy, Archbishop of Quebec, issued a personal statement saying it would be painful to be deprived of "someone who has for so many years been such a worthy adviser and very dear friend. I can speak for all my colleagues in the church in saying that we are all dismayed at losing a pastor in whom lives zeal, lucidity and common sense."

Within a year of Léger's moving to Cameroon, various news sources were reporting on his frustration and disillusionment. These reports were denied by his Sulpician Order superiors in Rome, who admitted he was "very tired and is badly in need of a rest after his first year in Africa." In a special report to *Fame Pereo* at this time, he said, "My first experience with missionary activity has taught me the necessity of those two virtues, patience and constancy."

And now, a year later, comfortably ensconced in a Canadian hotel suite, the television lights making his eyes seem darker and even more sunken than usual, Cardinal Léger told me about his initiation into a new and sometimes bewildering culture.

"When you arrive in a new country, you have to change your plans and adapt yourself to them. These are new countries and very independent. I found I had to be very careful because they have their own organizations, their own Ministry of Health and if you give the impression that you are there to change things or teach them what to do, you can find yourself in a very awkward position. I found I had to take a few months, even a year, as a novice to realize I was no more in Montreal, that I was in Africa. But of course there were lepers to care for and I spent my first while with them in a colony north of Cameroon.

"We had to become organized and build a community where the lepers could be helped. With the help of generous donors from Canada, we were able to build houses for them and treatment facilities. There are a number of villages being supported by Protestant and Catholic charities or humanitarian groups. We have trained sisters who go around the community and we are able to look after three thousand people now, but we know there are another ten thousand in the bush who need our care."

He talked about the problems of reaching the bush-dwellers and bringing medical aid and comfort to remote regions. "I have been in the bush there in the last few months, driving from place to place over the muddiest and the most primitive roads imaginable. I drove a car when I was young, but that was many years ago and I had to practically learn all over again, but one re-adapts."

I was interested in the people's reaction to his arrival in Cameroon. Was he looked upon as just another priest or recognized as a high prince of the Church?

"Well, of course there was ambiguity in my situation. I tried by all means to have people forget what I was, but it was impossible. I am always a chief. I am always the *Koo Koo Ma,* which means the "man who has power". You should realize that Cameroon is a very, very funny country. First of all it was a German colony, organized by Bismarck. He was a very systematic person. He took a ruler and divided up the country — in the north, Moslems; in the centre, Catholics; in the south, Protestants. It went on that way until the war, then it became a French colony and then independent. I am living and working now in the centre of a very huge and heavily Christian community. When I arrive at a village for confirmation, say, the people just stand there, they won't budge. They are waiting to see what my attitude is. They have a marvellous sense of observation and can judge their man after five minutes. We begin to sing and they like to sing every hymn they know for me, which takes hours. After the ceremony, it takes me a half-hour to walk from the church to the nearby rectory (which is just the same as the other houses) because they all want to touch me. They do not think or act in abstract. They say, 'He is the man who came to give us something.' They don't kiss my ring as people do in Canada. They bite my fingers instead. They are straightforward and real. I have to take all the children in my arms and bless them and kiss them. There is much joy and happiness and simplicity with them."

Léger has described Africans as twenty years ahead of the rest of the Roman Catholic world in their fervor, their under-

183

standing and devotion. He said, "Theirs is the heart of Christian reality."

"What is the attitude of the government to your being there?" I asked.

"When I left Canada I just wanted to serve in the Third World. I really had no special destination. But I met the President of Cameroon through the bishop and he said he would be very glad if I stayed there. He said he would give me a permanent visa, as if I was one of his citizens. He is a very humble, simple and dedicated man, also very intelligent. He speaks knowingly about the problems of the world and of Africa. He asked, with tears in his eyes, 'Can you do something for my country?' So I have worked now for two years and this is my first holiday. When I left, the President gave me a letter for the Prime Minister of Canada. It is about a project to build a secondary school. It would be really nothing for us to build. I am acting as an ambassador between the two countries."

Cardinal Léger said it was difficult to make people believe when he spoke of conditions in Africa. He told of showing a film to a select group of a dozen businessmen in Canada which described a hospital where there was no running water and patients and staff had to wash in water brought in pails from neighboring homes. He said eleven of the twelve Canadians didn't believe that conditions like that existed. The twelfth believed because his daughter-in-law was one of the nurses. Léger deplored plans that were initiated on a grand scale and claimed the best way was to give aid on the more direct person-to-person level.

"I met a representative from the United Nations in Cameroon and asked him what he was planning to do. He was obviously planning to do something since he had come all that way to see us. He said he was working on a project to build a highway between two towns. That's not a bad idea but he told me they had already spent two million dollars on the drafts; you see, they hadn't even started it yet. So I asked when it would be built. He said probably never. That is no help to the person in need. We must give directly to the people who are there and who are suffering."

"When you went to Africa, you wanted to work with the lepers," I pointed out. "Now it seems to me you have broadened your view to the problems of other nations, the needs of the whole globe."

"Yes, I'm not speaking only of Africa. I'm speaking of all the

Third World. I'm speaking of the two billion people trying to live on an annual income of about a hundred dollars a year. They have to live. They have to educate their children. What can we do? We must reflect on this. The biggest problem in the world, maybe the only problem, is how to bring these two groups together — those who have so little and those who live in such abundance. I realize that presidents and statesmen and governments are sincere, but when you are living in a country where ninety-five percent of the population is working on small farms with primitive tools, why bring them large tractors and television sets and jet planes? It may be good for our prestige but is it good for the man or woman living in the bush?"

Léger insisted that time was running out and that the West would have to concentrate its efforts on the problems of the Third World. "After all, it took only ten years for Kennedy to set up NASA and, with the concentrated efforts of thousands of scientists, to put a man on the moon. In my humble opinion, if we want man to walk with dignity on earth, we should have enough imagination to accomplish that, too. I think we have to be careful when we judge scientific performance. It is a worthy thing, the advancement of science, but at the same time I think we can do more for our fellow human beings. Maybe we don't need so many nuclear centres, but more schools and hospitals and agricultural facilities. So many young people want to go to the moon, want to go to the stars and, of course, I hope everybody wants to go to heaven, but our first obligation is to those who are still here on earth."

Léger hopes the young people in the western world will follow his example and devote their energies to working for and in the Third World. "I will not see the end of it. I am too old. If I was young again, twenty-five or thirty, I could do so much more. Something has to be done. A new world has to be built and it is really worth it to give your life in building it. I have the impression that the youth of today are not content, not satisfied with the world in which they live, but they are talking about the world where they live. I would like to have them understand that other world which is far bigger and more complicated than theirs."

I asked him what was required for a person to work effectively in the Third World and what changes he had made.

"You have to be very humble and get rid of all your feelings of pride. You are not going there to teach them what we do at home. That is no good at all. Do not impose what you think is truth, but try and find truth in the minds of these people. I found a great serenity in Africa. That wisdom of man who is 'in front of life'. You must change your way of thinking about time. For us time is money, for the African time is just time. When an African sees you glancing at your wristwatch, he will ask, 'Why are you trying to make the sun faster?' If you ask, 'Is the road good? Will it save me time in getting to the next village?,' he will answer, 'Ah, brother, let us go and find out.' There is a wisdom of life we do not have. They believe in their God and in all the spirits. There are no cemeteries. Their mothers and fathers are buried very near to their houses and they continue to speak and to live with them. There is a great deal of love.

"There is always a little house empty for the man who is traveling and when you arrive at night, no matter who you are, this little house is yours with some fruit, like bananas, there for 'the brother' to eat. You are called brother and treated as a brother. It is a tribal society and you must learn that blood is thicker than water. Of course, when you hear them calling each other brother, you also learn that in many cases this is literally true. A father will perhaps have twenty-five to fifty women, so a lot are indeed brothers."

Léger spoke of the special place that Canada held in the minds of people he worked with in Cameroon. He said there wasn't the same suspicion felt for Canada as for other countries and because of this good relationship we were in a unique position to do more. While he was in Canada he planned to raise money beyond his $50,000 bank award. In his tour in 1969 and 1970, Léger raised $2,930,400 in Canada and the United States. A charity organization called *Le Cardinal Léger et ses œuvres* (Cardinal Léger's Endeavors) was set up after his visit to administer future donations. Their first objective was the building of a rehabilitation centre for children suffering from polio, leprosy or any of the other diseases rife in Cameroon. The centre would consist of fifteen pavilions and the projected cost was $1.3 million. They were also optimistic about raising funds for forty-five other projects, including three schools, dispensaries and clinics, orphanages and farm developments.

A few weeks prior to my interview with Cardinal Léger, I had interviewed Barbara Ward, the noted British economist and humanitarian. In our talk she had angrily proclaimed, "Some day we will be called before God and he will ask, 'Did you clothe the naked? Did you feed the hungry? Did you give them shelter?' and if we can only say 'No, but we gave them .1% of our gross

186

national product', God will say, 'That's not enough.' "

I repeated Barbara Ward's quotation to Cardinal Léger and waited for his reaction. There was a long pause. His eyes seemed to grow darker as he pondered the words. Finally he said, "Perhaps we are already judged, not by God, but by man."

Later in the week, Léger spoke to the Empire Club in Toronto and that evening the newspapers carried a front page story in which he was quoted as saying, "Some day we will be called before God and he will ask, 'Did you clothe the naked . . .?' " I had really liked the Barbara Ward quotation. Cardinal Léger must have liked it too.

At seventy-nine, Paul Émile, Cardinal Léger, the Canadian who rose to be a prince of the Church and was even considered for the papacy, still serves the sick and homeless in Africa's Cameroon. For Léger the walls of the church were just too confining for the expression of his faith. By reaching in another direction for fulfilment, he has found personal peace in the simple joys of helping the less fortunate.

BISHOP JAMES PIKE

Bishop James Pike was an anomaly. On the one hand he was a caring, faithful and highly intelligent man; on the other he was involved in situations which were morally questionable, became an agnostic for a short while and toward the end of his life believed in communication with the dead.

When I met him, I was immediately struck by his amazing energy. His mind seemed to work at such a rate that his words could not keep pace, making him stutter or speak in non sequiturs. This, plus a deep raspy voice, often made him difficult to understand, yet his turn of phrase and exceptional insight made the effort of listening worthwhile. Pike seemed to be pushing himself all the time, but to what end I was never sure.

He was born in California on February 14, 1913 into a Roman Catholic family. As a boy he was an acolyte and later attended the Jesuit University of Santa Clara. Always a thoughtful man, he began questioning the papal stands on birth control and infallibility. As a result he transferred to UCLA and in 1936 attained a degree in Arts and Law. Two years later he received a Doctor of Sciences of Law degree from Yale University and later became a lawyer for the Securities and Exchange Commission in Washington. He wrote *Cases and Other Materials on New Federal and Code Procedures,* which later became a law textbook. He was then married but this marriage lasted only two years.

It was in this period that Pike became an agnostic. In 1942, he married Esther Yanovsky, one of his students at George Washington University. They wrote their own ceremony in which there was no mention of God.

During World War II, Pike joined Naval Intelligence and in 1944, still in uniform, rediscovered religion and joined the Episcopal Church. After the war, he attended the Virginia Theological Seminary and became tutor and fellow of the General Theological College. He studied theology and ethics with instructors such as Paul Tillich and Reinhold Niebuhr. Ordained in 1946, he was assigned to Christ Church in Poughkeepsie and the chaplaincy of Vassar. On the Pikes' first Sunday in their new parish, two people attended the early communion, with only seventy-five at the eleven o'clock service. After a few months, church attendance had risen to four hundred every Sunday.

Within ten years he had become chaplain at the University of Columbia and Chairman of their department of religion; contributed articles on conventional theology to the six-volume work, *The Church's Teaching;* become Dean of New York's Cathedral of St. John the Divine; had his own television show which ran for five years on fifty ABC stations; and been consecrated Bishop of California.

Although he had a somewhat unorthodox beginning, his career so far had created little controversy. In 1960, all this changed. As part of the *Christian Century* series, Pike wrote an article called *How My Mind Has Changed.* This was the first hint that he was questioning the basic precepts of the Trinity, the Virgin Birth and salvation through Christ alone. In that year Pike also fought to amend Church orthodoxy during a meeting of the House of Bishops but was able to achieve only one concession. The bishops granted that "St. Luke was an evangelist more than a historiographer."

Concerns about Pike became widespread. In January, 1961, clergy in Georgia called for him to be fired because of his "expressed doubts". Pike responded in an editorial in *The New York Times* saying that he was well within bounds. In February the Georgian Chapter as a whole demanded that formal charges be presented at the next meeting of the House of Bishops; however, their own Bishop, Albert R. Stuart, did not agree. But the problems for Pike and the entire Church were just beginning.

Within the House of Bishops he had support from those who thought him brilliant and were not afraid of questioning existing dogma; but others objected to his publicized liberal stance on social issues like McCarthyism, birth control, censorship and human rights. These battles were waged on a national scale, yet Pike's record as Bishop of California attests to his ability and popularity. While Bishop, the number of parishes in his diocese increased from 112 to 124; membership grew by nearly twenty thousand and, through voluntary contributions alone, the income of the Cathedral in San Francisco tripled. He also oversaw the construction of Grace Cathedral in San Francisco. Its windows include portraits of "secular saints" Albert Einstein, John Glenn and Thurgood Marshall; theological reformers Paul Tillich, Martin Buber and Fr. Karl Rahner SJ; church reformers Pope John XXIII, Dr. Geoffrey Fisher (Archbishop of Canterbury) and Arthur Lichtenberger (Presiding Bishop of the Episcopal Church).

During Lent in 1962, Eugene Exman of *Harper's* magazine heard a sermon by Pike and suggested the bishop write a book on doctrine. That summer he began *I Believe* but, after completing several chapters, put the project aside. In 1963, he received an advance copy of Bishop John Robinson's *Honest to God*. Pike told of his reaction: "I admired his courage; I felt he was getting somehow closer to the point. And it gave me the courage to throw away all the chapters I had written except the one on belief, and to write an entirely different kind of book, which is quite iconoclastic ... I decided not to try to come out smelling like a rose on orthodoxy."

That summer, in Mexico, Pike reorganized his book, now titled *A Time for Christian Candor*. In it he affirmed only one absolute — the existence of God. Everything else he maintained was historically conditional. Throughout this year, both his press coverage and congregation increased. The book was published in 1964.

A month before its publication, Pike gave two sermons at the 61st General Convention of the Protestant Episcopal Church in St. Louis. The first denounced racism and the inaction of the southern bishops. The second concerned itself with matters of dogma. He described the Trinity as an "irrelevancy" and called for an end to "outdated, incomprehensible and non-essential doctrinal statements, traditions and codes." A new controversy was in the making.

Again the House of Bishops was divided. Bishop George Leslie Cadigan, for example, supported Pike but Bishop Edward Randolph Welles dubbed him a "publicity seeker" with a "deep-rooted martyr complex", who was "thirsting" for a heresy trial. Bishop Louittit formally demanded an apology for the first sermon. Pike refused. A special committee was formed on how to disavow him without including heresy in their charges.

Years later, Bishop Pike told me that this was one of the crucial points in his life. We were talking about "peak experiences" and how they can change one's direction. He described them as mini-conversions that contributed not only to internal satisfaction and joy but to external health and effectiveness.

"The General Convention of the Episcopal Church in St. Louis was our worst convention on every score ... Coming back from it I was bitterly depressed about the Church. In addition I was being bugged by heresy charges which had taken a lot of time in the executive sessions. I was exhausted and tormented. The radio, television and press were at me all the time. I was very much involved with a couple of social struggles that were going badly and there were budget cuts and pledges not coming in because of stands I was taking. Our diocese was up to its hilt in mortgages with not many endowments. Everything was going wrong at home. The result was when I got on the plane to fly back I was in a considerable state of anxiety. These peak experiences are very quiet sometimes and they can come with religious images or not. Very quietly the following came to me — 'It doesn't matter, does it? What are you in this for, anyway? What is my whole corps of clergy in it for?' And then a very good line came to me. It was almost as though it were being told to me. I don't want to sound spooky about this. I'm quite willing to take credit for it, but the line just came out and rang around the world after I used it when I got back. The line was, 'We have tables, bread and wine, the word of God, voices and pens. What can they take away from us?' Let 'em have the buildings. Let the banks foreclose. We can worship in the park. We can rent halls or use homes. What is this about anyway? Is it buildings? Is it budgets? Is it great growth statistics and graphs? No. That's all nice, but it doesn't matter. At that point I became free of the idolatry of the success of the institutional church."

Following the St. Louis meeting, Father Frank M. Brunton became Pike's greatest enemy, writing editorial after editorial accusing him of heresy. Brunton was admonished by his bishop but continued his attacks. The action which would bring this confrontation to a head was Pike's ordination of Mrs. Phyllis Edwards as a deaconess. Previously deaconesses had to be celibate and could not participate in the eucharist. Mrs. Edwards became the first American woman to be recognized as a full minister. As a result, Brunton — supported by fourteen other clergymen — started a petition charging Pike with heresy. Though it contained no evidence or documentation, it was forwarded to the House of Bishops. Pike was charged in the petition with repudiation of the Virgin Birth, denial of the Trinity and other basic Christian precepts such as the Incarnation, the empty tomb, bodily resurrection and the Ascension of Christ. He was also charged with failing to celebrate the Feast of Annunciation, even though his verger, Charles Agneau, stated that six services had been celebrated that day. Pike published a complete point-by-point refutation of the charges in the *Churchman* newspaper.

In September 1965, during a meeting of the House of Bishops in Glacier Park, Montana, Pike was denied his usual seat on the Theological Committee and was not allowed to respond to the charges levied against him. When the committee presented its report to the general house, it put aside the charges of heresy but accused Pike of "self-aggrandizement and publicity seeking". Pike tried to interrupt the reading of the report by introducing his new book, *What is this Treasure?*, as evidence of his continued faith, but the committee would hear no arguments. They called for Pike to "reaffirm his loyalty to the doctrine, discipline and worship of the Episcopal Church." Pike compared this to "an immigrant taking the oath of citizenship a second time because someone raised a question about his belonging to left wing political groups."

Earlier that year, Pike, his marriage breaking up, had moved out of his official residence. A year previously he had met Maren Bergrud, who worked from time to time as his secretary. During their relationship, Pike paid her hospital bills and used his episcopal discretionary funds to pay her debts. In the spring of 1965, he set up an apartment for her and eventually moved in himself, although insisting that he did not wish to marry her.

On July 2, 1965, Luci Baines Johnson, daughter of the President, was rebaptized into the Roman Catholic Church. While Pike did not object to her switching churches, he publicly commented on the ceremony, calling it "a deliberate act denigrating another branch of Christendom." This started a most unusual controversy: this time Pike was accused of being too conservative. Though many church people agreed with him, they thought his statement too harsh.

That September, Pike took a six-month sabbatical to study at Cambridge University. His son, James Jr., accompanied him. Maren followed a short time later.

From England, Pike flew to Rhodesia on a visit to California's "companion" diocese, Matabeleland. Fr. Brunton wrote to Prime Minister Ian Smith regarding Pike's social stands, calling him a "notorious racial agitator". As a result Pike's hotel room was bugged and at the airport he was held incommunicado for three hours and denied access to the lawyer hired for him by Rhodesian bishop Kenneth Skelton. Pike was ordered out of the country by the authorities and put on a plane for London. Pike and Skelton then formally requested that canonical proceedings take place against Brunton for placing both of them in jeopardy. Their request was denied.

At Christmas, Pike and James Jr. made an extensive tour of the Holy Land, returning to San Francisco in February. James Jr. went by himself to New York. On February 4, 1966, Pike was informed that James Jr. had shot himself while in a drug-induced depression. Fr. Brunton was quoted as saying, "Thank God for one less Pike". Pike moved back into his official residence with his wife Esther, though maintaining separate bedrooms, and attempted to break off his relationship with Maren.

The tragedy of his son's suicide did not lessen the criticism and, if anything, increased the interest of the press. *Look* magazine published an article titled *Search for a Space-Age God*. In it, Pike was quoted as saying that "the Muslims offer one God and three wives; we offer three Gods and one wife". Pike wrote a denial and *Look* published it but the harm had already been done. Many more bishops were now against Pike. They scheduled a meeting of the presiding bishop and metropolitans for March 5th, so Pike could quell their fears. There, they requested him to write another letter to *Look* clarifying his position. The letter was to be distributed to all bishops as well. Though Pike wrote the letter, *Look* did not publish it, nor was it distributed to the bishops, who thus remained ignorant of his detailed position.

His diocese was also under attack for the participation of his priests in demonstrations against the war in Vietnam and for better race relationships, etc. Pike was rather conservative in his attitude toward civil disobedience but supported his priests' involvement. Large corporations withdrew their financial support of the cathedral, forcing Pike to look elsewhere for funds. With his own personal charisma and hard work, he succeeded in recovering the lost revenue from individuals.

On May 9, 1966, Bishop James Pike submitted his resignation in order to pursue his theological studies. It was accepted. He remained a bishop but without the administrative duties attached to a diocese. He became, as he said, "a worker priest in the purple". He joined Dr. Robert Maynard Hutchins at the Center for the Study of Democratic Institutions in Santa Barbara, a think tank comprised of twenty scholars from many disciplines. He was their first theologian. The New York *Daily News* headlined the move "Mind over Miter".

Esther did not want to make the move to Santa Barbara and publicly announced dual residences. Then Pike's mother offered to share her home with him and he accepted, installing Maren in an upstairs apartment. On August 13, Pike visitèd his former parish and in his final words to his congregation said, "It will be nice some day to be remembered as that conservative bishop you had here once".

At the meeting of the Georgian district in September, 1966, Bishop Louittit suggested that heresy charges finally be laid against Pike. He sent a presentment to all the bishops except Pike and released the information to the press. The other bishops asked to postpone the issue until the forthcoming full meeting of the House of Bishops. Louittit agreed to this but stated that he believed he had 90% support from laity, 95% from clergy and 90% from bishops. The presiding bishop, John Hines, was concerned about the public's opinion of a heresy trial. He conducted a private survey which indicated that the effects of such a trial would be disastrous, but this did not dissuade Louittit or his twenty-eight co-signers from proceeding. The bishops received a tremendous amount of mail, both pro and con, and the diocese of California was receiving the bulk of the criticism. Pike therefore resigned as Auxiliary Bishop to protect the diocese. Louittit responded, "That's a step in the right direction. But what we want is for him to resign the episcopate. The common word is unfrocked. I want him to admit that he does not accept the faith."

On October 18, Bishop Hines appointed an *ad hoc* committee led by retired bishop Angus Dun to investigate the controversy and present their findings to the meeting scheduled for October 23 in Wheeling, West Virginia. At the meeting, they discovered they did not have a quorum; therefore no trial could take place for at least a year. They did, however, proceed with the report, resulting in a severe censure. Resigned bishops usually have no seat, no voice and no vote in the House of Bishops; in Pike's case, the presiding bishop gave him a seat and a voice but no vote. Throughout the presentation of the report and later discussion, only two motions were carried: (1) that the word "totally" be omitted, leaving Pike "irresponsible" but not "totally irresponsible" and (2) that the rider, "we take this action aware of our common need for redemption, forgiveness and love" be added. Pike tried to speak in his own defence, saying that he was on trial, even though the bishops chose not to call it a trial. Bishop Hines said he would have ten minutes in which to present his side during the one hour allotted to debate. That hour went by without Pike being allowed to speak. There was much protest, so Pike's presentation was scheduled in a separate session at 9.30 that evening. Finally, at 11.00, Pike spoke for approximately eighteen minutes. The final vote was 103 for censure, 36 against.

The majority view was indeed harsh. In part it read, "It is our opinion that this proposed trial would not solve the problem presented to the Church by this minister, but in fact would be detrimental to the Church's mission and witness.... Having taken this position regarding a trial, nevertheless, we feel bound to reject the tone and manner of much that Bishop Pike has said as being offensive and highly disturbing within the communion and fellowship of the Church.... We are more deeply concerned with the irresponsibility revealed in many of his utterances... Finally we do not think his often obscure and contradictory utterances warrant the time and work and the wounds of a trial. The Church has more important things to get on with."

The minority view in part read: " ... there are frontiers of political and social and technological and theological thought and action confronting Christ's Church; and our mission is to pierce them. Few of us have done so, in large part because of the risk involved and because of the danger of the task. Bishop Pike has faced, often hurriedly, the demands, intellectual and theological, of our time in history, and we commend him for doing so. If he has to be a casualty ... we regret that this is so."

After the vote, Pike rose on a point of privilege and demanded a formal trial in order to defend himself properly.

After the meeting, he returned to his apartment in Santa Barbara where his relationship with Maren deteriorated even further. She began to take more and more medication and became completely incompetent at her job. Finally, on the evening of June 14, 1967, Pike asked her to leave. She did, but returned early the next morning, stating she had taken 55 pills. Pike steered her into her own apartment, where she collapsed. He called a doctor and ambulance, then made every effort to conceal his involvement with her by moving her personal belongings upstairs and even altering her suicide note to delete a reference to himself. Help came too late. She died in Cottage Hospital that morning.

At this time, I was producing radio programs for the United Church of Canada from Vancouver, B.C. I was also the host of an open line show on CKWX Vancouver and was at times asked to conduct interviews for the *7 o'clock show* for CBC-TV in that city. It was the CBC that first told me Bishop Pike would be coming to Vancouver from Santa Barbara for a brief visit to promote his new book, *If This Be Heresy.* Arrangements were made for the television interview but the bishop's schedule was changed at the last minute and his later arrival couldn't be accommodated by the studio. There was time for a radio interview, however, and so I proceeded with plans to conduct it at CKWX.

Although it was mid-afternoon, Pike had not lunched, so we met at a restaurant across from the radio station. After a brief handshake, we slid into a booth.

He enjoyed his role of theologian at the Santa Barbara think tank, he said, and was excited about its possibilities but decried the amount of time the media demanded of him. "I'm constantly being pressured into giving interviews.... Everyone wants to talk about the heresy thing and why I hate the church so much. Of course I don't hate the Church; I love it. It is absolutely necessary to God's work, but we mustn't make an idol out of it. I want to conserve the Church, but to conserve it we need to reform it. But the media is constantly looking for outrageous statements and I suppose one should always be careful."

He paused only long enough for a breath and a quick sip of rapidly cooling soup, then was off again on another topic. "Have you ever considered how important origins are to really shed light on understanding?" he asked. "I was in Israel on sabbatical, trying to discover a sense of where I should go in my work and studies. I was on Masada, the plateau above the Dead Sea where the Zealots held out for years against the Roman soldiers. It's a tremendous view. You feel as though you are standing on top of the world. It's really quite eerie ... a realization comes over you that here 860 people held out for four years expecting God to come down from the skies and rescue them. He didn't. Rather than become slaves, they left a suicide note. It was an honorable thing to do, at least the Roman commander thought so, because when he arrived he respected their decision. He wept."

Pike's own eyes misted over and he stared out of the window for a moment at the afternoon traffic on Burrard Street. I did not want to interrupt.

"It was a psychedelic experience for me, only no drugs were involved. I could feel all that courage. Years of sheer belief, courage and faith. This was the turning point I had been seeking. I had a new insight in how my studies could go forward and where I should go from there."

Normally I do most of the talking before a radio or TV interview in order to prevent the guest from repeating anecdotes or information. I always want them to save their best lines so that they'll be fresh for the program. But with Bishop Pike, there was no fear of him running dry or becoming stale.

"Linus Pauling agrees with me," he continued. "As you know, he works with me at the *Center for the Study of Democratic Institutions*. He says that science certainly isn't confined to laboratory work. Quite suddenly there can be a flash of illumination and you can continue your work without just struggling through all the data. The Center is a most interesting place. I've been there a year now. It's a kind of graduate facility without students."

While I enjoyed listening to Pike's dissertation, I was a bit worried about his lunch which he had hardly stopped to eat. "Perhaps I should tell you about the program we'll be doing," I ventured, hoping this would give him pause to work on his meal. "It's distributed to eighteen stations throughout British Columbia and a shorter edited version will go across Canada. These are joint ventures of the Anglican, Roman Catholic and United Churches of Canada. The stations provide free air time and ..."

"Aha!" he interrupted, "You don't find that kind of ecumenism in broadcasting in America. There, it is everyone for themselves. Of course the major churches have production facilities, but they don't turn out much relevant material and can't really present anti-establishment views because the station wouldn't carry them. They can't afford to buy time to say what they want, so the only way to communicate is through the newscasts which generally distort what you say. Well, I'm ready when you are."

We walked across the street to the radio station, where I introduced him to the manager and some of the staff. We recorded for about half an hour, but I don't remember asking more than one or two questions.

Following the interview, I accompanied him the short distance back to his hotel, where a press conference had been arranged. He said he felt the media had a great role to play in "explaining God to this generation. God is always trying to communicate — trying to get through. We must give him the opportunity whenever we can and recognize him when he does."

We paused at Burrard and Georgia where some young people were dancing and playing guitars on the street corner. "I have great sympathy for this hippie thing," he said. "They are so direct and open. They are seeking meaning away from our chrome-plated society. It's very much like the drop-out subculture of the Franciscans who were saying that the rich, corrupt Renaissance wasn't good and they wanted to go a different direction."

He said he hoped to visit the Holy Land again and study "origins" further. "If we can explore where we started, we can find where we went off the track."

I told him I hoped to see him at a scheduled conference in Banff that October and we parted.

In August, still another committee convened to compile a report to the House of Bishops concerning Pike's demand for a trial. Their report viewed heresy as "anachronistic" and suggested that no one should be able to make such charges so easily. They wrote, "Any risks the Church may run for fostering a climate of genuine freedom are minor compared to the dangers it surely will encounter from any attempts at suppression, censorship or thought control ... God made men free. It does not behoove His Church to hobble their minds or inhibit their search for new insights into truth."

That September, the general convention was held in Seattle. They agreed there should be an openness in theological inquiry and social witness. They also enacted canonical reforms safeguarding due process in ecclesiastical proceedings. Although they did not remove the previous censure, this constituted a vindication for Pike and he withdrew his demand for a trial.

In October of 1967, Pike was the theme speaker at the Banff Men's Conference. Hundreds of laymen from British Columbia and the prairie provinces had gathered at the Alberta resort town annually for the past 13 years to hear special speakers discuss theological issues that they hoped would inspire the delegates to return with renewed enthusiasm to their local churches. Pike delivered three major addresses. Each session was overflowing with attentive and appreciative laymen.

It was vintage Pike. At times warm and personal, tough and challenging, irreverent and humorous. "We are deep in an authority crisis. People don't accept things today because other people say so in essays or books found in motel rooms, or because a council of bishops met in the fourth or fifth century or because of some confession of faith, or because some Greek said so. This is not our way today. We want to see the facts and draw conclusions from these facts and we will make faith affirmations when they seem plausible ...

"What about the emotional necessity of God? He's been a prop to our security. We say 'don't worry, God will provide, he won't let you down.' If a lot of people were to report to a Gallup Poll about their belief in God, we'd find that their actual involvement with God is limited to emergencies ...

"We have in our *Book of Common Prayer* a prayer for rain and also a prayer for turning it off. I learned from a scientist at the Center the other day about satellites that can cover two or three small countries or a good chunk of a big country like yours and mine, and when geared to computers can tell you precisely the weather for two weeks ahead for any locale you want. Why would you ask the priest or minister to pray about it? You would get the facts. Again, *that* God is dead — the God that was going to rearrange the meteorology when we prayed for it.

"The real question is, is there any sense in which we can affirm faith in God? Any positive basis? The transcendent element which we see emerging with the evolution of man suggests that element is the universe itself. The "more" within man than "all the parts" — the fact that the total is greater than the sum of the parts — is true of the whole universe. We see it in people, the "more" than we could know of them through medical examination or psychiatric history — that which makes that individual person utterly different from any other person."

At one point Bishop Pike took a five dollar bill out of his pocket and waved it so all could see. He said we were entitled to believe that he had five dollars, we could even believe that he had more in his pocket, but we could not on the basis of the five dollar bill believe he was a millionaire — that would be "over belief."

"Look how often we engage in 'over belief' in regard to theology. We see some order, we see some purpose, we see some beauty, then suddenly announce He is omnipotent, omniscient, omnibenevolent — extrapolating all the way up to the skies. That's rather far-fetched, isn't it?

"Do we need to know as many things as we used to affirm? I don't think so. If there is a personal reality in, and through, and under all things, who is unchanging, who is without variables, who doesn't tinker around, we can at least say that a relationship is possible if we are willing to open ourselves to His revelation, if we are willing to listen. I don't have to assert more dogmas. I don't have to know all that much. I don't know as much about God as when I was ordained or about religion either. I find that I fall far short of being the exemplar of the few things I do affirm — hence I am not looking for more dogma to conquer yet. My motto for some time has been — fewer beliefs, more belief."

The previous May, Allen Spraggett, then religion editor for the *Toronto Star*, had talked with Pike in Geneva during a *Pacem in Terris* (Peace on Earth) conference. There Pike related mysterious events which had occurred after the suicide of James Jr. Pike described poltergeist activity in his apartment near Cambridge — objects moving around and letters from James Jr. suddenly appearing. This meeting prompted Spraggett to invite Pike to an on-air seance with the renowned medium Arthur Ford. Pike agreed and the seance was taped on September 3rd at CFTO-TV for the program *W-5*. The program reinforced Pike's belief in communication with the dead. He said, "Yes, I believe, very much so . . . the sensible affirmation to make is: one, that there is continuity of life after death and two, that on occasion, not invariably but on occasion, there can be communication with those beyond."

The Banff Men's Conference took place a few weeks after Pike's television seance. The publicity surrounding his session with Arthur Ford had not yet subsided. Many of us at the conference wondered if Pike would even refer to it, since press reports and editorial comment had for the most part held Pike up to ridicule. In his second address to the gathering, Pike met the issue head on.

"If any of you is going to live past death, it means there is something in you now of that nature. So we should look at what man is like now to see if we can perceive a transcendence of the space and time limitations. There is an enormous amount of data pointing to a quite plausible inference that everyone of us transcends space and time right now."

He talked about the university research programs into extrasensory perception and the many incidents recorded under laboratory conditions. He said that testing in the field of precognition showed the same thing. Clairvoyance, too, was being proven in research programs currently being conducted. Pike admitted that there was a considerable amount of charlatanry in the area of spiritualism but maintained there was hard evidence of communication with the dead.

"There are those who are dogmatic about this and say it can't be. I believe that in a fast growing world where the margins of knowledge are spreading so quickly, it's very unwise to say that something cannot be. It's interesting that in the last few years so much new evidence has come out about what seems to be communication with the beyond that many people will say immediately, 'Oh, that's ESP.' Those same people five years ago thought ESP was nonsense.

"On the first Sunday in September, I taped a program in Toronto with the Reverend Dr. Arthur Ford, member of the Disciples of Christ denomination and noted American medium. He was the avenue through which I received a lot of detailed information about people I had not thought about for a long time. What came through from my son might not seem so unusual, but other things certainly were. This has evoked in my mail an enormous amount of illustrative material describing similar experiences. Some of the details which came through Dr. Ford could have come from extrasensory perception, a little bit from direct knowledge on his own part (he did know my son was dead and a few other things) but too many obscure facts were revealed for me to believe in 'Super ESP' or detailed research alone. So what's the explanation?

"I find sufficient basis for affirming, by faith not proof, because I recognize the possibility of other explanations — the ongoingness of personal, individual life and, in addition, the possibility from time to time of communication with the dead. I affirm this as being natural to us as human beings. I do not believe in the supernatural at all. I believe it's natural. I believe in God, so I believe it is natural for him to *be*. Looking at the universe from a point of view that leaves him out would be a subnatural way of looking at things. Life after death is not a supernatural gift to the elect. It is of the nature of man. It is for everybody or it's for nobody. St. Paul put it this way: 'If the dead do not rise, then Jesus is not risen and we have no message.' If it is not natural for man to do this, then it did not happen to the man Jesus."

Pike pointed out that he did not believe in the physical resurrection of Jesus and claimed that all early accounts also denied this. He said all experience between Jesus and his survivors suggests a spiritual means of communication with the absence of space and time limitations.

"To say something is spiritual doesn't mean to say it is not real. Some people have been disturbed when their ministers on Easter Day talk about Jesus having spiritually gone on and say, 'Oh, you mean it's just the memory of the disciples?' No, it doesn't mean just that. I take seriously the accounts of communication between Jesus and his disciples after his death.

"If there is a series of contacts with the same person, it is not assumed that that person is omniscient, God or an oracle who can tell you what to do. The person may come through with advice, but it's rarely worth heeding. It's just another opinion. People make mistakes and think 'I must follow this advice because my mother told me from beyond the grave.' Well, your mother wasn't always entirely smart when she was living. In other words, we are talking about human beings who are finite. What dies is not an object, but a person and a person means that there's freedom — freedom of choice, freedom of reacting to encounters either positively or defensively.

"What happens to the concepts of heaven or hell? It became very difficult to localize them after Copernicus. We were not quite sure where to fit them in on the map. Then we said, 'Well, it's a state of being.' OK, let's go further and say that hell is an image of being self-centered and blocked in and heaven is being fulfilled and related and at peace with the source, the one, the all, namely God. The idea of a heaven of infinite bliss and a hell of infinite torment is a contradiction in terms. The kind of persons who would qualify for a heaven of infinite bliss would not be in bliss, knowing that a lot of people were deprived and suffering. At the least they would stage a demonstration in front of the throne of the Most High on behalf of these people or they would organize a rescue party — Operation Head Start — or failing that, and I mean this seriously, if they are the kind of people who should be up there, if they are anything like Jesus, they would go to hell and He'd be there too. That would leave God pretty lonely up there. He might even join them.

"One message that came through when I was communicating

with my son was that he was in great distress about what he had done. He hoped that we would understand. He thought he was understood by his new companions. Now this is a very touching message. If it didn't come through from him, they are great words anyway. He said, 'Dad, I still wish I hadn't done it.' You see, he didn't believe in anything then. He was part of the generation where everything was up for grabs, which is all right, it's the way faith becomes firm in due time. But he said, 'I wanted out and I found there is no out. And I wish I had stayed and worked out my problems in more familiar surroundings.' I think that is a firm message for a 'here and now' approach to life. Don't put off changing, don't put off reconciling, don't put off removing a barrier between you and another person. Get the scene cleared up as fast as you can. You don't know when your time is going to come. And when you enter the next scene, it's just as well to be as clear-headed and as big-hearted as possible. That's why I believe in *life after birth*. I think *this* is eternal life now. This is a call to live now, grow now, to keep on going, to justify getting up in the morning. We've hardly explored the fullness and the joy of interpersonal relations with those around us. We've hardly explored what our talents can achieve. Indeed, never has there been a time when there was so much potential joy in being alive."

Many viewers were amazed by Pike's willingness to believe in communication with the dead; others were themselves convinced after viewing the *W-5* program.

Later, evidence emerged that pointed towards a hoax. In his book *Arthur Ford: The Man who Talked with the Dead*, Bill Raucher uncovered the existence of papers containing information which could have been used to supply Ford with his supernatural communications. In his book *The Bishop Pike Story*, Allen Spraggett wrote, "What the TV seance did amount to was a brilliant display of Arthur Ford's talents as a medium in the sense of his having been able to litter the video tape with tantalizing evidentiary tidbits."

A year later, in February 1968, Spraggett introduced Pike to Dr. Ian Stevenson from the University of Virginia. He suggested that suppressed emotions had caused the poltergeist activity experienced by Pike. Neither the existence of Ford's papers nor this meeting did much to shake Pike's belief. He continued to attend seances with noted mediums such as Britain's Ena Twigg and continued to believe in communication with the dead.

Throughout the conference in Banff, Bishop Pike took time to speak to as many of the men as he could. In informal discussion groups he answered questions about his beliefs and about his personal life with surprising frankness.

"I never had a conversion experience," he stated in answer to one question. "What has happened to me especially in the last few years is a series of segmental conversions. One in particular may be one you have had, or a friend of yours. Before it happened, I seemed much older than I am now, much less freed up, not in nearly as good health and much, much plumper. Warning signs were being given by my physician about all kinds of things — cholesterol, fatty liver and everything else. I discovered, fortunately without any public event having to herald it, that I am an alcoholic."

Pike had been invited to lunch by a very prominent San Francisco woman who headed many social service agencies in that city. Twelve years earlier she had joined Alcoholics Anonymous and had climbed from "the gutter" to her present professional standing.

"I assumed our lunch was to discuss one of our episcopal institutions or to help get backing from various quarters for some new endeavor. We had done this kind of thing before. Instead, she said she had observed enough and heard enough and she thought I was too valuable to the community, to the Church and to myself to let it go any longer. She said, 'You are an alcoholic. So am I. Let me tell you my story.' She did and I identified with it. Everything she said I recognized. Then her story began to get rather grim. Nothing like she described had ever happened to me. She said, 'Look, if an elevator is cut loose from its moorings and it's rushing fast down to the basement and it happens to stop at the fifth floor, I think it's wise to get off. Don't you?' I pulled the old line, 'Well, you see, I have problems,' and she said, 'Yeah, I know, Jim, and some day I'd like to hear about them but, as long as you've got this problem, you're not going to be able to solve any other problem.' So I said, 'OK. I'm an alcoholic, what do I do about it?' The answer was AA.

"I've learned something about the Church out of this. An AA meeting is a liturgy of recall by the sharing of experience. One remembers death and resurrection. One remembers how bad it was and how good it is. The reason why people fail who try this on their own, is because they forget. They drop back into social drinking because they feel so good. I've also strengthened my own perseverance in this regard by helping others. Without all

203

this having been straightened out, nothing else could have happened."

Pike's stature with the public grew in the late 1960s and he became much in demand as a high profile supporter of various causes. He was, for example, asked to attend the trial of the Catonsville Nine — Philip and Daniel Berrigan and seven of their friends accused of destroying draft records during the Vietnam War. He agreed, but knew virtually nothing about the trial. Pike sat with defence counsellor William Kunstler and after a day became convinced that the case was central to the anti-war effort. He spoke that night on their behalf. "I supported that damned war in the beginning because I believed the lies we were told about it ... but I was wrong and you were right.... I opposed burning draft cards when that started to happen because I thought it was childish ... but I was wrong and you were right.... I declined to support Benjamin Spock and Bill Coffin and the others when they were on trial for conspiracy to incite draft refusal because I thought they were being irresponsible ... but I was wrong and they were right ... and I came to Baltimore last night certain in my own mind that the Catonsville Nine should not have burned draft records because it was illegal ... but I was wrong and they were right."

In 1966 Pike had met Diane Kennedy who was studying at the Pacific School of Religion at Berkeley. She took two courses from Pike — *The New Morality* and *The New Theology* — and was an excellent student. Pike later hired her as a research assistant.

In December 1968, the now divorced Pike married Diane Kennedy. Because of the church's attitude to remarriage, this caused yet another controversy. The factions both for and against him grew and the situation became so uncomfortable for the Pikes that they chose to leave the church formally. This process would take six months.

The Pikes decided to visit the Holy Land in the fall of 1969. They were both extremely interested in the Dead Sea Scrolls and wished to study the area in which they were found. They had arranged for a guided tour to the area of the Qumran caves, but decided to rent a car in Jerusalem and get a feel of the area before the tour. The car became stuck in the middle of the wilderness. After working on the car for an hour, they decided that it would be closer to walk on toward the Dead Sea rather than turn back. They were approximately six miles west of the Sea.

By 6 p.m., in the middle of a very deep canyon, Pike could not go on. Diane went to get help, leaving Pike to continue more slowly. Diane climbed for six hours before eventually finding her way out of the canyon. She kept walking, but found no one until she happened upon an Arab work camp ten hours later. They insisted Diane wait until the arrival of their Israeli army overseers the next day. The army patrol arrived at 8.30 a.m. and the search party finally set out at 12.45 . The car was soon found but the search for Pike continued from dawn to dusk every day until Sunday September 7, almost a week later, when his body was found sprawled on an outcropping of rocks. Pike had fallen while trying to climb out of the canyon.

One would have thought that the death of James Pike would put an end to the controversies which dominated his life. This was not the case, because he upset too many people. He upset the faithful through his criticism of the church hierarchy. He upset conservatives for his liberal social attitudes illustrated in his comments: "I've advised people to go to prison for the sake of their conscience rather than commit murder in Vietnam ..." and "How can a father, who's just finished his fourth martini, lecture his son about smoking pot?" He upset liberals with his orthodoxy on many issues, like that of Luci Baines Johnson. He upset many because of his complicated and problem-ridden private life and perhaps most of all because every move he made became public. He was accused many times of being a publicity seeker. Critics would cite his unique turn of phrase as proof, as when he characterized the rhythm method of birth control as "Vatican roulette" or the work of the John Birch Society as "political necrophilia". This was good press but his biographers believe that the press sought Pike more than the other way round. Either way he remains a mystery. To encourage and horrify so many in a relatively short ecclesiastical career is indeed extraordinary.

Bishop Pike gained prominence during a time of crisis for the Christian church. He joined liberal theologians throughout the world in questioning basic doctrine and emphasizing the Church as a socially as well as morally conscious institution. This was the era that produced some of the most challenging writing on the role of the Church in the 20th century. Through the perspective of time we can now see that the ideas expressed by Pike and his contemporaries, such as Bishop John Robinson, were not far removed from the previous generation, as represented by Reinhold Niebuhr and Paul Tillich. The then revolutionary ideas are now seen as rather conservative, if not orthodox. I only wish that Pike had lived through the turmoil of the 1960s. He might well have been granted his wish to be known as that "conservative bishop you had here once".

ARCHBISHOP "TED" SCOTT

Ted Scott and I were old friends by the time the 1971 General Synod of the Anglican Church of Canada took place in Niagara Falls. We had served on committees together, spoken at the same conferences, done a great deal of radio and television work and traveled thousands of miles in each other's company. Increasingly, I heard talk of Ted being Primate material. I wasn't sure the Church was ready for what appeared to be a very progressive — if not radical — bishop occupying the top job.

In 1970 Archbishop Howard Clark announced his wish to retire from the Primacy. A kindly, dedicated and learned man, Clark was in poor health and wished to lay down the burdens of office so as to enjoy his later years. His last hurrah would be at the upcoming Synod where a successor would be elected.

At this time, the push for union between the Anglican and United Churches was at its strongest. In a symbolic gesture of togetherness, it was decided that the two Canadian communions would hold their national meetings at the same time and place. This was the first time it had ever happened. It may well have been the last.

Niagara Falls was chosen as the site for eight days in January and February. The Anglicans moved into the Foxhead Hotel while the United Church representatives encamped at the nearby Sheraton Brock. Some sessions were combined, but for the most part, each communion went about its own business.

I was finishing up a tour of duty as National Radio Coordinator for the Anglican, United and Roman Catholic Churches in Canada and had been asked by the United Church to report on their General Council meeting to a network of Canadian stations.

The top news story at both events would be the election of the head person. The United Church changes its moderator every two years. The Anglican Primacy can be for life. I had planned on dividing my time between the two hotels so that I could watch both elections, but I suddenly became very busy. I was in the broadcasting room at the Sheraton Brock listening to the monitor which was carrying the proceedings live from the floor of the court when I heard my name mentioned. Someone had made a motion that before the election of moderator, each candidate be interviewed in front of the commissioners so that a knowledgeable vote could then be cast. It was also moved that I be asked to conduct the interviews. A church committee official came rushing into the broadcast room to ask if I would indeed conduct the interviews, since no one had thought to clear it with me first. I readily agreed and so began a tradition that still continues at every United Church General Council.

That year Dr. Bob McClure, the feisty and popular medical missionary, was retiring as moderator. He had been the first layman ever to hold that high office. His down-to-earth, outspoken and sometimes audacious manner had stirred the Church and the nation during his tenure and he was leaving large shoes to be filled. There were six candidates for moderator. It took only two ballots, however, to elect a successor that afternoon: Arthur B.B. Moore, Dean of Victoria College and one of the main architects of the proposed union with the Anglican Church.

When I emerged from the conference court, there was a phone call from CBC radio, Toronto asking me if I could get them an interview with the new Primate of the Anglican Church in time for the 6 o'clock network news. I explained that I had been so busy I didn't even know who it was. They told me that the name had come over the wire a few minutes earlier and that the new Primate was a bishop from B.C. called Edward Walter Scott.

When I entered the ballroom of the Foxhead, the Synod was in session and the new Primate, the Right Reverend E.W. "Ted" Scott, Bishop of the Diocese of Kootenay, was in the chair. I scribbled a note and handed it to a page who slipped it in front of Ted. He looked up, caught my eye and handed the gavel to the secretary, announcing to the assemblage that he would be back shortly, then joined me at the back of the room. After congratulating him, I apologized for the interruption and asked if he could come over to the broadcast room at the Brock for a brief interview.

We walked together this crisp, cold, sunny day, pausing for a moment to look toward the falls where the massive ice bridges were forming, almost covering the deep blue raging torrent of the river. I wondered what thoughts were in the mind of this seemingly simple priest who had suddenly been thrust into the top position of his church. Was it the thorny question of union with the United Church? The issue of women clergy? The ache he felt so keenly for his beloved native people? He turned from the beauty of Niagara, then answered my unspoken question. He quietly said, "I'm going to miss the Kootenays."

I first met Ted Scott on a Sunday morning in 1966 in Vancouver. At that time I was Director of Broadcasting in British Columbia for the United Church of Canada. Part of my responsibility was to look after four hours a week of air time of CKWX radio. The radio station had at one time been owned by the Church and the four hours remained as part of a deal made when the station was sold to private interests.

The Sunday morning time period had been a problem for me because it was filled with a church service broadcast which drew extremely small audiences and also went against my personal views on religious broadcasting. I have never thought that the mere airing of a church service was of any real value to the audience or the station. I removed the service from the schedule and started an open line program called *God Talk* which was originally run at the traditional church service time of 11 a.m. to noon but was expanded because of its rapidly increasing popularity. The format was quite simple. An Anglican priest, a Roman Catholic priest and a United Church minister formed the panel with myself as moderator. From time to time other denominations joined us as well as atheists, agnostics and non-Christian representatives. The program's popularity was due in large part to the frankness and openness of the panel who held nothing back in their encounters with the on-the-air callers.

God Talk was a breath of fresh air in an otherwise dull Sunday morning broadcasting scene. Audiences increased to such an extent that the station's sales department asked if they could sell advertising on it. Ministers discovered some members of their congregations listening to *God Talk* on their portable radios with one ear and the sermon with the other.

One Sunday morning the dialogue with a caller was well under way when I glanced into the control room and noticed a flash of purple. Recognizing the vestments of a bishop I tiptoed out of the studio while the call was in progress, entered the control room and introduced myself. I was greeted by a short, bespectacled man with slightly greying hair and warm, inquisitive eyes. He said that he was listening to the program on his car radio and wanted to find out who was producing it. Knowing the station's call letters, he had asked directions at a gas station. He then introduced himself as Ted Scott from the Kootenays. I asked him to join the panel for the remainder of the show. He said he would be delighted to take part. This was my first meeting with the man whose path would cross mine many times over the years and whose gentle strength and wisdom has guided not only the Anglican Church of Canada, but all communions on the national and international religious scene.

Ted Scott was born the son of a minister in Edmonton, Alberta in 1919. It was difficult then for a parish priest with a wife and four children to eke out more than a meagre living.

Recently we talked about those early days. "My father wasn't making very much in those days as a minister, but we didn't feel poor because everyone else was in the same boat," he said. "Dad had a parish in a little town called Caron, Saskatchewan. Our clothing came from church donations and all of the parish work was in the low income and poverty areas. It was when we moved to Vancouver during the Depression that I noticed the difference. We lived in the east end of Vancouver, North Burnaby, and I remember one day, as I went to the post office to mail some things for my father, I saw standing in the unemployment line two of the boys I had gone to school with in Caron. I remember thinking how much better my chances were than theirs because I was a minister's son. I was able to get educational bursaries and other breaks because my father was a minister."

His early life on the prairies and in Vancouver during the 1930s made a lasting impression on him. He attributes his concern for the poor and the alienation of native people to his experiences growing up in a relatively poor, but caring family.

"I remember Christmas when well over half of my father's congregation was on Welfare. We worked a great deal with Indian people and I saw the kind of conditions they lived under. I saw people trapped in situations of great difficulty, unable to enjoy the things that most of us take for granted."

"When and why did you decide to become a priest?" I asked.

"I think it was in my third year of university. I had been working that summer and reflecting quite a bit on the political situation in Vancouver during the Depression time and became convinced that it didn't make any difference what kind of system you had unless you had responsible people within that system. The Church had a concern about developing responsible, self-reliant persons who then had a responsibility in terms of the structures of society. It was the concern for people and their potential in the world that made me decide for the church."

After university Ted enrolled at the Anglican Theological

College in Vancouver. He also became active in the Student Christian Movement, a fellowship that brought people of all denominations together to examine issues of faith.

"This confronted one with the realities of life, much more than theological education did," he said. "The academic world was concerned with the Church in a very narrow sense. Here we saw how the Church could be a major factor in the world around us."

After ordination in 1942, Ted was sent to Prince Rupert to serve in the mission field. War had turned this northern British Columbia seaport into a boom-town with the population leaping from 7,000 to 20,000 in one year. Recently married, Ted and Isobel found a considerable lack of privacy because of the housing shortage.

"We had to share houses and make room for many military couples. But there was a real sense of community since we were all in the same situation together," he recalls.

In 1945, he was asked to become general secretary of the Student Christian Movement at the University of Manitoba in Winnipeg. For the next five years he would throw himself into the ecumenical movement that was forever to influence his life. Considering his future appointment as Chairman of the Central Committee of the World Council of Churches, a statement he made in Winnipeg in 1947 takes on added importance:

"Another great religious development of our time is that of the ecumenical movement, which has reached one culminating point in our day in the formation of the World Council of Churches. If this movement provides a means for formal organizational relationships between Christian bodies, either on a basis of intellectual discussion only or a basis of negative reaction to other ideologies, then it will be of no real value. If, on the other hand (and I am convinced that this is and can be made the case), it is an honest attempt to bring together Christian individuals and groups of various historical traditions that may seek to understand each other's heritage and seek together for a more positive understanding of their faith and of the things to which the living God is calling us in these days, then it will become one of the most hopeful developments of our time, and worthy of our full support."

He returned to parish work in 1950 as rector of the Church of St. John in Fort Gary and in 1955, rector of St. Jude's in Winnipeg. In 1960 the Diocese of Rupert's Land was looking for a priest to take charge of its Indian work and to fill the position of

Director of Social Service. Ted Scott took the job. In co-operation with government and welfare agencies, he helped establish Canada's first Indian and Metis Friendship Centre which served as a cultural centre helping native people adjust to urban living. In 1964 he accepted the position of Associate Secretary of the National Office's Council for Social Service in Toronto, a post he held until his election as Bishop of Kootenay on January 25, 1966.

Before I left Vancouver in 1967, I got to know what a dynamic churchman and compassionate human being Ted is. I heard him speak many times at rallies, conferences and seminars, some of which we had jointly arranged. It is in small groups, though, that Ted is most effective. He has the rare ability to listen intently to each individual opinion, to steer discussion until everyone has a chance to contribute and to crystallize the feelings of the group concisely and accurately, usually gearing it to some positive action. I have seen him talking compassionately on a one-to-one basis with strangers on the streets of Vancouver, Toronto, Nairobi — counseling and giving comfort or direction. As bishop he pioneered joint ministries in his diocese — United Church and Anglican ministers serving the same pastorate, sharing the same facilities. He led his denomination and others in special programs to help native people and provide services for the underprivileged.

I remember him speaking out repeatedly in those days in support of youth movements protesting the Vietnam War and on behalf of groups organized to support Cesar Chavez and his farmworkers. He preferred shirts and ties to formal clerical garb and wore beaded pectoral crosses presented to him by Indian bands instead of the usual gold-plated ones. He was, and still is, what we call in media circles 'good copy'. If a quotation was needed to spruce up a story on some contentious issue, or a taped comment required for a radio or television program, which included the church's position in any area of society, we could always call Bishop Scott. This often brought him more attention than he wanted. He was not a publicity seeker. I have often thought his ready response to the media was partly because he felt an obligation as bishop to make the Church's presence felt, but mostly because he was earnestly trying to help journalists do their job.

I recall a scene at the 1967 General Synod of the Anglican Church held in Ottawa, where the subject of church union was to be one of the major items discussed. From my seat at the press table I watched as speaker after speaker pointed out the wisdom of the two churches proceeding to organic union. A local television crew was waiting patiently until a Canon, a well-known opponent of union, rose to speak. The producer then went into action. The television lights came on and the cameraman began filming. As soon as the Canon sat down, the lights were unplugged, the camera switched off and the crew began packing up the rest of the equipment.

I got to the press room at the same time as the producer. I told him I thought his actions were stupid in not attempting to cover the other side of the issue. He replied simply that he had filmed what he had been told to. At that moment the press room door flew open and in strode Bishop Scott. His normally grey demeanor was florid with emotion. He asked if the crew realized what they had done. His quiet voice surprised me, but the tone made me glad he wasn't speaking to me.

Scott argued that they had, in just a few minutes, confirmed the suspicions of many members of the church hierarchy who claim the media misrepresents and distorts. He admitted that the decision, as to what to broadcast, was ultimately theirs, but that they at least could have had the courtesy to appear impartial. He was enraged because he and others had worked hard to defend the rights of the press in Canada and felt that the crew's actions made his support difficult to give. Not waiting for a reply, he turned and left the room. The producer turned to me and asked, "Who the hell was that?" I told him it was Bishop Ted Scott of the Kootenays. Missing the point completely, the producer reduced Scott's argument to one simply in favor of church union.

It was my turn to get angry. I wasn't sure if the producer paid any attention as I reiterated Ted's argument and none too patiently explained that the bishop was in favor of fair play and responsible reporting and that he was the kind of good friend Canadian journalism could ill affort to lose.

Ted's reprimand had its effect. I noted with satisfaction that the news that night carried a balanced report. The producer had asked a pro-union spokesman to appear and respond to the Canon's speech.

Ted Scott has perhaps become more wary of the press since becoming Primate because he knows the general public believes, erroneously, that the Primate speaks for the whole church, and also because he has been 'burned' too often for his outspoken remarks. Certainly, as moderator of the Central Com-

mittee of the World Council of Churches, he has endured vitri-
olic attacks by the press of many countries, mainly because of
his support of the money sent by WCC's Special Fund of the
Program to Combat Racism to places like Zimbabwe and Nami-
bia. He's been called "communist", "pinko" and "fellow trav-
eler". These names and others were also applied to him, and
quoted in the press, by angry Canadian businessmen because of
his questioning of their rights to push through the Mackenzie
Valley Natural Gas Pipeline without regard to the rights of some
15,000 Indians. When he led his church through its Task Force
on the Churches and Corporate Responsibility and into the
boardrooms of the nation's largest businesses, demanding
moral and ethical consideration for their investments, the bar-
ons of Bay Street, many of them members of the Anglican
Church, were furious. One Anglican businessman we spoke to
exclaimed, "Ted Scott was fine until the communists got
to him."

I commented to Ted once, "What's all this about you being a
communist?"

He answered, "I wouldn't even say I was a socialist. I was just
thinking the other night at a meeting when someone raised that
question, that in terms of my record of voting, I have voted for all
three Canadian parties, but likely in both provincial and federal
elections I have voted for the Conservatives more than any other
group; but that probably is not the image a lot of people have
of me."

Ted's election to the Primacy was greeted with great ap-
proval, but a certain amount of surprise. After all, he was one of
the "junior" bishops, relatively young — at 51 the youngest
person elected to the Primacy — and with a reputation as a
social activist and a progressive. There had, of course, been
enthusiastic talk prior to the General Synod of the possibility of
his election, but it wasn't until the morning of the election that
Ted decided to let his nomination go forward. His wife, Isobel,
found out the results of the election by accident when her call
was inadvertently put through to the press room where an
excited journalist told her what had happened. Ted vowed not to
let this happen again. Five years later, when we were both in
Nairobi at the World Council of Churches meeting, Ted stood for
hours in a telephone booth in the huge Kenyatta Centre placing
a call to Canada to discuss with Isobel his nomination to head
the Central Committee.

When I quoted to Ted Cardinal Léger's statement that you

have to believe in God who would make a Cardinal out of a poor Canadian boy from St-Anicet. I asked if he felt that way about his accomplishments.

"Well, my aspirations were never that high and not in that area. When you have not been part of the basic establishment — have even been critical of it — then find yourself in a key role in it, you have to make demands on yourself that are fairly high. People both in the House of Bishops and at the general meeting that day have said it showed pretty clearly that I never anticipated it would happen to me. Certainly not in the case of the World Council of Churches either. When I went to Nairobi, I had no idea that would come up. I didn't seek the office."

In that office Ted soon found himself admidst swirling controversy. The Program to Combat Racism was started in 1969 by the World Council's Central Committee and quickly became the target of criticism all around the world. It had become a program not only to combat racism but to expose it and in so doing revealed the complicity of governments in the oppression of certain people. The biggest storm broke in 1977 when Ted and his committee authorized a grant in the name of the World Council to the Patriotic Front in Zimbabwe. The money was to be used for humanitarian purposes, specifically for the thousands of refugees driven from their homes by the war then raging.

With charges that the money was being used by Robert Mugabe and his guerrilla forces to buy arms, the press had a field day. The grant was labeled "blood money" and Ted and his colleagues were called "ecclesiastical murderers". The conservative wings of the member churches began questioning their involvement in the World Council. In the storm of publicity the Salvation Army suspended its membership. Ted defended his committee's actions on the ground that the money was used for health purposes and educational needs. I asked him at the time if he could issue a promise that the money was not used to buy arms.

"No, not in the total sense I can't," he admitted. "The money is given on the basis of trust and on the basis of networks of people who can watch what happens to the use of it. There has never been any case where there was proof that it was used for other than the purpose for which it was given. I'm confident, personally, that it has been used properly, but I can't give you ultimate proof that this was the case."

Ted Scott's trust was vindicated the following year when it

was discovered that much of the information used against him and the Program to Combat Racism came from the discredited South African Department of Information and was deliberately used to destroy the Church's credibility. The world press had also done a complete about-face in regard to Mugabe, transforming his image from terrorist to responsible statesman.

When Ted steps down from his post as moderator of the Central Committee, certain wounds will remain. I asked him about the criticism and abuse he took. Did it hurt?

"A person would be lying to say it didn't cause you pain. But when you experience pain yourself, it can give you an image of the pain in others. In my worst moments I would have given anything to be removed from some of the situations I was in, but there were certain issues behind them that were fundamentally important and had to be worked at. I'm not sure the World Council has always found the best way to work at those issues. We haven't always explained our work to people effectively and have therefore laid ourselves open to too much easy misinterpretation."

"Are you disappointed in the reaction of people, especially church people?" I asked.

"I think my biggest disappointment came in my earlier years in my father's congregation. It seemed to me that often Christian people cared little about what happened to other people in that congregation. Cities can become ghettoized and people can live in one place and not know what's going on in other parts of that city. It's the same thing I see in the world situation. The world becomes ghettoized. We can live here in Canada surrounded by so many things we just automatically take for granted and not think of the implications to people in other parts of the world. I guess that my disappointment is that, to me, being a baptised Christian means to be a member of a worldwide community concern. Very often I don't see that concern made visible and expressed."

When Ted Scott was elected Primate, he made a promise which, since then, no one has really wanted him to keep. He said he would resign the office in ten years to make room for a new man. At the seven-year mark I asked him if he planned to stick to his pledge. He said he was looking at the situation very seriously, but wasn't prepared to announce his intentions at that time. After twelve years in office I asked what had happened.

"I really struggled with that one, Roy. I finally said to the

Archbishops in the central group that I would stay on if they could suggest concrete things that I could do that would not be done otherwise." He listed several programs that were pending in the Canadian Anglican community and with his time freed from World Council duties he expected to be able to pay more attention to these matters.

I suggested that his staying on the job indicated he still had a considerable amount of faith in the Church.

"Yes, very much. People ask me if I'm optimistic and I say no, not when you look at the realities of the world situation. The next two or three decades are going to be an extremely difficult time. I am only hopeful because I have a faith to base hope on. I believe in the reality of God. Now that's not always easy to hang on to. There are moments when we have to struggle. One of the things I find most difficult is older people who seem unable to sense the difficulty youth has in coming to faith today with the complexities of our world. Some young people, in trying to escape these complexities, slide into a very simplistic faith. We've seen a lot of that developing. To have a mature faith and a responsible faith is not easy. One has to nurture faith and work at it all the time and the Church must help people do this."

Ted had worked very hard on the Plan of Union which would have joined the Anglican and United Churches into one body. That he was very confident of its success made its failure even harder to accept. In 1975, after ten years of negotiations, it fell to Ted to announce the statement from the House of Bishops to the National Executive Council. The statement said, "We find our-selves agreed that the Plan of Union in its present form is unacceptable ... and we think that the climate of feeling, at least in our constituency, seems at the present time less favorable to organic union and more disposed towards other expressions of unity."

I asked Ted if the failure of that union had been difficult for him to accept.

"It was a major disappointment at the time. In the long haul it has become evident, from what is happening elsewhere, that churches can come together through growing consensus, rather than structural plans. People are pretty well disillusioned with structural patterns even within their own Church. There's a little book called *The Authority of the Laity* containing a poem that goes like this: 'A strange thing happened on the way to the Kingdom. The Church, the people of God, became the church, the institution.'

"I see the Church as the people of God and the kind of relationships developed there can't be achieved through structures. In many cases I'm much closer to the members of other churches than to some Anglicans and this is true in reverse, but at the time I was very disappointed with the failure of union."

I asked about the impact of the institutional church on society during his years as Primate.

"I think it could have been a lot better than it was, but I do believe that the Churches are now beginning to address the issues. For a long time we were not doing that. For example, if the Churches had, much earlier, begun to address the whole issue of the Christian attitude toward nature, a lot of the ecological crises need not have happened. If we had begun, much earlier, to address the way in which we relate to other people and struggle for personal relationships so that people are subjects, not just objects, then I think a lot of things might have been different. I happen to believe, rightly or wrongly, that we're at the end of a historical era. The era of enlightenment is coming to an end. The Church is beginning to enunciate some of the values that are apparent and I'm happy to see this concern. It's persons nurturing persons and helping a new vista to develop."

Ted's high profile in Canada and his leadership in the World Council have given him a pre-eminent position in the world church scene. In 1979 he was seriously considered as a candidate for Archbishop of Canterbury. Coincidentally my wife and I were touring Canterbury the day we noticed a press report of this consideration, so we promptly bought a postcard showing the magnificent old cathedral and sent it to Ted in Canada with the message, "Having a wonderful time. Wish you were here."

Archbishop Scott travels hundreds of thousands of miles each year across Canada and around the world. The pressures of an exhausting schedule of executive meetings and international conferences have affected him very little. His face is more deeply lined and the hair completely grey now, but his energy level and vibrant personality seem the same as when I first met him in the control room of that Vancouver radio station. I asked him recently how he was able to keep going — what sustained him?

"Two groups," he answered, "one group includes the national staff, our House of Bishops and our National Executive Council. We work in a very close relationship. The fact you know you are supported by these people right across the country is tremendous. The other group is my family. Our family keeps in close touch. We have three of our children living here in Toronto and four of our grandchildren. We have regular family events. All of my children are better at different fields than I am and they are a great help to me. My wife is incredible. Nobody could give more kinds of support, put up with more things and yet push at certain times when a push is needed, and that's very good."

Several years ago in an interview, I asked Ted what personally provided the impetus for all his work. He answered, "One of the essential things for me in the Anglican Church has always been the Baptismal service and the exhortation of the parents and god-parents at the end. This is our profession — to follow Jesus Christ and do the best we can. That has always meant a great deal to me. There is a sense of responsibility and of having some focus on the kind of person I would like to try to be. I'm prepared to look hard at my shortcomings and try to do something about them, but I take seriously the fact that nothing I do will ever make God stop loving me."

I couldn't count the number of times I have interviewed Ted Scott over the years. I've thrust a microphone under his nose on street corners, in crowded boardrooms, even on airplanes. We've stood in front of cameras at packed convention centres and under the blazing sun in Kenya. I've interviewed him for *Man Alive* on the ordination of women, Church union, homosexuality, Third World aid, Indian land rights and numerous other subjects. *Man Alive* produced a special profile of him called *Scott of Canada* in 1978. We showed him addressing the Lambeth conference in Canterbury and globe-hopping for his Central Committee work. We showed him in church basements and in his own home workshop, where he relaxes making furniture. His only stipulation was that in preparing the program, we not only listen to his friends but to those who disapproved of his approach to the Primacy. We complied.

A few days after his election as Primate, I interviewed him and the new moderator of the United Church, Dr. A.B.B. Moore, in the Jarvis Street television studios of the CBC for an upcoming *Man Alive* program. The two men had known each other for twenty-five years and worked together on the church union commission. You could feel the mutual friendship and respect throughout the two-hour taping session.

As we left the studio, Ted asked where I was going. I told him I was on my way to Union Station to catch a train to my home in Trenton. It was such a nice night, I had decided to walk. Ted decided to join me. We were hardly out of the building when Dr. Moore called out that he would walk with us, then take the subway home.

The three of us proceeded abreast down Jarvis Street talking about the interview and catching up on personal news. When we reached the corner at Dundas Street, Dr. Moore was in the middle of a rather long story, so we waited on the corner until he finished, since he planned to catch the subway a few blocks west.

We didn't notice where we were standing until we said our goodnights. We looked up and saw flashing signs proclaiming "Girls, Girls, Girls", "Nude Strippers Live on Stage", "Come in for Sexorama".

We were suddenly aware of what a juicy bit of gossip this scene would make for a passing reporter — the moderator of the United Church, the Primate of the Anglican Church and the host of *Man Alive* standing together late at night on the doorstep of one of Toronto's oldest and most active strip joints.

Many times my interviews with Ted have been conducted under the pressure of journalistic exigencies, "I need a quote now" or "What's your reaction to this?" Other times, under extreme time limitations, Ted has waited patiently for malfunctioning cameras and overly functioning producers. Through it all his sincerity and good humor has never flagged. His answers to my questions have always been straightforward and honest, but I have often had the feeling that his major concern is that the interviewer is doing his best job. He frequently asks your opinion of the same issue you have presented to him. He never fails to inquire about your personal well-being and that of your family and mutual acquaintances. Parting is difficult for Ted. He sincerely hates to see you go. In fact one of his greatest regrets about his job is his inability to spend more time with treasured friends and former colleagues.

Hugh McCullum, editor of the *United Church Observer*, says, "Like many others, when I need a pastor, Ted is the one I go to. At a personal level he makes me feel that my problems, and mine alone, are his deepest concern. He's a great problem-solver, listener and confessor." Anyone who has spent much time with Ted would say the same.

Like Léger and Pike, Ted Scott has been honored by his church with a position of prominence. Like both of them, I'm sure Ted has often found the structure confining and cumbersome, but he has chosen to remain within the system and make it work.

Pike's search for meaning led him away from the institution, but along the way he inspired and changed individuals who saw their relationship to others and to their God more clearly.

Léger's sacrifice and devotion presented an example which helped many realize that faith without action is a barren faith indeed.

Scott's quiet employment of the church machinery to bring relief and hope to desperate corners of the world humanized the system and made it more relevant.

In all three we can observe a dedication to mankind and a striving toward understanding and compassion. We can learn from all three that no matter what course we choose, conviction can lead us in similar directions and faith can bring us to the same goals.